Pinky Extension and Eye Gaze

Ceil Lucas, General Editor

Pinky Extension and Eye Gaze

Language Use

in Deaf Communities

Ceil Lucas, Editor

GALLAUDET UNIVERSITY PRESS

Washington, D.C.

Sociolinguistics in Deaf Communities

A Series Edited by Ceil Lucas

Gallaudet University Press
Washington, D.C. 20002

ISBN 1-56368-070-X

ISSN 1080–5494

Cover design by Joseph Kolb
Interior design by Richard Hendel
Composition by G&S Typesetters, Inc.

♾ The paper used in this publication meets the minimum requirements of
American National Standard for Information Sciences—Permanence of Paper
for Printed Library Materials, ANSI Z39.48–1984.

Contents

Editorial Advisory Board

Contributors

Jean Ann
Department of ASL, Linguistics,
    and Interpretation
Gallaudet University
Washington, D.C.

Sarah E. Burns
18B Strand Road
Sandymount
Dublin, Ireland

Steven Collins
Department of ASL, Linguistics,
    and Interpretation
Gallaudet University
Washington, D.C.

Valerie L. Dively
Department of ASL, Linguistics,
    and Interpretation
Gallaudet University
Washington, D.C.

Priscilla Shannon Gutierrez
37259 Downing Street
Palmdale, California

Rob Hoopes
Department of Linguistics
Georgetown University
Washington, D.C.

Mike Kemp
Department of ASL, Linguistics,
    and Interpretation
Gallaudet University
Washington, D.C.

Susan Mather
Department of ASL, Linguistics,
    and Interpretation
Gallaudet University
Washington, D.C.

Melanie Metzger
Department of ASL, Linguistics,
    and Interpretation
Gallaudet University
Washington, D.C.

Karen Petronio
Interpreter Training Program
Eastern Kentucky University
245 Wallace Building
Richmond, Kentucky

Rachel Sutton-Spence
Centre for Deaf Studies
University of Bristol
22 Berkeley Square
Bristol, United Kingdom

Elizabeth A. Winston
Educational Linguistics Research
    Center
Loveland, Colorado

Introduction

The title of volume 4 of the Sociolinguistics in Deaf Communities series focuses on an aspect of variation in sign languages—pinky extension—and an aspect of sign language discourse—eye gaze—in order to evoke the richness and uniqueness of language use in Deaf communities. *Pinky Extension and Eye Gaze: Language Use in Deaf Communities* is a collection of data-based studies that show the variety and range of sociolinguistic issues currently facing Deaf communities around the world. The topics of the studies range from variation in ASL and tactile (Deaf-Blind) signing to language contact outcomes in British Sign Language (BSL) and Taiwan Sign Language (TSL), and from language policy and language-teaching issues to sign language discourse and language attitudes. As always, it is my hope that the volumes in this series will enhance our understanding of the richness and complexity of sociolinguistics in Deaf communities.

I am grateful to the contributors of this volume and to the members of the editorial advisory board for their work in putting this book together. I also gratefully acknowledge Ivey Pittle Wallace (managing editor, Gallaudet University Press), Jenelle Walthour (editor, Gallaudet University Press), and Carol Hoke (copy editor, WriteOn!) for their support, hard work, and good humor.

Part I Variation

A Preliminary Examination of Pinky Extension:

Suggestions regarding Its Occurrence,

Constraints, and Function

Rob Hoopes

Studies of the phonological and phonetic structure of signed languages have indicated both parallels with and contrasts to the phonological structure of spoken languages. One interesting parallel is the description of the prosodic structure of signed languages. This paper presents findings of a preliminary study of a phonological characteristic of American Sign Language (ASL) referred to here as "pinky extension." Specifically, in certain social and linguistic environments, some signers extend their fifth digit (or "pinky") during particular signs despite the fact that the citation forms of these signs do not specify pinky extension. This study examines the signing of one such native ASL user in order to: (1) determine whether pinky extension is, in fact, an example of variation; (2) identify possible linguistic and social constraints for its occurrence; and (3) consider possible functions for its occurrence. The findings suggest that pinky extension is a phonological variable in ASL that is subject to social and linguistic constraints. The data further suggest that pinky extension functions as a prosodic feature of ASL.

Pinky extension (PE) is the extension of the fifth digit during a sign, contrary to the sign's citation form. Prior to this study, it had been observed that PE is characteristic of only certain signers (Lucas, personal communication, Spring 1995). Moreover, it had been observed that its occurrence in the speech of an individual signer seemed to be variable. For

This study was possible only because of invaluable help from Ms. Joyce Leary and patient guidance from Dr. Ceil Lucas. I would also like to thank Dr. Peter Patrick of Georgetown University for his insightful comments in reviewing the early drafts of this paper.

example, if a signer signs THINK several times during natural conversation, the pinky might be extended each time, some of the time, or not at all.

The purpose of this study has been to begin a systematic description of this phenomenon. The signing of one native ASL signer was examined in order to address questions such as: Does PE occur in free variation? If so, are there any constraints upon its occurrence that can be identified? If a pattern of occurrence can be discerned, does the pattern suggest any linguistic or sociolinguistic function of PE?

IMPORTANCE OF DESCRIBING PHONOLOGICAL STRUCTURE
AND VARIATION OF SIGNED LANGUAGES

The importance of describing the phonological structure and variation phenomena of signed languages cannot be overstated. Phonological and phonetic theoreticians commonly assert (or deny) that basic structural principles are grounded in properties of speech articulation and perception (Anderson 1981; Coulter 1993; Ohala and Kawasaki 1984). By examining languages whose articulatory and perceptual bases are visual rather than auditory, the phonological characteristics that are inherent attributes of the auditory modality are laid bare. Put differently, such studies provide independent confirmation of theories first developed purely on the basis of spoken language (Padden and Perlmutter 1987).

Of particular interest to this study is recent research concerning the prosodic structure of ASL. Surprisingly, these studies suggest that intonational patterns in signed language are comparable in many respects to the intonational patterns of spoken languages. It would seem that aspects of a language concerned with the modality of the signal (such as phonological structure) would be modality dependent, whereas structural aspects not closely related to the nature of the signal would likely be modality independent (Coulter 1993). Thus, one would expect that the prosodic structure of a language would be particularly likely to exhibit modality specificities. However, although the signal itself certainly exhibits modality specificities, abstract generalizations about the nature of prosodic structure are likely to be modality independent (Coulter 1993).

Research into the prosodic structure of ASL illustrates this point. For example, Grosjean (1979) demonstrated that phrase-final lengthening, universally found in spoken languages, is also found in ASL. Later Coulter (1993) demonstrated lengthening before phrase and sentence boundaries. He also demonstrated a hand-height contour in certain phrases (i.e., listing of numerals), which peaks at the position of the stressed sign. This is analogous to phrase-level accents in spoken languages that form the inflection points of phrase-level intonation patterns. Coulter (1990) presented evidence that, just as in spoken languages, the phonetic correlates of emphatic stress in ASL are predictable from the notion of greater articulatory effort. Finally, a number of researchers have suggested that ASL phonological segments are grouped into basic prosodic units analogous to syllables of spoken languages (Coulter 1992, 1990; Liddell 1984; Perlmutter 1993; Wilbur 1992).

A description of the phonology of ASL, including phonological variation, also informs our understanding of sociolinguistic phenomena. It has been demonstrated for spoken languages that minute phonological variations can have far-reaching social consequences, the variations being used by members of a linguistic community to mark group identity, group solidarity, and social distance and also to define the social environment (Fasold 1984). The question becomes whether this obtains in the Deaf community, which Padden and Humphries (1988) describe as a distinct cultural and linguistic group that coexists with American culture. They detail the striking differences of this community from the culture of hearing Americans due to their unique education, language, interaction with authority figures, and comparative lack of access to radio, TV, and English language print media. Thus one would expect phonological variations in the signing of members of this community to correlate with social factors.

Several researchers have examined this issue in signed languages. Zimmer (1989) and Roy (1989) both describe variation at all levels of ASL as a function of the formality of the social context. Others describe lexical variation related to ethnic background (Aramburo 1989; Woodward and De Santis 1977; and Woodward and Erting 1975). Further, Lucas and Valli (1992) describe in-depth morphological, lexical, and syntactic features that vary between ASL and a type of signing used by Deaf signers in particular situations known as "contact sign." (For a review of variation studies in ASL, see Lucas 1995.)

The full sociolinguistic consequences of PE are beyond the scope of this study. However, a description of this variable in individual signing styles, as well as suggestions of possible social constraints, are the first steps of such inquiry.

PROCEDURE

Subject

The subject for this study was a fifty-five-year-old Deaf woman whom I will refer to as Helen. Born in eastern Kentucky, Helen was deafened in infancy as the result of spinal meningitis. She was the only Deaf person of her immediate family.

Helen attended the Kentucky School for the Deaf (KSD) in Danville, Kentucky, for all of her primary and secondary education. Because of the distance of KSD from her home, she lived in the dormitory throughout her education at KSD. After graduation, she attended Gallaudet College for two years and then moved to the Midwest to marry a KSD classmate.

Helen's husband was a linotype operator, while Helen worked in a hospital cytology lab, viewing slides, for nearly twenty-four years. She and her husband had three daughters, all hearing. After approximately fifteen years of marriage, they divorced.

Helen has been a member of the local Deaf club for thirty-five years and has remained in close contact with many of her Deaf classmates from KSD as well.

Data Collection

Data collection consisted of videotaping Helen on four occasions. Three of the sessions lasted approximately two hours each. The fourth session lasted approximately one hour. During the first session, Helen was videotaped talking with a Deaf friend whom Helen has known since her high school days at KSD. During the second session, she was video-taped talking with a Deaf graduate student from Gallaudet University, a person whom Helen has seen occasionally during the past year. During the third session, she was again videotaped with her Deaf friend from KSD. And for the final session, she was videotaped with a hearing inter-preter who has been a good friend of hers for several years.

The sessions, videotaped in Helen's home, were purposely kept as un-structured as possible to encourage naturalistic signing. For the first three sessions, Helen and the other participant were asked to "just chat." No topics of discussion were prescribed. Only during the final session were topics suggested (which, incidentally, made no difference in the frequency of PE).

Analysis

One hundred occurrences of PE were culled from approximately seven hours of videotaped discourse. Each occurrence was analyzed for handshape, syntactic category, preceding and subsequent handshape, topic, and sentential context. A subset of occurrences was also timed according to number of frames. These were then averaged and compared with occurrences of the same lexemes without PE. Finally, to determine if occurrences were socially constrained by level of intimacy with the other signer, the frequency and diversity of occurrences during the first session (between Helen and her longtime friend) were compared to those during the second session (between Helen and a relatively recent acquaintance).

Several issues that arose during data analysis should be noted. First, it was observed that the pinky was often extended during fingerspelling, for example during all the letters in the fingerspelled words I-T and L-I-L-L-Y. However, the extension in this case appears to be the result of a process distinct from that of PE during lexemes. In particular, PE during fingerspelling occurs only when the fingerspelled words contain the letter *i*. As will be demonstrated, this is a constraint unrelated to PE during lexical signs. Moreover, the constraints identified for PE during lexemes are inapplicable to fingerspelling. Therefore, it was concluded that PE during fingerspelling is a separate phenomenon with separate constraints. Accordingly, all examples of fingerspelling were excluded from analysis.

Also excluded were instances of "lexicalized" PE. These include signs such as YESTERDAY and KID. The older forms of these signs did not specify extension of the pinky. However, PE for these signs may now have become lexicalized, with the result that PE may not vary within the signing of an individual, native ASL signer. For instance, signers consistently sign YESTERDAY either with or without extension.

Finally, clear examples of phonological assimilation were also excluded. In these instances, it was observed that the extension of the pinky occurred (or spread) gradually over only certain segments of the target sign. For example, in the sentence THINK ABOUT I-T, the pinky began to be extended after the initial formation of the sign ABOUT and then continued into the following sign "I." This was in sharp contrast to the

100 examples of PE where the extension of the pinky attached to all segments of the target sign and acted in concert with the specified fingers of the sign.

FINDINGS AND DISCUSSION

As indicated, each occurrence of PE was analyzed for handshape, preceding and subsequent handshape, sign, syntactic category, topic, sentential context, and formality. In addition, a subset of occurrences was analyzed for duration as measured by frames. We will discuss the findings for each of these factors, beginning with those that appear to have no relationship to the occurrence of PE and concluding with those that do.

Factors with No Relationship to Pinky Extension

PRECEDING AND SUBSEQUENT HANDSHAPE

At the outset of this study, it was expected that if the handshape of the sign immediately preceding or following the target sign included an extended pinky (either as specified by the citation form or as a result of PE), then PE on the target sign would be more likely. However, the findings indicate that preceding and subsequent finger configurations have no effect upon the occurrence of PE in the target sign.

As Table 1 illustrates, 95 percent of the occurrences of PE follow signs in which the pinky is not extended. Moreover, 97 percent of the occurrences of PE precede signs in which the pinky is not extended.

Thus, in most instances, PE occurred despite the fact that the pinky was not extended during either the preceding or the subsequent sign. The converse is also true (i.e., although the pinky may be extended during the preceding or subsequent sign, the target sign is often formed without PE). For instance, in one sentence, the sign WONDER occurred immediately after the sign WAIT. Both of these signs can exhibit PE, as indicated by other examples in the data. However, in this instance, PE occurred only during the sign WAIT. The following sign, WONDER, was signed in its citation form. The sentential context in which this occurred was as follows:

```
                t
```
TEACHER: REALLY FIRST WAIT (w/PE). WONDER (w/o PE). LONG BOY PUT-THERE (continuative aspect).

TABLE 1. *Phonological Assimilation Analysis*

Context	Number of Occurrences	Percentage
Pinky extended in preceding handshape	5	5
Pinky not extended in preceding handshape	95	95
Pinky extended in subsequent handshape	3	3
Pinky not extended in subsequent handshape	97	97

"The teacher, at first he waited. Then he started wondering. He thought that boy has been putting things there for a long time."

Thus, hand configurations of the preceding and subsequent signs appear to have no influence upon the occurrence of PE on the target sign. It is worth noting again the distinction between PE as observed in my data and instances of phonological assimilation of the pinky between contiguous signs (which were excluded from this study). In contrast to PE in which the extension continues throughout the sign, the extension of the pinky in instances of assimilation is a gradual opening (in the case of regressive assimilation) or closing (in the case of progressive assimilation) during only a portion of the target sign.

SIGN

As Table 2 shows, PE occurred in twenty-six lexemes. It is impossible to determine in this preliminary study whether PE is subject to lexical constraints (other than syntactic category, which will be discussed later). More examples are needed and from more than one signer to determine if extension occurs only for a closed set of lexemes (i.e., whether PE can occur on any lexeme as long as linguistic and social constraints are satisfied).

TOPIC

The topic of conversation seems to have no effect upon the occurrence of PE. This was indicated by the frequent occurrence of a single lexeme being signed with *and* without PE within the discussion of a single topic. For example, when comparing the use of facial expression by Deaf individuals who grew up in residential schools with those used by Deaf individuals who grew up in oral schools, Helen used the sign FACIAL-EXPRESS seven times. Three times she extended the pinky; four times she did not. Here are two examples from that discussion signed *without* PE:

TABLE 2. *Occurrence of PE in Twenty-Six Lexemes*

Lexeme	Number of Occurrences
1ASK3	1
CL-FEET-WALKING	3
CONTINUE	21
CRY	1
DOLL	1
EXPRESS	4
GO	2
GO-AROUND	1
LAZY	1
LIE	1
LIMIT	1
MOVE	1
MULL-OVER	2
NOTICE	1
NOT-GUILTY	7
NUDGE	1
SMILE	1
SUCKER	1
SWALLOW	1
THINK	10
TIME-GO-ON	1
TOLERATE	3
3TOLD1	1
VARIOUS	9
WAIT	3
WONDER	21
TOTAL	100

WHO DEAF GREW-UP RIGHT, **FACIAL-EXPRESS** APPROPRIATE.

"Deaf individuals who grew-up in the Deaf community use appropriate facial expression when they sign."

NOW SEE ORAL PRO-3 [pause]. THINK EXAGGERATED **FACIAL-EXPRESS**

"Now I see Deaf people who grew up oral. I think their facial expression is too exaggerated when they sign."

Here are two examples from the same discussion *with* PE:

KNOW THAT MAN **FACIAL-EXPRESS** TOO-MUCH?

"You know that man who uses too much facial expression?"

I THINK TOO-MUCH. FACIAL-EXPRESSION [signed with exaggeration and scowl]. NEED LESS.

"I think it is too much. His facial expression is too exaggerated. He needs to use less."

These examples and others in the data also illustrate that PE is not related to "feminine" topics, as is commonly thought. Frequency of PE did not increase when the conversational topics were "feminine" (e.g., cooking, or babies).

Factors That Constrain Pinky Extension

My findings suggest that handshape, syntactic category, and duration are linguistic constraints upon PE. Level of intimacy between signers appears to be a social constraint.

HANDSHAPE
Prior to collecting data, I compiled a list of handshapes for which PE was physically possible. These were based in part on the taxonomy of ASL hand configurations identified by Liddell and Johnson (1984). The handshapes identified were A, S, 1, H, V, K, D, R, T, N, M, E, L, O, and X. During data analysis, I also noticed several "bent" handshapes (e.g., LIMIT) that I had not identified. It had not occurred to me that a bent hand configuration would provide enough visual contrast to make PE possible. The following rounded and bent configurations were then added as physically possible hand configurations: C, bent B (e.g., HOUSE), bent 1 (e.g., VARIOUS).

Pinky extension actually occurred with far fewer hand configurations than those identified as physically possible. Table 3 sets forth the handshapes for which PE *actually* occurred and the number of occurrences for each. These findings suggest at least three phonological constraints. First, PE cannot occur with hand configurations in which the middle finger is extended (e.g., CL: VEHICLE or SEE). However, if all the fingers are extended but bent (e.g., WAIT or NUDGE), PE may occur.

Second, if the fingers are closed, and the pinky is not extended in the underlying lexical sign, then PE cannot occur if the thumb is also in a closed position. For example, it does not seem to occur on S handshapes (e.g., SAVE) or T handshapes (e.g., TRY). Rather, PE can occur with the fingers in a closed position only if the thumb is extended and away from

TABLE 3. *Occurrences of PE by Handshape*

Hand Configuration	Number of Occurrences
A	24
bent B	13
bent B th. ext.	6
L	1
flat O	1
1	31
bent 1	12
bent 5	3
X	9

the hand (e.g., CONTINUE, LAZY) or extended and touching the hand (e.g., TOLERATE). I would suggest that this constraint may be necessary to prevent merging with the handshape I.

Finally, there were no occurrences of PE with rounded handshapes such as O or C. The flat O configuration of MOVE, however, did permit extension. Thus it appears that, if the fingers are all specified for a non-closed position, the fingers must be in a bent or flattened position to permit PE. PE cannot occur if the fingers are specified for either fully extended (e.g., PROVE) or rounded positions (e.g. BE-WIDE-AWAKE).

SYNTACTIC CATEGORY

The data suggest that syntactic category is also a constraint. Table 4 shows the occurrences of PE by syntactic category. As Table 4 indicates, of the 100 occurrences of PE, 99 occurred with verbs. Clearly, this suggests that syntactic category is a constraint or, at the very least, another process is at work causing PE to co-occur with verbs.

It should be noted that signs such as LAZY, SUCKER, and NOT-GUILTY were classified as verbs. In ASL these lexemes can act as adjectival and nominal predicates. Two examples from the data illustrate this usage:

PRO-3 LAZY PRO-3.
"He is lazy."
PRO-1 SUCKER. PAY FULL S-E-A-S-O-N
"I am a sucker. I paid for a full season."

When the sign VARIOUS occurred with PE, it was also used as a predicate. Specifically, it occurred at the end of a listing of verbal predicates

TABLE 4. *Occurrences of PE by Syntactic Category*

Syntactic Category	Number of Lexemes	Number of Occurrences
Noun	1	1
Verb	99	25
Plain verb	76	17
Indicating verb	2	2
Classifier predicate	3	1
Adverbial predicate	18	5
Other (adj., adv., prep., special)	0	0
TOTAL	100	26

in place of a complete predicate. For example, it occurred in the following sentence:

STUDENT INVOLVE WITH SIGN. SIGN-SONG, SIGN-CHOIR, VARIOUS.
"The student was involved with sign language. He would sign songs, sign choir songs, and sign various things."

Thus, the occurrences of VARIOUS were also considered verbal units. The only occurrence of PE with a lexeme other than a verb was during the sign DOLL. The sentence in which this occurred was:

DONT-WANT GIVE MY KIDS THAT KIND DOLL

Clearly DOLL acts as a noun in this context. Because there was only one occurrence of this sign in the data, I cannot determine whether Helen always signs DOLL with pinky extension. I suspect that PE for DOLL has become lexicalized for this signer so that it is always signed with PE. If so, it would be similar to YESTERDAY and KID, where PE has become lexicalized. These cases are not really instances of the PE variation process observed in the data whereby there is variation in PE if the requisite constraints are satisfied.

LEVEL OF INTIMACY

The level of intimacy also seemed to play a role in the occurrence of PE. When Helen signed with her longtime friend, PE began occurring in Helen's first extended turn. When Helen signed with the graduate student with whom she was only superficially acquainted, the first occurrence of PE was not until 20 minutes after the beginning of the conversation. The overall frequency of PE with the friend was higher than with the acquaintance (i.e., 29 tokens in 29 bar-code increments as opposed to 26 tokens in 37 bar-code increments). The lexemes with which PE occurred were also more diverse with the friend than with the acquaintance.

Factors Indicating Prosodic Function

Three other factors — duration, pauses, and word repetitions — were also examined. All three seem to be related to PE. Thus one might conclude that these are also constraints upon PE. However, I would suggest that a more productive way to view these factors is as prosodic features of ASL indicating stress. Further, I suggest that PE *is also* a prosodic feature indicating stress that co-occurs with other prosodic features indicating stress if linguistic and social constraints are satisfied. In other words, it is more likely that the prosodic structure of ASL results in the co-occurence of PE with these features, rather than one being constrained by the other.

DURATION

When the duration of signs with PE was compared with the duration of the same signs without PE, the difference was striking. For example, the average duration of the sign WONDER with PE was 20.5 frames. The average duration of the sign WONDER without PE was 9.3 frames.

When the duration of several signs with PE was averaged, the average length was 17.9 frames. The average of the same signs without PE was 9 frames. The breakdown of these averages is set forth in Table 5.

PAUSES

PE most often occurred immediately before a pause. During a pause, the hands were held motionless for a short time or were returned to the rest position. Often, but not always, these pauses occurred at the end of the sentence. The following are a few examples:

WHAT D-O WHAT. [Pause]. WONDER. [Pause]. GET-UP.
"What should I do? I wondered about it. Then I got up."
EAT. SWALLOW [pause]. BLACK DROOL. [Shivers and scowls].
"He put it in his mouth. And he swallowed it. Then drooled black drool. Yuck!"

As mentioned, Coulter (1993) demonstrated that ASL exhibits lengthening before phrase and sentence boundaries. I suggest that PE can co-

TABLE 5. *Duration of Signs with and without PE*

Lexeme	Number of Frames	
	With Extension	Without Extension
WONDER	21	9
	17	13
	25	9
	18	11
Total for WONDER	82/4	56/61
Average frames for WONDER	20.5	9.3
VARIOUS	9	9
	12	—
THINK	—	5
		6
CRY	14	14
CONTINUE	17	—
LIMIT	25	—
SMILE	19	—
Total for all lexemes	178/10	90/10
Average frames for lexemes	17.9	9

occur with phrase final lengthening, the greater articulatory effort signaling a kind of discourse focus or stress.

REPETITION

Finally, PE often occurred with a verb that was repeated several times within a single topic. Such repetition suggests that the activity denoted by the verb was a primary focus of the signer's discourse and that PE acts as a marker of this focus.

SUMMARY AND CONCLUSIONS

PE did in fact vary in the signing of the native signer studied. This variation appears to be subject to linguistic and social constraints. The linguistic constraints that seem to influence the occurrence of PE include phonological constraints (handshape) and syntactic constraints (syntactic category). This study also provides a list of lexemes that accept PE but does not draw any conclusions regarding lexical constraints.

PE seems to respond to at least one social constraint. When the level of intimacy was low, PE occurred the least. As intimacy increased, the frequency of PE increased.

An equally important finding of this study was the factors that appear to have no influence upon the occurrence of PE. Topic seems to play no role. Nor does preceding or subsequent handshape seem to have an effect. This is contrary to my initial hypothesis that assimilation would account for much or all of PE.

Perhaps the most intriguing finding is the tendency of PE to co-occur with prosodic features of ASL that indicate a kind of stress. The data show that PE tended to occur (1) with lexemes often repeated throughout a topic; (2) before pauses; and (3) with lexemes lengthened to almost twice their usual duration. This is evidence that PE itself is a prosodic feature of ASL that indicates a type of emphatic stress or focus. Although in the visual modality, an extended pinky in sign language to indicate stress is analogous to stress in spoken languages indicated by a stronger signal as a result of greater articulatory effort.

Finally, it should be noted that the findings here are of a single study of a single native signer. These findings are presented as suggested starting points for a more in-depth study utilizing more tokens and more subjects.

REFERENCES

Anderson, S. R. 1980. Problems and perspectives in the description of vowel harmony. In *Issues in vowel harmony,* ed. R. Vago, 1–48. Amsterdam: Benjamin Publishers.

Aramburo, A. 1989. Sociolinguistic aspects of the black Deaf community. In *The sociolinguistics of the Deaf community,* ed. C. Lucas, 103–22. San Diego: Academic Press.

Coulter, G. 1990. Emphatic stress in ASL. In *Theoretical issues in sign language research,* vol. 1, *Linguistics,* ed. S. Fischer and P. Siple, 109–25. Chicago: University of Chicago Press.

———. 1993. Phrase level prosody in ASL: Final lengthening and phrasal contours. In *Phonetics and phonology: Current issues in ASL phonology,* vol. 3, ed. G. Coulter, pp. 263–72. San Diego: Academic Press.

Fasold, R. 1984. *The sociolinguistics of society.* Cambridge, Mass.: Blackwell Publishers.

Grosjean, F. 1979. A study of timing in a manual and a spoken language: American Sign Language and English. *Journal of Psycholinguistic Research* 8(4):379–405.

Labov, W. 1972. *Language in the inner city*. Philadelphia: University of Pennsylvania Press.

Liddell, S. 1984. THINK and BELIEVE: Sequentiality in American Sign Language. *Language* 60(2):372–99.

Lucas, C. 1995. Sociolinguistic variation in ASL: The case of DEAF. In *Sociolinguistics in Deaf communities*, vol. 1, ed. Ceil Lucas, 3–25. Washington, D.C.: Gallaudet University Press.

Lucas, C., and C. Valli. 1992. *Language contact in the American Deaf community*. San Diego: Academic Press.

Milroy, J. 1992. *Linguistic variation and change*. Oxford, UK: Blackwell Publishers.

Ohala, J., and H. Kawasaki. 1984. Prosodic phonology and phonetics. *Phonology Yearbook*, 113–27.

Padden, C., and T. Humphries. 1988. *Deaf in America: Voices from a culture*. Cambridge: Harvard University Press.

Padden, C., and D. Perlmutter. 1987. American sign language and the architecture of phonological theory. *Natural Language and Linguistic Theory* 5:335–75.

Perlmutter, D. 1993. Sonority and syllable structure in American Sign Language. In *Phonetics and phonology: Current issues in ASL phonology*, vol. 3, ed. G. Coulter, 227–61. San Diego: Academic Press.

Roy, C. B. 1989. Features of discourse in an American Sign Language lecture. In *The sociolinguistics of the Deaf community*, ed. Ceil Lucas, 231–51. San Diego: Academic Press.

Sankoff, D. 1978. *Linguistic variation: Models and methods*. New York: Academic Press.

Schiffrin, D. 1994. *Approaches to discourse*. Oxford, UK: Blackwell Publishers.

Wilbur, R. 1992. Why syllables? In *Theoretical issues in sign language research*, vol. 1, *Linguistics*, ed. S. Fischer and P. Siple, 81–108. Chicago: University of Chicago Press.

Wolfram, W. 1993. Identifying and interpreting variables. In *American dialect research*, ed. D. Preston, 193–221. Philadelphia: John Benjamins.

Woodward, J. C., and S. DeSantis. 1977. Two to one it happens: Dynamic phonology in two sign languages. *Sign Language Studies* 17:329–46.

Woodward, J., and C. Erting. 1975. Synchronic variation and historical change in American Sign Language. *Language Science* 37:9–12.

Zimmer, J. 1989. Toward a description of register variation in American Sign Language. In *The sociolinguistics of the Deaf community*, ed. Ceil Lucas, 253–72. San Diego: Academic Press.

What Happens in Tactile ASL?

Steven Collins and Karen Petronio

In American Sign Language (ASL), the receiver watches the signer and receives the communication through a visual mode. However, many Deaf-Blind people use ASL even though they are unable to see the signer. Instead, these Deaf-Blind people put one hand on top of the signer's hand and receive ASL tactilely. What happens when a language that was designed for a visual mode is used in a tactile mode?

This question is of interest for two reasons. The first reason, which is the focus of this study, concerns the sociolinguistic changes ASL undergoes as it is adapted to a tactile mode. In the past 30 years, many studies have focused on ASL phonology, morphology, syntax, and discourse. These studies were done on visual ASL; few studies have been done on tactile ASL. The study of ASL in tactile mode is of sociolinguistic interest because it describes a variety of ASL, that is, the language used by a very particular and clearly defined community of users. It is a variety shaped largely by the characteristics of its users and therefore is not only linguistic but also sociolinguistic. The second reason concerns the needs of interpreters who interpret for Deaf-Blind ASL users. Knowledge gained by studying the tactile signing of skilled Deaf-Blind ASL users will contribute to the improvement of Deaf-Blind interpreting services.

What linguistic changes, if any, occur when ASL is used in a tactile mode? To answer this question, skilled Deaf-Blind ASL users[1] were videotaped as they conversed tactilely with other skilled Deaf-Blind ASL users. Specific linguistic features were selected and studied. Previous studies on these features in visual ASL were compared and contrasted with what occurred in tactile ASL. The selected features from different linguistic areas and the questions addressed are as follows:

1. We would like to thank all the Deaf-Blind people who were involved in and made this research possible. We also thank the two anonymous reviewers for their helpful comments and suggestions.

In this paper we follow the usage of the AADB and of other organizations of the convention Deaf-Blind.

- Phonology: Signs can be broken into smaller parts (Battison 1978; Liddell and Johnson 1989; Stokoe et al. 1965; and others). The basic parameters include handshape, movement, location, and orientation. In tactile ASL, the receiver's hand is placed on the signer's hand. Does this result in any changes in these four parameters?
- Morphology: Many adjectives and adverbs are composed of nonmanual facial configurations in visual ASL (Liddell 1980; Padden 1988). In tactile ASL, the Deaf-Blind receiver is unable to see these nonmanual adverbs and adjectives. How are these nonmanual morphemes conveyed in tactile ASL?
- Syntax: Questions can occur with a variety of different word orders in visual ASL (Humphries, Padden, O'Rourke 1980; Petronio and Lillo-Martin 1997). What word orders occur in questions in tactile ASL?
- Discourse: In visual ASL, a receiver gives back-channel feedback to the signer by using head nods, head tilts, and different facial configurations. This information is inaccessible to Deaf-Blind signers. What type of back-channel feedback is used in tactile ASL?

DATA

The data came from videotapes of two different situations involving fourteen Deaf-Blind adults. One set of data came from videotapes made during an informal social event that took place in Seattle, Washington. This event included eleven Deaf-Blind adults who knew and regularly socialized with each other. An 8mm camcorder with zoom capacities was used to videotape different tactile ASL conversations during the 4-hour event.

The second set of data was from videotapes made by one of the authors from an earlier study in Washington, D.C. These videotapes included three Deaf-Blind adults using tactile ASL to tell stories to each other. In contrast to the informal setting described above, this was a more formal testing situation. These videotapes were recorded on two VHS cameras, each shooting from a different angle.

When receiving ASL tactilely, a Deaf-Blind receiver can use one or two hands. With one-handed tactile ASL reception, the receiver puts a hand on the top of the signer's dominant hand; with two-hand reception, the receiver puts one hand on top of the signer's dominant hand and the other hand on top of the signer's nondominant hand.[2] Most of the tactile conversations in the videotaped data involved the receiver using one-handed tactile reception. It is possible that receiving tactile ASL with either one or two hands could affect the way a person signed. In order to avoid this confounding factor, the data examined were limited to the signing of Deaf-Blind signers who were communicating with Deaf-Blind receivers using one-handed tactile reception.

PARTICIPANTS

The fourteen Deaf-Blind adults involved in this study all had Ushers Syndrome 1. Ushers Syndrome 1 is a genetic condition in which individuals are born deaf and later, usually in their teen years, start losing vision in varying degrees due to retinitis pigmentosa.[3] Although all fourteen participants are classified as legally blind, they varied with regard to how much they could see. For example, six people did not have enough remaining vision to see ASL; they always received ASL tactilely. The other eight informants had enough remaining vision that, under the right conditions (e.g., lighting and distance), they used visual ASL as their primary receptive mode. However, when the lighting and/or distance was not adequate, these eight Deaf-Blind adults would switch to tactile ASL. The following characteristics were shared by the fourteen adults:

- all had Ushers Syndrome 1;
- all used ASL (tactile or visual) as their primary means of communication;
- all knew and used ASL before becoming legally blind;
- all regularly socialized with Deaf-Blind adults who used tactile ASL; and

2. If a signer is right-handed, the right hand is usually the dominant hand. Conversely, if the signer is left-handed, the left hand is usually the dominant hand.

3. Retinitis pigmentosa is a hereditary degenerative disease of the retina, characterized by night blindness, pigmentary changes within the retina, a narrowing of the visual field, and eventual loss of vision (*American Heritage College Dictionary* 1993).

- all were comfortable with and experienced at signing tactilely with other Deaf-Blind adults.

Although all the participants shared the preceding traits, they varied in other characteristics. For example, ten of the participants had attended residential schools for deaf children. The other four attended special classes for deaf children in public schools. Three participants had a master's degree, several had an associate of arts degree, and others had a high school diploma. The ages of the fourteen participants ranged from 28 to 48 years. Six of the participants were women, and eight were men. At the time of the taping, twelve people were working, one was a full-time student, and one was looking for a job.

It is important to note that all the participants were skilled at expressing themselves using tactile ASL. That is, this is a study of the characteristics of tactile ASL as used by skilled Deaf-Blind ASL users when communicating with other skilled Deaf-Blind ASL users.

FINDINGS

The findings are presented in the next four sections. The first section discusses phonology and is followed by sections on morphology, syntax, and discourse.

Phonology

This section presents findings on differences and similarities of the phonological form of signs used in visual and tactile ASL. Signs were examined in terms of their handshape, location, movement, and orientation.[4]

Early studies on visual ASL sought minimal pairs to determine the distinctive parts of signs. Minimal pairs were interpreted as providing evidence for three parameters: handshape, movement, and location. For instance, the signs DONKEY and HORSE use the same location and movement but differ in handshape; MOTHER and FATHER use the same handshape and movement but differ in location; and SICK and TO-BECOME-SICK use the same handshape and location but differ in movement. Battison (1978) later identified a fourth parameter, orientation, based on pairs

4. Although nonmanuals are considered another parameter of a sign, this parameter was not focused on in this section.

such as CHILDREN and THINGS. These two signs have identical handshape, movement, and location; they differ, however, in palm orientation: The palm of the hand faces upward for THINGS but toward the floor for CHILDREN.

Signs in the tactile ASL data were examined for these four parameters to determine whether a sign exhibited any phonological differences when used in visual ASL.

HANDSHAPE

Throughout the tactile ASL data, signs had the same handshape as in visual ASL. The same handshapes were used despite the fact that those of a few signs were difficult for Deaf-Blind receivers to recognize tactilely. These included the signs for SIX, SEVEN, EIGHT, and NINE. In these signs the tip of the index, middle, ring finger, or pinkie contacted the tip of the thumb—all handshapes that are difficult to perceive when one's hand is on top of the signer's hand. Skilled Deaf-Blind ASL signers tended to hold these signs a fraction of a second longer for the receiver; however, the actual handshapes were not altered.

LOCATION

Signs in ASL can be categorized by location. One category includes signs that do not contact the signer's body; another includes signs that do contact the signer's body, including the head and arms. Findings for these two categories are presented separately.

Signs without Body Contact

The signing space for visual ASL is described as a circular area in front of the signer's body (Frishberg and Gough 1973; Klima and Bellugi 1979). The top of the circle is slightly higher than the signer's head, the bottom is about at waist level, and the sides are approximately the width of the signer's elbows when the arms are extended sideways. Signs that do not contact the signer's body are located within this area. Information about a sign's location includes specification about the sign's height (e.g., chest or chin level) and the distance from the body (e.g., a few inches from the body or farther away).

Under certain conditions, the signing space (the circle) can shift in visual ASL. For instance, if a signer is standing in the street and signing to someone who is looking out a second-floor window, the circle shifts upward. When the signing space shifts, the location of signs shifts in relation to the signer's body. For example, the citation form of NOW is located about lower chest level. When the signing space shifts upward as the signer communicates with someone on the second floor, the location of NOW shifts upward to about chin level from the normal chest level.

The size of the circle can also be reduced or enlarged in visual ASL. If two people want to have a private conversation and "whisper," they will greatly reduce their signing space. If a person signs to someone very far away, the signing space will be noticeably increased.

Upon first looking at tactile ASL signs that did not contact the body, many signs appeared to be articulated in locations that differed from those of the corresponding signs in visual ASL. However, closer inspection showed that the apparent differences were the result of shifting and size changes of the signing circle. This was similar to the shifting and size changes that can occur in visual ASL; however, the shifting and size changes occurred more frequently and for different reasons in tactile ASL. In tactile ASL, the shifting and size changes of the signing space were influenced by the positions of the Deaf-Blind signer and receiver. The data contained many examples of tactile conversations with the signer and receiver in different positions. Varying positions included the following: both standing face-to-face; both sitting side-by-side; the signer sitting and the receiver standing, or vice versa; and in some cases the signer and receiver leaning across a table or another person as they communicated tactilely. The signing space, the circle, in effect, shifted to the area where the signer's and receiver's hands came into contact. In cases where both the signer and receiver were standing face-to-face and both were about the same height, the signing space used for tactile ASL was often the same space used for the signs in visual ASL. When the signer and receiver were in other positions, however, the signing space shifted to the area where the signer's and receiver's hands touched. Table 1 shows some location shifts that occurred with the sign NOW. As illustrated in Table 1, the positions of both the signer and receiver influenced the location of the sign NOW.

In tactile ASL, because the receiver's hand is on top of the signer's hand, the signer and the receiver are generally closer to each other than they are in visual ASL. Because of this closeness, the signing space for tactile ASL is usually smaller than that for visual ASL. This affects the locations of signs articulated near the outer edges of the signing space in visual ASL; because of the smaller signing space, these signs are articulated within a smaller space in tactile ASL.

TABLE 1. *Variation with Location of* NOW

Sign	Positions	Location
NOW	Signer and receiver stand facing each other; both are about the same height	Signer's lower chest level
NOW	Signer standing, receiver sitting	Signer's waist level
NOW	Signer sitting, receiver standing	Signer's nose level
NOW	Signer and receiver sitting across a table; both are leaning forward with arms almost fully extended; hands are in contact over the table	Signer's shoulder height, about 25 inches in front of body

Signs with Body Contact

Many signs in ASL are articulated at a specific location on the signer's body. For instance, DISAPPOINT is located in the center of the signer's chin, THINK is located on the side of the signer's forehead, and NEAT is located on the signer's lower cheek. In visual ASL, the signer's head tends to remain in an upright neutral position while the signer's hand rises and contacts the head.

The tactile ASL data contained many examples of signs involving contact with the signer's body. Although contact was maintained, an interesting adaptation often occurred. Instead of just the signer's hand moving to contact the required body part, the body part also moved toward the signer's hand. For instance, in the sign EAT, the signer's head leaned forward as the hand rose to contact the mouth; thus, the receiver's hand did not have to reach so far. By moving the body part toward the signing hand, the Deaf-Blind signer made it more comfortable and/or possible for the Deaf-Blind receiver to maintain contact with the signer's hand. In one occurrence, two people were leaning across a table. Both had their arms almost completely outstretched; their hands touched over the table. The signer signed NEAT, a sign located on the lower cheek. As NEAT was signed, the signer leaned forward and shortened the distance the hand had to move to contact the lower cheek. Because of the shortened distance, the receiver was able to remain connected with the signer's hand. If the signer's head had remained in the neutral position, the receiver could not have maintained contact.

In particular, this adaptation occurred when the two signers were at different heights or when they were not positioned close to one another. Table 2 illustrates other examples where the body part moved toward the signer's hand.

TABLE 2. *Variation with Signs That Contacted the Body*

Sign	Citation Form	Positions	Variation
Name-sign "D"	Contact with inside of left elbow; left arm stays at side	Signer sitting; receiver standing	Signer's left arm rises to shoulder height to meet signer's hand
FOOD	Contact with mouth; signer's head remains upright	Signer standing; receiver sitting	Signer's head leans forward to meet the upward-moving hand
CL:CC "Stuff food into the mouth"	Contact with mouth; signer's head remains upright	Both signer and receiver are sitting face-to-face	Signer's head leans forward to meet the upward-moving hands

MOVEMENT

Movement in ASL signs is quite complex. Many signs are distinguished from each other only by subtle differences in movement (Supalla and Newport 1978). Liddell and Johnson (1989) distinguish several movement contours (e.g., straight, arc, circle) and secondary local movements (e.g., wiggling, flattening, hooking). In addition, the degree of muscle tension during the articulation of the movement can affect a sign's meaning.

In comparing the phonological forms of signs in tactile ASL and visual ASL, we investigated the same movement contours, secondary movements, and muscle tension. In general, the size of the movement path in tactile ASL was generally shorter than in visual ASL. As we discussed earlier, the signing space in tactile ASL is often smaller than that in visual ASL because the Deaf-Blind receiver and the signer are physically closer to each other. This smaller signing space resulted in shorter movement paths than what typically occurs in visual ASL.

ORIENTATION

More variation took place in the orientation parameter of tactile ASL than usually occurs in visual ASL. In visual ASL, under certain conditions, phonological assimilation can cause a sign's orientation to assimilate to the orientation of the preceding and/or following sign (Liddell and Johnson 1986). For example, in citation form, CAN has a downward palm orientation. However, in one visual ASL story, CAN occurred between the signs BIG and PLAY and had a sideways orientation. Both BIG and PLAY had a sideways orientation; the orientation of CAN clearly assimilated to the orientation of its environment.

In addition to displaying the same kind of phonological assimilation that occurs in visual ASL, tactile ASL also showed orientation variation that resulted from the receiver's hand being placed on top of the signer's hand. For example, one Deaf-Blind signer used the classifier sign with the V handshape when talking about a person who was walking straight down a hallway, turned left, and then continued walking. In visual ASL, the tips of the fingers typically face downward throughout this whole sequence. In tactile ASL, the fingertips faced downward when the person was walking straight ahead, but after making the left turn, the fingertips were parallel to the floor and remained in that orientation for the remainder of the sequence. This variation, from a downward to a sideways orientation, appears to result from the receiver's hand being placed on the top of the signer's hand. If the signer had maintained the fingertip-downward orientation, the receiver's wrist would have had to twist awkwardly. To accommodate the receiver, the signer modified the sign's orientation. A similar modification occurred with the sign WAIT. In visual ASL, WAIT is signed with the palms angled upward. In tactile ASL, it was often signed with the palms facing the body, a more comfortable orientation for the tactile receiver.

In other instances, variation occurred in the orientation parameter that may result from a combination of the receiver's hand being placed on the signer's hand and normal phonological assimilation processes. An example of this occurred with the sign NOW, a sign with an upward palm orientation in citation form. Throughout the tactile data, there were many instances of NOW with the regular upward palm orientation. However, in one instance two Deaf-Blind people were sitting next to each other at a dinner table when the sign NOW occurred with a downward orientation. One of the dinner partners informed the other that the appetizers had just arrived at the table by signing.

(1) A-P-P-E-T-I-Z-E-R NOW INDEX-arc
"The appetizers are here now."

NOW had a downward orientation in (1). It is unlikely that this orientation change was due solely to the receiver's hand resting on the signer's hand because of the numerous other tactile examples of NOW having the regular upward orientation. In (1), the orientation of the signs preceding and following NOW ("R" and INDEX) had a palm-downward orientation; the downward orientation of NOW may have been due to phonological assimilation to the preceding and following signs. However, in visual ASL, as far as we are aware, NOW does not occur with a downward orientation, even in sentences like (1). Thus, the change to a downward orientation of NOW in (1) seems to be due to neither phonological assimilation nor the receiver's hand's position atop the signer's hand alone; it appears instead to be due to a combination of the two.

In summary, the following variations occurred for the orientation parameter:

- orientation variation due to regular phonological assimilation,
- orientation variation due to placement of the receiver's hand atop the signer's hand, and
- variation resulting from a combination of the preceding.

Morphology: Nonmanual Adjectives and Adverbs

Visual ASL has numerous adjectival and adverbial morphemes that consist of nonmanual configurations of the lower part of the face (Baker 1976; Baker and Padden 1978; Liddell 1980; Padden 1988). Some examples of nonmanual adverbs are listed in Table 3. When nonmanual adverbs or adjectives co-occur with a manual sign, their meaning combines with the sign's meaning. For instance, if the nonmanual adverb referred to as "mm" co-occurs with the verb DRIVE, the combination means "to drive in a casual manner," but if the nonmanual "ee" co-occurs with DRIVE, the meaning becomes "to drive in a very intense manner" ("ee" has clenched teeth with open lips).[5] In visual ASL, sighted receivers are able to see this nonmanual information.

Deaf-Blind receivers, on the other hand, are unable to see the configuration on the signer's face. To determine what happens to these nonmanual morphemes in ASL, the data were first examined for all instances of lower-face, nonmanual configurations. Several examples were found. For instance, when a Deaf-Blind signer articulated a classifier sign for describing something long and narrow,[6] she simultaneously used the non-

5. See Baker and Cokely (1980) pages 20–21 for illustration of the morpheme "ee." They called it "intense."

6. The classifier sign used two hands, each with an open 8 handshape. The hands started near the signer's body and moved straight outward.

TABLE 3. *Examples of Nonmanual Adverbs*

Symbol	Physical Properties	Function
"mm"	Lips together and pushed out without puckering; slight head tilt	Adverb
"cs"	Shoulder raised, head turned to side; special facial expression	Adverb
"th"	Lips apart and pushed out; tongue protruding	Adverb

Source: Liddell 1980, 189.

manual "oo" (i.e., rounded lips). The combination of the manual sign and the nonmanual configuration results in the meaning "something very long and very narrow."

How was the Deaf-Blind receiver, who was unable to see the nonmanual configuration, receiving the adverbial information? Closer examination of the signs co-occurring with these nonmanual morphemes revealed subtle difference in the sign's articulation. For example, when the classifier sign co-occurred with "oo," the sign was articulated more slowly and with more muscle tension than would typically occur in its citation form. This phenomenon is further illustrated in differences in DRIVE when it co-occurs with "ee" or "mm." When DRIVE occurred with "ee," the movement of the sign became quicker and more tense. In contrast, when "mm" co-occurred with DRIVE, the movement of the sign became slower, and the muscle tension was lax.

Another example occurred when a Deaf-Blind signer used the lower-face configuration associated with the nonmanual adjective "cha" while using a classifier sign CL:CC to represent "a big blob of peanut butter" ("cha" involves a quick opening of the mouth).[7] In addition to using the nonmanual configuration, there were also changes to the classifier sign: The sign started with a lax movement and ended with a very quick, tense, abrupt stop that caused a fast bounce. In other words, these nonmanual morphemes also involved a manual component that was imposed on the manual sign and caused changes in muscle tension and movement. Deaf-Blind receivers, although unable to see the nonmanual facial configuration, received the adverbial or adjectival information by tactilely perceiving the muscle tension and movement patterns that affected the manual sign.

7. See Baker and Cokely (1980) page 25 for illustration of "cha."

Previous research on visual ASL does not mention corresponding muscle and movement patterns that occur when nonmanual adjectives and adverbs were used. Do these changes occur only in tactile ASL, or do they also occur in visual ASL? Informal observations of ASL discourses showed that the muscle tension and movement patterns noted in the tactile ASL data also occurred when these nonmanual morphemes were used in visual ASL.

This leads to another question. If a Deaf-Blind receiver is able to tactilely perceive the "mm," "cha," "oo," and "ee" morphemes from corresponding muscle and movement patterns, are there instances where the Deaf-Blind signer will eliminate the facial configuration and use only the muscle tension and movement component? The data were reexamined for instances in which the muscle and movement patterns associated with "mm," "cha," "oo," and "ee" occurred without the corresponding nonmanual facial configuration. It was found that in tactile ASL, the signer more commonly eliminated the associated facial configuration and used only the muscle tension and movement patterns for these nonmanual adjectives and adverbs.[8]

Syntax: Questions

Questions in visual ASL can have a variety of word orders (Humphries, Padden, and O'Rourke 1987; Petronio and Lillo-Martin 1997). Under certain conditions, wh-questions in visual ASL can have a wh-word at the beginning or end of the sentence or at both the beginning and end. Wh-questions have a wh-question marker that co-occurs with the signs within the sentence (Baker-Shenk 1983). This marker consists of a head tilt, eyebrow squint, and possible forward body and shoulder rise (Valli and Lucas 1995). In visual ASL, under certain conditions, a wh-question can occur without an overt wh-word, as shown in (2) (Lillo-Martin and Fischer 1992).

$$\overline{\quad wh\text{-}q \quad}$$
(2) TIME
"What time is it?"

In visual ASL, the receiver knows this is a wh-question because she or he can see the nonmanual wh-question marker.

---

8. More research is needed on the other nonmanual adverbs and adjectives.

In tactile ASL, the Deaf-Blind receiver is unable to see the nonmanual wh-question marker. Within the tactile ASL data, all the instances of wh-questions had an overt wh-sign; sentences such as (2) did not occur. The many wh-questions that did occur followed the same syntactic patterns as in visual ASL. For example, as shown in the following examples, there were initial wh-words (e.g., [3]), final wh-words (e.g., [4]), and wh-words at both the beginning and the end (e.g., [5]).[9]

(3) WHAT-FOR INDEX
"What is (this thing) for?"
(4) SIGN YOUR NAME O-R NOT, WHAT
"Do you or don't you want to sign your name?"
(5) WHAT PLANE LOOK-LIKE WHAT
"What did the plane look like?"

Many wh-questions in tactile ASL were preceded by an index sign directed toward the receiver (glossed as YOU). The function of this sign appeared to alert the receiver that something would be directed toward him/her, a forewarning that a question will follow. This use of YOU is illustrated in the following sentences.

(6) YOU WHY VISIT 7 FLOOR, GIRL WANT VISIT 7 FLOOR FOR++
"Why did the girl want to visit the seventh floor?"
(7) YOU WHAT PLANE WHAT
"What kind of a plane was it?"
(8) YOU HOW YOU
"How are you?"

Notice that in (6) and (7), the sign YOU is neither subject nor object.

Petronio (1988) noted that when using interpreters, several Deaf-Blind people reported being confused and unaware when a question was directed toward them. The initial use of YOU appears to be a way that skilled Deaf-Blind signers clearly informed the Deaf-Blind receivers that a question was directed to them.

In visual ASL, yes/no questions are indicated by the use of the non-manual q-marker. This marker consists of a raised eyebrow, a widening

9. The remaining sentences in this section also included nonmanual question markers. However, because they were not the focus of this section, they are not included.

of the eyes, a forward tilting of the head and body, and possibly raised shoulders (Valli and Lucas 1995). Yes/no questions in visual ASL may end with the sign glossed as QUESTION (crooked index finger that wiggles). This sign is optional in visual ASL and usually adds further meaning, such as emphasis.

In tactile ASL, as with the wh-marker, Deaf-Blind receivers are unable to see the nonmanual q-marker. Yes/no questions in tactile ASL ended with the sign QUESTION, as in examples 9–11.

(9) AADB QUESTION
"You mean AADB?"
(10) DRINK QUESTION
"Is it for drinking?"
(11) NOW QUESTION
"Right now?"

To summarize, we observed three characteristics of questions in tactile ASL:

- Every wh-question had an overt wh-sign,
- Questions were often preceded by the sign YOU, and
- Yes/no questions ended with the manual sign QUESTION.

Discourse

BACK-CHANNEL FEEDBACK

An important element of any conversation, signed or spoken, is the back-channel feedback that the receiver gives to the sender. In visual ASL, back-channel feedback is given by facial signals such as head nods and raised eyebrows. Back-channel feedback can also be given by manual signs such as OH-I-SEE (a nodding Y hand), KNOW, REALLY, and so on. This feedback, given as the signer continues to sign, lets the signer know that the receiver is understanding, agreeing, disagreeing, doubting, puzzled, and so forth. This allows the signer to constantly monitor the communication to meet the receiver's needs.

The head nods and other facial signals used as back-channel feedback in visual ASL would not be effective in tactile ASL because Deaf-Blind signers can not see them. Similarly, if the receiver signed OH-I-SEE with the free hand, the Deaf-Blind signer would miss this sign since the signer is not in tactile contact with the receiver's free hand.

The Deaf-Blind receiver might give back-channel feedback by removing her/his hand from the top of the signer's hand and placing it under the signer's hand, signing a response, and then returning that hand to the top of the signer's hand. However, by definition, back-channel feedback (in both signed and spoken languages) occurs while the sender is relaying the message. The switching method just described requires the receiver and signer to take turns; the receiver cannot give feedback as the signer continues to sign. In addition to being slower, this switching method interrupts the signer in a way that "regular" back-channel feedback does not. This method rarely showed up in the tactile ASL data.

As described earlier, the most common method of communication that occurred in the tactile data, and the method this research focuses on, involved the Deaf-Blind receiver using one-handed tactile reception. In the remainder of this section we will describe some of the ways fluent Deaf-Blind ASL receivers gave tactile back-channel feedback to fluent Deaf-Blind ASL signers. The types of back-channel feedback that the receivers used are unique to tactile ASL; they do not occur in visual ASL.

Two types of tactile finger taps occurred: the one-finger tap (Figure 1) and the four-finger tap (Figure 2).

The one-finger tap expressed a meaning of "I understand." This meaning was subtly changed by speed or number of repetitions of the tap. Table 4 shows examples of occurrences of the one-finger tap. The tap is indicated by the dotted lines. (Although the table does not indicate the fact, the signer continued to sign.)

The four-finger tap was another very common way the receiver gave back-channel feedback to the Deaf-Blind signer. The four-finger tap, which also showed variation in the speed of the tap and the number of repetitions, was used to convey meanings such as "OK," "Oh, I see," and "I agree." The dotted lines in Table 5 show where the four-finger tap occurred.

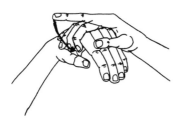

FIGURE 1. *One-Finger Tap*

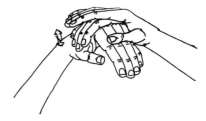

FIGURE 2. *Four-Finger Tap*

TABLE 4. *Examples of the One-Finger Tap*

Signer (English interpretation)	Receiver's Response
"They have squid (yuk)...."	One-finger tap (slow)
"Yes, I planned to but then changed my mind...."	One-finger tap
"I'll inform you when the water is there...."	One-finger tap

TABLE 5. *Examples of the Four-Finger Tap*

Signer (English Interpretation)	Receiver's Response
"We will see you later...."	Four-finger tap
"She was really lucky...."	Four-finger tap
"He is a really good cook...."	Four-finger tap

Deaf-Blind receivers also used a "tactile nod" to indicate "yes" or to show agreement. In visual ASL, the sign YES used the handshape A and a nodding movement from the wrist. In the tactile nod, the receiver, whose hand was on the top of the signer's hand, lightly grasped the signer's hand and used the same nodding movement. This resulted in the signer's hand being slightly raised and lowered by the receiver. Examples of occurrences of the tactile nod are shown in Table 6.

Squeezes to the signer's hand were another way that receivers gave feedback to the signer. These came in two varieties. A gentle, repeated squeeze functioned similarly to the tactile nod and indicated "yes" or "I understand." A single, firmer grasp was used to indicate that the receiver had missed something and needed it repeated. Examples of the single squeeze requesting repetition are shown in Table 7. The underline indicates where the tactile squeeze occurred. As Table 7 illustrates, the signer repeated the missed information after the receiver used the single, tactile squeeze. Although not shown in the table, after the signer repeated the information, the receiver usually indicated understanding with a tactile tap or nod.

After collecting our videotaped data, we showed the results to many of the Deaf-Blind informants. All of these people were unaware and surprised that they were using these different means of tactile feedback. That this tactile feedback system is widespread in the Deaf-Blind community is shown by the fact that all the signers used it and it appears in the data from both the East and West coasts.[10]

10. Further research is needed on the variety of tactile feedback that is used and on the subtle differences in meaning that are possible.

TABLE 6. *Examples of the Tactile Nod*

Signer (English Interpretation)	Receiver's Response
"I'm very curious about that. . . ."	Tactile nod
"It seems it is true. . . ."	Tactile nod
"It should be right now. . . ."	Tactile nod

TABLE 7. *Use of the Tactile Squeeze Requesting Repetition*

Signer	Signer Feedback
". . . PEANUT BUTTER, PEANUT BUTTER. . . ."	Tactile squeeze
". . . PLANE NUMBER 707 707. . . ."	Tactile squeeze
". . . 7th FLOOR 7th. . . ."	Tactile squeeze

CONCLUSIONS

This study focused on tactile ASL as it was used by fluent Deaf-Blind ASL signers when they communicated tactilely with other fluent Deaf-Blind ASL signers. Selected linguistic features from four subfields of linguistics (phonology, morphology, syntax, and discourse) were studied. Previous findings on these features in visual ASL were compared and contrasted with what occurred in the tactile ASL data. Comparing visual ASL with tactile ASL provided a unique opportunity to observe the variation and change that occurred when a community of fluent Deaf-Blind ASL signers used a visual language in a tactile mode.

Regarding the four phonological parameters, no variation or changes were noted in the handshape parameter. The other three parameters (movement, orientation, and location) displayed the same type of variation due to phonological assimilation that occurs in visual ASL. However, although the same forms of variation occurred in tactile ASL, this variation was sometimes due to: (1) the receiver's hand being on the signer's hand and (2) the signer and receiver being physically closer to each other than they generally are in visual ASL. For example, because of the physical closeness, the signing space used in tactile ASL was generally smaller than that used in visual ASL. This smaller space usually results in smaller movement paths in signs. In addition, because the signer's and receiver's hands are in contact, the signing space shifted to the area where the hands were in contact; correspondingly, the location of signs articulated in neutral space also shifted to this area. The orientation parameter showed some variation that resulted from modifications the signer made to better accommodate the receiver. One change, unique to tactile ASL, occurred with signs that included body contact. In addition to the signer's hand moving toward the body part, the body part often moved toward the hand in tactile ASL. This adaptation allowed the receiver to maintain more comfortable tactile contact with the signer.

Examples of the nonmanual adverbial and adjectival morphemes "mm," "oo," "ee," and "cha" were examined. It was noted that these morphemes consisted of at least two components: (1) a specific facial configuration and (2) specific muscle tension and movement patterns that were imposed on the sign that co-occurs with the morpheme. Deaf-Blind receivers, although they could not see the first component (the specific facial configuration), perceived these adverbial and adjectival morphemes from the second component (the specific muscle tension and movement patterns that co-occurred with the sign). In visual ASL, these morphemes use both components. In tactile ASL, Deaf-Blind signers sometimes used both components; at other times they eliminated the facial configuration and used only the muscle tension and movement component.

In the area of syntax, question word order was examined. With one exception, the same variety of word order typical of wh-questions in visual ASL also occurred in tactile ASL. The one exception involved the use of covert wh-signs that, under certain conditions, are permitted in visual ASL. In contrast, all the wh-questions in the tactile ASL data had an overt wh-sign. In visual ASL, a yes/no question can optionally end with the sign QUESTION. In contrast, the sign QUESTION occurred after each yes/no question that appeared in the tactile ASL data. Another interesting finding involved the sign YOU, which preceded many questions in tactile ASL. In visual ASL, a signer looks directly at the receiver when directing a question to him/her. In tactile ASL, the receiver cannot see the signer's face to perceive toward whom the question is directed. The use of YOU before the question appears to function as a substitute for the signer's eye gaze; it informs the receiver that something is being directed toward him/her. Although the use of an overt wh-sign, the final QUESTION sign, and an initial YOU sign can all occur in visual ASL, they all were used much more frequently in tactile ASL. In tactile ASL, their use appears to function as a substitute for the nonmanuals, which the Deaf-Blind receiver cannot see.

The last area examined, back-channel feedback, provided clear examples of language change that has occurred in tactile ASL. In this case, it appears that signers were unable to modify or adapt the back-channel feedback used in visual ASL to meet the needs of tactile ASL users. Instead, a new tactile system of back-channel feedback has evolved in the Deaf-Blind community. Even though this system of tactile nods, squeezes, and taps is unique to tactile ASL, it serves the same function as the visual feedback system does in visual ASL. Interestingly, although all the Deaf-Blind participants from both the East and West coasts used tactile feedback, none were consciously aware they were doing it or even that such a system has evolved.

The variation, adaptations, and changes described in this paper are examples of linguistic change that has and is occurring in the Deaf-Blind community within the United States. In the past several years, in addition to an expansion of the American Association of the Deaf-Blind, there has been growth in many state chapters of this organization. Deaf-Blind people are increasing their contact with other Deaf-Blind people. The opportunity for Deaf-Blind people to get together and form communities has resulted in ASL's undergoing sociolinguistic changes as Deaf-Blind people modify it to meet their needs. From a linguistic viewpoint, tactile ASL provides us with a unique opportunity to witness the linguistic changes ASL is experiencing as the Deaf-Blind community adapts the language to a tactile mode.

REFERENCES

Baker, C. 1976. What's not on the other hand in ASL. In *Papers from the Twelfth Regional Meeting of the Chicago Linguistic Society.* Chicago: University of Chicago Press.

Baker, C., and D. Cokely. 1980. *American Sign Language: A teacher's resource text on grammar and culture.* Silver Spring, Md.: T. J. Publishers. Reprint, Washington, D.C.: Gallaudet University Press, 1991.

Baker, C., and C. Padden. 1978. Focusing on the non-manual components of American sign languages. In *Understanding language through sign language research,* ed. P. Siple, 27–57. New York: Academic Press.

Baker-Shenk, C. 1983. A micro-analysis of the nonmanual components of questions in American Sign Language. Ph.D. diss., University of California, Berkeley.

Battison, R. 1978. *Lexical borrowing in American Sign Language: Phonological and morphological restructuring.* Silver Spring, Md.: Linstok Press.

Frishberg, N., and B. Gough. 1973. Morphology in American Sign Language. Working paper, Salk Institute for Biological Studies, La Jolla, Calif.

Humphries, T., C. Padden, and T. J. O'Rourke. 1980. *A basic course in American Sign Language.* Silver Spring, Md.: T. J. Publishers.

Klima E. S., and U. Bellugi. 1979. *The signs of language.* Cambridge: Harvard University Press.

Liddell, S. 1977. Non-manual signals in American Sign Language: A many layered system. In *Proceedings of the First National Symposium in Sign Language Research and Teaching,* ed. W. C. Stokoe, 193–228. Silver Spring, Md.: National Association of the Deaf.

————. 1989. American Sign Language: The phonological base. *Sign Language Studies* 64:195–277.

————. 1980. *American Sign Language syntax.* The Hague: Mouton.

Liddell, S., and R. Johnson. 1986. American Sign Language compound formation processes, lexicalization, and phonological remnants. In *Natural language and linguistic theory,* vol. 4 (November).

Lillo-Martin D., and S. Fischer. 1992. Overt and covert wh-questions in American Sign Language. Paper presented at the Fifth International Symposium on Sign Language Research, Salamanca, Spain, May.

Padden, C. 1988. *Interaction of morphology and syntax in American Sign Language.* Outstanding Dissertations in Linguistics Series. New York: Garland. (from Padden 1983)

Petronio, K. 1988. Interpreting for Deaf-Blind students: Factors to consider. *American Annals of the Deaf,* 133(3):226–29.

Petronio, K., and D. Lillo-Martin. 1997. Wh-movement and the position of Spec CP: Evidence from American Sign Language. *Language* 73(1):18–58.

Stokoe, W. C. 1960. Sign language structure: An outline of the visual communication systems of the American Deaf. In *Studies in Linguistics: Occasional Papers 8.* New York: University of Buffalo.

Stokoe, W. C., D. Casterline, and C. Croneberg. 1965. *A dictionary of American Sign Language on linguistic principles.* Washington, D.C.: Gallaudet College Press. Reprint, Silver Spring, Md.: Linstock Press, 1976.

Supalla, T., and E. Newport. 1978. How many seats in a chair? The derivation of nouns and verbs in American Sign Language. In *Understanding language through sign language research,* ed. P. Siple, 91–132. New York: Academic Press.

Valli, C., and C. Lucas. 1995. *Linguistics of American Sign Language: A resource text for ASL users,* 2d ed. Washington, D.C.: Gallaudet University Press.

Part 2 Languages in Contact

Grammatical Constraints on Fingerspelled

English Verb Loans in BSL

Rachel Sutton-Spence

Fingerspelling is used in many countries in communication among and with the deaf community. It is an important part of sign languages in countries where deaf people receive regular education and are literate. It has been defined as "delivering a rapid sequence of hand-configurations, each corresponding to a letter of the alphabet" (Padden 1991b). In many European sign languages, and in American Sign Language (ASL), the influence of fingerspelling upon a deaf person's signing is frequently evident. However, for various reasons the function of fingerspelling in sign languages has been little researched.

Until recently, research on the role that fingerspelling plays within sign languages was very sparse. Sign linguists were, perhaps, more concerned with describing those features of sign languages that were independent of surrounding spoken languages and less concerned with features derived from the spoken languages, such as fingerspelling or the use of spoken language mouth patterns. The most notable exception to this is Battison's ground-breaking work of 1978, which described the processes of the lexicalization of fingerspelling loans in ASL. However, increasing research interest is now centering upon areas of language contact between sign languages and spoken languages. Wilcox (e.g., 1988) and Padden (1991a, 1991b) have both addressed questions concerning fingerspelling in ASL.

Research into fingerspelling in British Sign Language has not previously been conducted in any great depth, although Martin Colville conducted some, as yet unpublished, research in this area in the early 1980s. This paper is the result of a larger study into the role of the manual alphabet and fingerspelling in BSL during the 1980s and first part of the 1990s. The British manual alphabet may be seen in Figure 1.

This work was financially supported by a student scholarship from the Economic and Social Research Council, grant number R00429024933.

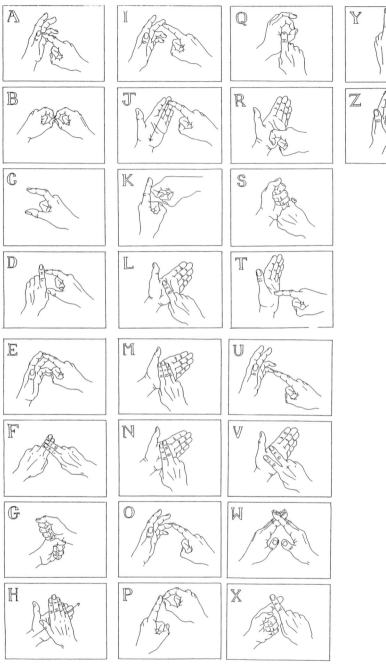

FIGURE I. *The British manual alphabet.*

The exact status of fingerspelling in British Sign Language is unclear, but its role is clearly complex and varied. The majority of signs in the BSL lexicon have developed naturally within the deaf community.[1] They are independent of English orthography and English grammar. The manual alphabet, on the other hand, was originally introduced to deaf people by hearing educators with the express purpose of representing English. Yet, fingerspelling is used for code-switching into English and borrowing from English, and it acts as a resource for new signs in BSL.

This paper briefly describes the uses of fingerspelling within BSL but also focuses particularly on the interesting constraints that operate upon fingerspelling loans in BSL, resulting in very few fingerspelled loan verbs. This issue was also raised by Carol Padden (1991a), whose research on ASL fingerspelling found that verbs were rarely borrowed from English through fingerspelling. The study of BSL reported here found exactly the same bias against fingerspelled verbs in BSL, and I propose explanations for this phenomenon.

BSL *borrows* from English and from other sign languages; one very common way of introducing new vocabulary into BSL is through finger-spelling. Fingerspelling allows the signer to borrow any English word (and even a word from another language so long as it is written using the same alphabet).[2] Because deaf signers are bilingual in BSL and English, they are able to use English loans freely within their signing. Sometimes the fingerspelling loans are only nonce loans (or instances of single word code-switching), but they sometimes become lexicalized and thus become a part of BSL.

Where fingerspelling is used in BSL, it may be only a temporary measure to introduce the use of a new concept and may later be dropped from regular use if an accepted sign emerges. For example, when facsimile

1. *Borrowing* refers to linguistic forms being taken over by one language from another (Crystal 1980). Most borrowing produces *loan words*, although sounds and grammatical structures are also borrowed. When signers fingerspell, they are using English (or another spoken language with a written form) as a source for an item in their sign language, and this may be termed borrowing. It should be noted that borrowing can take place in other ways in sign languages, for example, through loan translation or the use of spoken language components with manual components.

2. The *d* in *deaf* is lowercased in this paper because not all signers are culturally Deaf.

machines first came into use, the noun *fax* was fingerspelled, but a sign FAX has now developed that is in common use and serves as both a noun and a verb. The term *grass roots* (referring to the "rank and file" of the deaf community) was fingerspelled as a loan from English until the mid-to late 1980s but now has its own sign GRASSROOTS, which has arisen from the frequent use of the concept within BSL. Expression of the English word *community* used to exist solely as a fingerspelling, but most deaf people now understand the sign COMMUNITY (borrowed from ASL).

DATA CORPUS

In order to gain a real understanding of the use of fingerspelling and the manual alphabet in BSL, large amounts of signing were collected from many deaf people who interacted and conversed about many and varied topics.

Limited time and resources made it difficult to gather large amounts of signing data from many signers. Another problem was ensuring that the linguist's presence had little or no effect on the signs produced during linguistic observation. Labov's "Observer's Paradox" (1966)—a well-known pitfall—must be avoided, especially when a hearing linguist observes deaf signers, a situation in which there may be a supposed status imbalance. Deaf signers may still believe that they need to shift their style of signing to suit the perceived requirements of the researcher. Deuchar (1977, 1978) has already observed that the forms of BSL associated with hearing people may contain more fingerspelling than other forms, and this would be a particular problem for this research. Also, the signers may accommodate to the signing of conversational participants to ensure understanding, perhaps by altering the amount of fingerspelling they use.

To solve this problem, I employed data from eight years (1981–1989) of *See Hear!*, the BBC television magazine program for the deaf. These data are archived in the Centre for Deaf Studies at Bristol University.

Not even this corpus is completely satisfactory because it is possible that even if signers were not influenced by linguists, they may have been affected by the program's producers or other linguistic monitors. However, this source provides at least a single, large corpus of data collected under similar circumstances (in approximately the same formal television register) without the signers' being aware that someone would analyze their fingerspelling. Useful future research could examine signing from other registers.

See Hear! has been broadcast weekly or fortnightly since 1981, usually for 26 weeks each year. The program's topics are varied but include deaf community news, interviews with deaf and hearing people on subjects relevant to the deaf community, and information on current events, sports, and technology. There have also been several dramatic productions, especially of Christmas pantomimes. In the magazine programs analyzed, there were usually two full-time presenters who acted as anchorpersons. They interviewed guests and presented other items. Members of the deaf community have frequently appeared as guests, especially when the program has gone on location to deaf clubs around the country.

Involving participation of deaf signers from all backgrounds, the programs analyzed totaled almost 60 hours (not all of this, of course, was of deaf people signing). Analysis of the broadcasts yielded information from 504 deaf signers of all ages, backgrounds, and geographic parts of the country (including eighteen guest presenters), as well as five full-time program presenters. Any signer who was deaf and used signing alone or with speech was included in this corpus. The very few deaf people who used spoken English as their main form of communication but accompanied this speech with occasional signs or single-manual letters were not included in the corpus.

The total number of words in the transcription of the signing of the deaf people on *See Hear!* was calculated using the number of words in the transcripts of the subtitles translating the signing. There were 190,006 words in the transcripts, and the signing data provided 19,450 examples of uses of the manual alphabet. Those signs that have specialized movement or location as a result of extra BSL phonology were excluded from the original count. Given that this rough, conservative estimate reveals that an average of 10 percent of signing in this corpus involves fingerspelling, fingerspelling should not be ignored by linguists or denied its place within the language, if only for the frequency of its use within BSL. This proportion is not dissimilar to that found by Padden (1991a).

The types of words fingerspelled in this corpus may be seen in Table 1. The distribution of fingerspellings suggests many important points for discussion; however, we will now focus on the observation that, in all these fingerspellings, there are very few verbs.

TABLE 1. *Uses of Fingerspelling in BSL*

Type of Word	Percentage
Whole proper names	18.6
Whole other-content words	19.0
Acronyms	9.2
Whole-function words	20.5
Single-manual-letter signs	9.1
Abbreviated whole words	21.0
Manual letter with nonderived sign	2.6

Note: The data are from a corpus of 19,450 fingerspellings.

VERB FINGERSPELLINGS IN BSL

There are grammatical constraints upon what is borrowed into any language. Open-class words are more likely to be borrowed than closed-class, and of all the open-class categories, nouns are the most frequently occurring category (Bynon 1977).

Padden (1991a, 1991b) found that this is also true in ASL, when she calculated that fewer than 1 percent of all fingerspellings in her corpus of ASL signing were verbs. This same paucity of loan verbs may be seen in the BSL corpus from *See Hear!* Verbs formed only 0.8 percent of the entire fingerspelling corpus and only 2.2 percent of all whole English-content words that were fingerspelled. In the entire *See Hear!* corpus there were 512 examples of nonce single-manual-letter signs (i.e., a sign using only the manual letter corresponding to the first letter of the English word the sign represents). Of these 512 single-manual-letter signs, only 12 (2.3 percent) were verbs.

As there is not a complete prohibition on fingerspelled verbs in BSL, it is helpful to describe the situations in which they *are* permitted to occur.

Thirty-one percent of the verb fingerspellings in this corpus were produced by older Scottish, Irish, and Welsh people whose BSL involves considerable fingerspelling, often producing several fingerspelled words in sequence with no other BSL signs in between (e.g., I-L-O-V-E-D-T-H-A-T-D-O-L-L or T-H-E-R-E-I-S-G-O-I-N-G-T-O-B-E-A-H-A-P-P-Y-E-V-E-N-T) (Sutton-Spence and Woll 1990). This is better interpreted as code-switching rather than borrowing because the signers are producing representations of grammatically complete English, in English word order, rather than single lexical items within BSL.

A further 13 percent either had no commonly accepted sign synonym (e.g., the verb L-O-B-B-Y, as in "to lobby parliament," although there has since emerged a sign LOBBY) or accompanied a sign for clarification (e.g., I-N-S-U-L-A-T-E, INSULATE) or were being used in an unusual way (e.g., S-W-E-A-T as a culinary term). Almost all of these fingerspelled verbs were used in the infinitive form.

A further 5 percent were used as exact quotations of English, for example, the title of a television program, "H-A-N-D-L-E WITH CARE," or as an explanation of an English acronym, "T-A-C-K-L-I-N-G ACQUIRED-DEAFNESS."

Three percent were fingerspelled for emphasis (e.g., "HOW D-A-R-E YOU TELL-ME!" Another 3 percent were for explaining the meaning of a sign in English (e.g., "HIBERNATE. THAT SIGN H-I-B-E-R-N-A-T-E").

Four percent were verbs used as nouns, adjectives, or as part of noun or adjective phrases (e.g., doing lots of M-O-D-E-L-L-I-N-G at school).

The most noticeable point is that only the remaining 12 percent (e.g., C-O-P-E or H-E-L-P) have sign synonyms within BSL but were still fingerspelled and could not be readily explained away as code-switching into English.

Reasons for the Lack of Fingerspelled Verbs in BSL

Padden (1991a) has remarked that "fingerspelled items are overwhelmingly nouns, and almost never verbs. . . . [I]f fingerspelling is indeed supposed to be infiltration of English into ASL, why is it so constrained to one type of grammatical category?" (1991a, 3). The rest of this paper will consider the possible reasons for the predominance of fingerspelled noun loans in BSL, using the observations made concerning loans in other (mainly spoken) languages. I will argue that this lack of fingerspelled loan verbs is not peculiar to sign languages and is not caused by the unique situation of borrowing between languages in two modalities. Rather, the patterns observed are similar to those seen in borrowing between many world languages.

Many researchers argue that the main cause of this pattern is the structural constraint imposed upon borrowing by the donor and recipient languages, although we will investigate nonstructural constraints.

Nonstructural constraints depend on the degree of proficiency, the number and status of bilinguals in the language community, and the status of the two languages in the community (Maravcsik 1978). Bauer (1983) has further described the nonstructural, social factors influencing the acceptance and spread of a loan. These are: the status of the person using the loan; the attitude of the language community regarding the loan word and the need for the form; the prestige gained by and the convenience of using the loan form. He also notes that loans may be rejected on the grounds of aesthetics, etymology, perceived vulgarity, grammar, or semantics. These are all factors that may influence the use of a fingerspelled loan in BSL.

The *absolute amount* of borrowing between languages is dictated primarily by the nonstructural, social constraints described by Maravcsik and Bauer. However, the *types* of loans and the *grammatical categories* into which they are borrowed are constrained above all by the structural similarity of the languages.

BORROWING VERBS IN SPOKEN LANGUAGES

The percentage of verbs borrowed by different languages varies, but studies of various languages show that it frequently is small. Yau (1993) found that English words used in Hong Kong magazines were "overwhelmingly" nouns, although the exact numbers are not given. Kartunnen and Lockhart (1976) investigated borrowing from Spanish into Nahuatl in the sixteenth and seventeenth centuries and found that only 3.5 percent of all loans were verbs. Throughout the entire Colonial Period, noun loans outnumbered loans in all other grammatical categories by more than twelve to one. Arakawa (1931, cited in Higa 1979) found that loans from English into Japanese were mainly nouns, and only 2.1 percent of the loans were verbs. Cannon (1987) reviewed three dictionaries of American English and found 1,029 recent loans of foreign words from 84 languages into American English, of which only twelve (0.01 percent) were verbs.

One significant exception to these figures is Witney's finding (1881, cited in Haugen 1950) that verbs borrowed from English into American Norwegian and American Swedish made up 18.4 percent and 23.2 percent, respectively, of the total loans.

Class Size as a Factor

Some of the difference in borrowing may be due to the overall sizes of the classes (the number of words borrowed from each class could be proportional to the size of the class). Nouns make up approximately 60 percent of English vocabulary, whereas verbs account for only 14 percent, and adjectives, 12 percent. Consequently, we would expect that more nouns would be borrowed than any other class. However, the percentage of verb loans is frequently far smaller than one might expect even given the proportion of nouns and verbs in a language.

Size of class cannot completely account for the large numbers of nouns and the very small numbers of verbs that are sometimes borrowed. A number of other factors contribute to the constraining of verb loans.

Length of Contact Time as a Factor in Borrowing Verbs

The length of time the languages have been in contact affects the number of verbs borrowed. Nouns are borrowed first, and verbs only when the languages have been in contact for some time (Bynon 1977). This may be seen in the records of Spanish loans into Nahuatl after the Spanish contact with the Mexican people. In the entire sixteenth century, over 200 Spanish words were borrowed into Nahuatl; only one of these was a verb. By the end of the seventeenth century, over 700 words had been borrowed, and 33 of those were verbs. In the eighteenth century verb loans grew because a practice had developed to increase the degree of linguistic integration of verbs by borrowing the Spanish infinitive and adding a Nahuatl suffix.

Length of contact between languages is not especially important in the case of BSL and English, however. BSL and English have been in very close contact for as long as deaf people have received formal education (at least 200 years), so length of time does not adequately explain the rarity of loan verbs in BSL.

Grammatical Inflection as a Factor

A much more significant reason for resistance to verb loans is their grammatical inflection. To a considerable extent, the number of borrowed verbs is a reflection of the structural similarity between the two languages. Conversely, the structural dissimilarity between English and BSL can account for the small number of verbs borrowed from English into BSL through fingerspelling. Loan verbs account for approximately 18 percent of borrowed words into Norwegian American from English (Haugen 1950) but for only 2 percent of borrowed words into Japanese (Arakawa 1931, cited in Higa 1979). Norwegian and English are structurally much more similar than Japanese and English.

Maravcsik (1978) claims that it is a universal feature of language borrowing that an inflectional affix cannot be borrowed into a language unless a derivational affix has already been borrowed. As there are no derivational affixes borrowed from English into BSL, inflectional affixes cannot be borrowed, according to this rule.

These are reasons that a language may not find it structurally "convenient" to borrow verbs. However, it is also possible that the lack of loan verbs is due to a lack of need for them.

GENERAL APPLICABILITY OF WORDS
TO DESCRIBE ACTIONS

One possibility is that verbs are more applicable in new situations than nouns. Verbs may thus be said to be more versatile than nouns because a given verb may be generally applied to actions perceived as similar in some way, whereas nouns are applied specifically to name things. A consequence of this is that new verbs are *required* less often than new nouns. This means that fewer loans might be required, creating a disproportionate number of fingerspelled nouns.

This general applicability of verbal lexical items is seen in the records of loans into Nahuatl, in which verbs tended just to extend in meaning. By the seventeenth century, the convention of adding the native suffix *oa* to Spanish infinitives was established so that, in theory, any verb could be borrowed. Despite this, only specialized, technical verbs (e.g., verbs meaning *canonize* and *consecrate*) were borrowed. Kartunnen and Lockhart (1976) recorded that "[m]ore basic, colloquial, frequently used verbal concepts were rendered through meaning extension" (1976, 43).

Factors Constraining the Use of Fingerspelling in Loan Verbs

The previous section outlined reasons that languages do not borrow many verbs. One main reason was a lack of structural similarity between two languages. It may be broadly argued that the reason for the rarity of fingerspelled loan verbs in BSL lies in the grammatical differences between English and BSL.

The general dearth of verbs may have several explanations, all related to the different structures of English and BSL and the morphology of BSL and English verbs. For instance, a new, nonderived verb sign can easily be inflected using BSL morphology, whereas if a fingerspelled borrowed verb is to be inflected, a conflict between BSL and English grammatical morphology arises.

Verb Morphology

Two basic conflicts must account for the lack of verb borrowing: the different way that verb inflections are realized and the different morphological information contained in verbs in the two languages.

Inflection, or modulation, in BSL verbs is not realized by the addition of affixes as it is in English. Instead, morphological information is added by including a change in movement and location of the verb sign, a change in handshape, and additional (or a change in) nonmanual features. The changes in movement may be in its speed, size, and intensity, its number of repetitions, and its direction of movement.

The morphological information contained in BSL and English verbs is not the same. BSL verbs may contain information about person, number, location, and aspect, as well as manner and the physical form of the subject or object. The types of verbs that show different information have been described by Padden (1990). Unlike English, however, they do not show tense, which is realized lexically.

Many verbs in BSL inflect to show manner and aspect. Casual manner is expressed nonmanually by a lax "mm" mouth pattern (with the lips closed), while effort and tension are realized by tense, narrowly parted lips, frequently written as "ee." Thus, the BSL verb WORK-CASUALLY carries the lax "mm" mouth pattern during production of the manual sign WORK, and WORK-HARD carries the tense, narrow "ee" mouth pattern during the same manual sign. Repetitive aspect is shown by a slow repetition of the sign. In WORK-REGULARLY, movement in the sign WORK is repeated several times with a rapid, circular motion.

Some verbs also inflect for person and number, moving in syntactic space (e.g., ASK, GIVE). Inflection for number and person is shown by direction of movement. The verb sign moves away from the subject and toward the object. For example, in the verb ASK, the sign I-ASK-YOU (singular) moves from the signer toward the grammatical location of the second person, whereas the sign YOU (singular)-ASK-ME moves from the grammatical location of the second person toward the signer.

Other verbs do not show person or number but do show location, using real-world, topographical space (e.g., PUT, TOW). These spatial verbs (Padden 1990) frequently contain classifier predicates contained in the handshape. For example, in SOMETHING-MOVE-FROM-A-TO-B, the handshape varies depending on what is moving (e.g., a car, bicycle, or person). Another characteristic of BSL verbs is to incorporate information about the object into the handshape of the verb. For example, in the verb SMOKE, the handshape differs according to whether a pipe, cigarette, cigar, or joint (marijuana cigarette) is being smoked. The verbs GIVE and CARRY have handshapes dependent upon the object and its size, thus GIVE-A-BIG-BOX differs from GIVE-A-SMALL-BOX, and both differ from GIVE-A-PENCIL, GIVE-A-FLAG, GIVE-BUNCH-OF-FLOWERS, GIVE-A-TROPHY, or GIVE-A-BABY. These morphosyntactic differences can account for the pattern of BSL verb borrowing from English.

Using English inflections in fingerspelling loans results in the inclusion of information not naturally contained within a BSL verb inflection (e.g., tense) and the exclusion of information usually carried in BSL inflection (e.g., aspect, manner, and (sometimes) spatial location and object).

Another problem is that even the morphological information in the verbs of both languages is shown differently. In English, most verbs are inflected using a suffix, with some commonly used, notable exceptions (e.g., *sing* and *sang*). One common method of dealing with an unlexicalized loan in spoken languages is to borrow the root and use a native affix for the verb inflection. This happened in the Nahuatl of Mexican colonial times when the Spanish verbs were borrowed using the Nahuatl verb suffix *oa*. It also happens in modern Japanese (Akamatsu, personal communication, June 1992). The suffix *suru* is added to Japanese nouns to make verbs, for example, *sanpou* ("a stroll") becomes sanpou-suru ("to go for a stroll"). This suffix can be added to loan nouns to form verbs in the same way. The noun *furai* (from the American English word *fry* or *chip*) can become *furai-suru* ("to deep-fry") and *demo* ("a demonstration" or "protest") can become demo-suru ("to demonstrate").

This addition of a native affix is not possible in BSL because BSL does not have affixes. Even in the verbs used by the older signers from Scotland, Wales, and Ireland, the overriding characteristic shared by the fingerspelled verbs in the corpus is that they almost always appear in the infinitive form (or, less commonly, as the gerund). In other words, they are as grammatically neutral as possible.

It has already been mentioned that, instead of adding a suffix, the two means of verb inflection in BSL are movement of the sign and additional or changed nonmanual features that occur simultaneously with the sign.

It is not possible to use movement for inflection in a fingerspelled loan because BSL does not permit fingerspelling of more than two letters to move through signing space. The real difficulty for inflection of finger-spelled loans lies in the physical problems involved in moving the hands in any direction during the many changes in hand-configuration that oc-cur in the fingerspelling of a full word. In BSL signs, when two hands move and change shape, they are subject to the symmetry constraint of BSL, which requires both hands to take the same handshape (e.g., MAGIC, in which both hands open from the closed fist to a curved 5 hand). In BSL fingerspelling, the second, passive, hand often assumes a different shape from the active hand. For this reason BSL lexicalized verbs cannot change the handshape so that movement can be unhindered. For example, in GIVE, the signer cannot move the hands through the signing space easily while articulating the manual letters G-I-V-E. Other changes in movement such as speed, intensity, distance, and repetition are also impractical.

The ultimate effect of this is that it is unacceptable (and physically very difficult) to modify a fingerspelled verb using the natural morpho-logical processes of BSL to show the verb morphology required by BSL. Lexicalized loan verbs in ASL (discussed further in the next section) are notable for the fact that they are made using a single hand, which means they are not subject to the symmetry constraint of a two-handed finger-spelling.

A further, minor study of BSL signers confirmed that it is not accept-able for fingerspellings to move through signing space as part of the agree-ment of verbs. The average rating for all the fingerspellings moving through signing space was 2.8 on a scale where 3 was "totally unaccept-able." For many of the test items, all signers responded with a rating of 3, a complete and unequivocal rejection. This compared with an average rating of 1.5 for nonderived sign synonyms moving the same way through the signing space ($t = 30.2$, $df = 899$, $p < 0.001$).

Evidence for the claim that the *movement* makes the fingerspellings particularly unacceptable comes from comparing these sentences with those using a full fingerspelling articulated in neutral space, followed by an index to demonstrate verb agreement. The average rating for finger-spellings with a moving index was lower than the rating given for those fingerspellings that moved themselves (2.4 compared to 2.8; $t = 9.3$, $df = 819$, $p < 0.001$). Lower ratings were for items considered more acceptable, so items with a moving index were considered significantly more acceptable than items that moved.

Lexicalized Loan Verbs in BSL

Perhaps because of the small number of verbs borrowed on a temporary basis, there also seem to be very few lexicalized loan verbs of any type and even fewer that allow movement as agreement verbs. In view of the problems involved in the movement of the hands during two-handed fingerspelling, one might expect that most lexicalized fingerspelled verbs would be plain verbs that would not be required to move through inflection (e.g., LOVE and SMOKE). There seems to be only one lexicalized, plain loan verb, and that is two letters long: DO (D-O). So far there do not seem to be any lexicalized two-letter verbs that are not plain verbs, nor any lexicalized verbs of more than two letters.

Battison (1978) describes several ASL lexicalized loan verbs such as #OFF, #ON, #NO, #DO, and #SAY-NO-TO. In all cases these have been modified to match ASL phonology, being one-handed and reduced to two major changes in handshape or orientation. As a result, they may be seen as having only two parts that can change orientation and move through space to show grammatical information including person and number, just like any other nonderived verb sign.

The most common process for lexicalization of a loan fingerspelling into BSL is to take only the first letter of the English source word. Lexicalized loan agreement verbs involve only the one handshape of the first letter, so the verb may be inflected through movement for person and number. In some cases this manual letter handshape is made repeatedly as the sign moves through syntactic space. Two agreement verbs are QUESTION (Q) and ANSWER (A). Other agreement verbs include PROPOSE (P), RECOMMEND (R), REPRESENT (R), and VISIT (V). In all cases, these are accompanied by the appropriate spoken component from the corresponding English word. Some of these lexicalized signs have sign synonyms not based on letters from the manual alphabet, and these synonyms inflect in exactly the same way. The process is also similar to that in other BSL signs with similar handshapes and movements, for example, HELP (in which the fist is placed upon the upturned palm and both hands may be moved through the signing space). However, even these lexicalized "verb" loans tend to function more as nouns than as verbs, so that the signs are often better glossed as PROPOSAL, APPLICATION, REPRESENTATIVE, and so on. Thus we have single-manual-letter handshapes that are fully integrated into the phonology of BSL and should have no problems moving just as any other BSL verb sign, yet they still are very rare. I propose that the reason for this again lies in the other ways that BSL shows morphosyntactic information, namely by changes in handshape and addition of BSL mouth patterns. I further suggest that the problem is that the handshape of a single-manual-letter sign and its accompanying English mouth pattern are vital for its meaning.

Changing the handshape of a single-manual-letter sign totally removes its meaning because it is the link between the handshape of the manual letter and the English word that gives the sign its meaning. Consequently, verbs that incorporate the subject or object into the handshape cannot be single-manual-letter signs. The difficulties that would arise may be seen in the example of GIVE. There is no physical reason why the G handshape cannot be moved exactly as the handshapes used in GIVE. In fact, if the sign is GIVE-A-BUNCH-OF-FLOWERS, the handshape is practically the same. Consequently, it must be the inability of the sign to contain all the necessary morphological information that renders it unworkable.

A single-manual-letter sign in BSL also must have the English mouth pattern to give it meaning and to distinguish it from any other sign that might use the first letter of the English word (for example, as single-manual-letter signs using the manual letter *m*, the BSL signs MOTHER, MONTH, MEMBER, MINUTE, and MONDAY are manual homonyms). I have already mentioned that manner and aspect in BSL are frequently marked using BSL mouth patterns, including "mm," "ee," and "th," expressing ease, effort, boredom, length or duration, and so on. Here again, there is a conflict. The sign will need not only an English mouth pattern for full disambiguation but also a BSL mouth pattern to show morphological information about manner and aspect. As a result, it cannot show all the information necessary, and an alternative sign is used to resolve the potential conflict.

CONCLUSION

The grammatical differences between BSL and English constrain the number of fingerspelled verbs in BSL. Although these specific grammati-

cal constraints might be unique to BSL and English (or, at least, to a spoken language and a signed language), the general idea that grammatical
differences between languages prevents the loan of verbs is common to
many world languages. I would not argue that the low frequency of
fingerspelled loan verbs in BSL is specifically due to modality specific constraints. Were this the case, we should not see any fingerspelled loans with
high frequency, and we do see other content words borrowed in relatively
large numbers. Instead, this is a claim that the linguistic and sociolinguistic processes behind verb loans from English to BSL are the same as for
loans between any languages, whether spoken or signed. Of course, BSL
does use space to provide morphological information in its verbs, whereas
English does not. However, the point is that the languages are merely very
different, and in any interlinguistic situation where the grammatical systems are different, loans of verbs are few and far between. Where languages are similar, loan verbs are more likely, as I mentioned earlier with
the proportion of loan verbs from English into American-Norwegian. Indeed, BSL has borrowed the ASL lexicalized loan verb #SAY-NO-TO, which
fits well with this theory, because of the grammatical similarities between
ASL and BSL.

However, it is not enough merely to say that English and BSL are too
different to allow many loan verbs. It is also important to identify these
differences and explain precisely why they constrain the loan process. If a
fingerspelled verb is to be inflected, it needs to follow either English grammatical morphology or BSL morphology. There are problems with both
of these. Not only do the inflections of the two languages contain different information, but the movement required for BSL inflections is physically very hard to impose upon a fingerspelled sign. These two basic
difficulties may account for the lack of verb borrowing.

Using English inflections results in the inclusion of information not
naturally contained within a BSL verb inflection (e.g., tense), and the exclusion of information that can be carried in BSL inflection (e.g., aspect
and location). Thus it may be argued that it is not possible to add BSL
inflection to a fingerspelled loan because of the physical constraints involved in fingerspelling, so any verbs borrowed must either be borrowed
and used uninflected or borrowed complete with the English suffix so that
the utterance becomes a code-switch into English, complete with English
grammar.

In this latter case, there are no devices for showing the information that
would normally be carried in the BSL inflection, and there is redundant

information about tense in the loan fingerspelling. Consequently, we may conjecture, in order to avoid this, few verbs are borrowed, and alternative solutions are found.

Fingerspellings may become integrated into BSL, provided they can be changed to fit BSL morphology, and then they behave in a similar way to other BSL signs. There is a movement within the British deaf community away from use of fingerspelling for loans from English and toward using loans from other sign languages or other BSL resources (such as creation of iconic signs or loan translations). Despite this, it is clear that finger-spelling provides a lexical resource for a great many other signs in BSL. It is a rich resource for borrowing and is frequently used by the bilingual deaf community.

REFERENCES

Battison, R. 1978. *Lexical borrowing in American Sign Language*. Silver Spring, Md.: Linstok Press.

Bauer, L. 1983. *English word formation*. Cambridge: Cambridge University Press.

Bynon, T. 1977. *Historical linguistics*. Cambridge: Cambridge University Press.

Cannon, G. 1987. *Historical change and English word-formation*. New York: Peter Lang.

Crystal, D. 1980. *A dictionary of linguistics and phonetics*, 41. Oxford: Blackwell.

Deuchar, M. 1977. Sign language diglossia in a British deaf community. *Sign Language Studies* 17:347–56.

———. 1978. *Diglossia in British Sign Language*. Ph.D. diss., University of Stanford.

———. 1984. *British Sign Language*. London: Routledge and Kegan Paul.

Haugen, E. 1950. The analysis of linguistic borrowing. *Language* 26:210–31.

Higa, M. 1979. Sociolinguistic aspects of word-borrowing. In *Sociolinguistic studies in language contact*, ed.W. Mackey and J. Ornstein, 277–94. The Hague: Mouton.

Kartunnen, F., and J. Lockhart. 1976. *Nahuatl in the middle years*. California: University of California Press.

Labov, W. 1966. *The social stratification of English in New York City*. Washington, D.C.: Center for Applied Linguistics.

Maravcsik, E. 1978. Universals of language contact. In *Universals of human language, vol. 1*, ed. J. Greenberg, 93–122. Stanford, Calif.: Stanford University Press.

Padden, C. 1990. The relation between space and grammar in ASL verb morphology. In *Sign language research: Theoretical issues,* ed.C. Lucas, 118–32. Washington, D.C.: Gallaudet University Press.

———. 1991a. Rethinking fingerspelling. *Signpost: the newsletter of the International Sign Linguistics Association.* 4:2–4.

———. 1991b. The acquisition of fingerspelling by deaf children. In *Theoretical issues in sign language research,* vol. 2, ed. P. Siple and S. Fischer, 191–210. Chicago: University of Chicago Press.

———. In press. The ASL lexicon. *International Review of Sign Linguistics.*

Scotton, C. M., and J. Okeju. 1973. Neighbors and lexical borrowings. *Language* 49:871–89.

Sutton-Spence, R., and B. Woll. 1990. Variation and recent change in British Sign Language. *Language Variation and Change* 2:313–30.

Weinreich, U. 1966. *Languages in contact.* The Hague: Mouton.

Wilcox, S. E. 1988. The phonetics of fingerspelling. Ph.D. diss. University of New Mexico, Albuquerque.

Yau, M.-S. 1993. Functions of two codes in Hong Kong Chinese. *World Englishes* 12:25–34.

Contact between a Sign Language

and a Written Language:

Character Signs in Taiwan Sign Language

Jean Ann

This article examines a contact situation between Taiwan Sign Language (TSL) and written Chinese that has resulted in the invention of "character signs"—signs that are representations of Chinese characters. The specific claim of the article is that, phonologically, the character signs of TSL are somewhat outside the system. The article is divided into three parts. The first is an introduction to borrowing in general, TSL, written Chinese characters, and character signs. The second section shows how the phonological structure of character signs differs from that of native TSL signs. The third section spells out the relevance of these observations.

BORROWING AND LOANWORDS

By any yardstick, language contact is a rich area of sociolinguistic research. Languages come in contact under a myriad of circumstances that produce distinct linguistic outcomes (Davis 1989; Lucas 1989; and refer-

This chapter is a revised version of talks presented at the Linguistic Society of America annual meeting in 1995 in New Orleans and at the Fifth Theoretical Issues in Sign Language research conference in Montreal in 1996. I would like to acknowledge the assistance of Daisuke Hara, K. P. Mohanan, Tara Mohanan, Sew Jyh Wee, and Long Peng with various parts of this chapter. Three anonymous reviewers gave me helpful comments on an earlier draft. I am greatly indebted to Wayne Smith for sharing with me much of his unpublished work on TSL and for allowing me to reproduce the pictures of TSL signs and handshapes from his works coauthored with Ting Li-fen. I am grateful to Chiangsheng Yu for providences cited there). Among these are bilingualism (speakers/signers of one or perhaps both languages begin to speak the language of the other), invention of a pidgin (simplified speech to facilitate communication among speakers of different languages), or, perhaps less drastic, borrowing of syntactic structures, vocabulary items, or other linguistic features from one language to another. I focus on the borrowing of vocabulary items.

The spoken language literature has yielded interesting descriptions of borrowed words at all levels, including phonology, morphology, syntax, and semantics. This article (as well as much of the discussion in the literature [Heath 1994, 389]) focuses on the phonological properties of borrowings. In general, languages deal with borrowings in two ways. First, a borrowing might be required to obey the constraints of the new language; hence, it may change considerably from its original form. Second, a borrowing might be allowed to retain some or all of its original form, with the possible consequence that the loan would remain somewhat marked in the new language. (This property of remaining outside the native system is associated with recent loans, whereas older loans are thought of as not being recognizable as loans, so complete is their assimilation into the new language [Bynon 1977, 225]). Both of these scenarios are attested in the world's languages (Davis 1994, 2273).

A situation that requires that restructuring occur to make the borrowing fit into the new language can be illustrated by the case of English loanwords in Japanese. The syllable structures of English and Japanese are quite different, and Japanese requires that many English words change considerably to become licit Japanese words. Words such as *baseball* ([beis bɔl]), *MacDonald's* ([mək da nəlz]) and *strike* ([straik]) become [be yi sɯ bo rɯ], [ma kɯ do na lɯ do], and [sɯ to ra yi kɯ]. In these examples, added and deleted segments result in borrowings that display a CV pattern, conforming to the syllable structure and segmental inventory of Japanese. (For other examples, see Hock 1986, 394; Davis 1994, 2273–74; and references cited there.)

The scenario in which borrowings remain somewhat marked in the new language can be illustrated with a few examples. Malayalee English is a variety of English spoken by native speakers of Malayalam (Mohanan

---

ing the Chinese characters in the text, and to Min Li for providing a final character needed at press time. Finally, I thank Lin Fang Shi, Wang Tzuu Bin, and Cheng Ru Fang, who served as my TSL consultants. The shortcomings herein are my responsibility alone.

and Mohanan 1987).[1] When English words are borrowed into Malayalee English, the segments of English are matched to the segments of Malayalam where possible, with the result that the English word appears with as many segments as are the same in Malayalam and English. For example, English /tap/ would be pronounced /tap/ in Malayalee English since Malayalam has /t/, /a/, and /p/. When a perfect match cannot be made, the segment that is used in Malayalee English is a reanalysis of the English segment. For example, the English segment /θ/ (not present in Malayalam) is reanalyzed as /t̪/ in Malayalee English. Most strikingly, /f/, an English segment that does not occur in Malayalam and that Malayalam has no phonetically similar sound for, itself becomes a segment of Malayalee English (Mohanan and Mohanan 1987, 17–19).

Another example of this phenomenon concerns Malay, the national language of Malaysia, which has accepted a great number of lexical borrowings from various sources in its long history of contact with other spoken languages. Asmah (1987, 8–9) discusses the case of Arabic loan words that contain phonemes nonnative to Malay. Of these, some were retained in Malay: /ʃ/ and /z/. Another (/f/) is variously changed to /p/ or retained as /f/. Asmah (1987, 8) identifies the words in which /f/ remains as those belonging to semantic domains involving religion. Other phonemes borrowed into Malay through words dealing with religion are /dʰ/ and /gʰ/. The phoneme /v/ is borrowed from English in words such as *novel* and *varian* (Asmah 1987).

The classic example of a phoneme borrowed into English from another language is /ʒ/, borrowed from French. It can occur as the final sound in *beige* and *garage* (discussed, for example, in Sandler 1989, 83–84; Davis 1994, 2274; and Bynon 1977, 225). Clearly, these examples illustrate that borrowings are not all restructured to fit into the new language; rather, borrowings sometimes have properties that cause them to stand out from the native words of the new language.

The question of what happens to a word when it is borrowed into another language can be asked at the morphological level as well. Yiddish,

1. Clearly, the data bring up questions, since English loanwords in Malayalee English, one of a number of Indian English varieties, occur in a different sociolinguistic context from English loanwords in Japanese. However, because the generalizations about Malayalee English hold for English borrowings into Malayalam (K. P. Mohanan and T. Mohanan, personal communication), I consider the English borrowings into Malayalam (and Malayalee English) comparable to English borrowings into Japanese.

a Germanic language, has a subset of words borrowed from Hebrew, which takes certain Hebrew affixes rather than Germanic ones (cited in Sandler 1989, 83–84). Singapore English, a variety of English spoken in Singapore, includes words borrowed from Malay, Tamil, and Chinese languages such as Hokkien and Teochew. One Malay borrowing, *buaya* "crocodile," functions only as a noun in Malay. In Singapore English, *buaya* refers to "a lecherous male" and has additional syntactic possibilities (and the attending morphological possibilities).[2] In addition to functioning as a noun (*the buaya, two buayas,* and *of the buaya* are all grammatical in Singapore English), *buaya* can also function as a verb (*he likes to buaya, he buayas every day*) and an adjective (*he is very buaya, the most buaya guy*). The ability of *buaya* to belong to different grammatical categories is typical of other nouns in English such as *table* and *square*. *Buaya* accepts much of the expected English morphology given its syntactic functions. However, Singapore English also has borrowings that, like *buaya*, are syntactically regular but, unlike *buaya*, resist English morphology, such as the verb *tahan* "tolerate" and the adjective *shiok* "enjoyable." Forms such as **tahans, *tahaning, *tahaned, *shioker,* and **shiokest* are all ungrammatical, but bare forms in the same sentences are grammatical. Thus, at the morphological level, too, borrowed words are not necessarily adapted completely to the new language. (For more discussion, see Heath 1994, 386). To my knowledge, English loanwords in Japanese and Malayalee English and loanwords in Malay behave syntactically as any native word.

Turning our attention to sign languages, I note first that the term *borrowing* in the traditional sense would describe a case in which one sign language incorporates a sign that originally came from another sign language. However, as Davis (1989, 97) observes, borrowing does not adequately describe what happens, for example, in the ASL-English situation. A fingerspelled English word is not English, but rather a signed depiction of a written representation of an English word. Therefore, although it is clear that ASL represents the words of written English as signs via its fingerspelling system (see for example, Battison 1978), it is not obvious that these are indeed borrowings from English to ASL.

2. All these grammaticality judgments come from students enrolled in the Structure of English course at the National University of Singapore from 1993–1995.

In order for the correct terminology and an accurate typology of such signs to emerge, we must carefully examine as many as possible. Clearly, sign languages that represent words of spoken languages with alphabetic writing systems have been discussed in the literature, yet little published material deals with sign languages that incorporate words from writing systems that are not alphabetic. Analysis of the character signs of TSL provides just such an opportunity because the writing system of what we will call "Chinese," for the moment, is not an alphabetic one but is a syllabary—that is, it represents its syllables, not its phonemes.[3] Before describing the formation of the character signs of TSL, I begin with a brief history of TSL, followed by an explanation of the relevant aspects of the "Chinese" language, Chinese characters, and character signs.

A BRIEF HISTORY OF TSL

The sign languages of the People's Republic of China (mainland China) and Hong Kong (a once British colony that returned to mainland Chinese rule in 1997) have a history distinct from the sign language of the Republic of China (Taiwan). Political rivals since 1949, Taiwan and mainland China clearly share many aspects of a common culture and history. Despite this, there is no evidence to suggest that they have ever shared a sign language. Prior to the Japanese occupation of Taiwan, deaf people were often isolated by their families and certainly not formally educated (Smith, conversation 1991). Under such conditions, there was no chance for a sign language to develop. The Japanese, believed to have been the first in Asia to provide education for deaf people (Hodgson 1953, 267), brought formal education of deaf people to Taiwan. Today

TSL can be fairly neatly divided into two dialects, one centering around Tainan in the south where the first school for deaf children in Taiwan was established in 1915, and the other in the Taipei area, where Taiwan's second school was established in 1917. Both of these

3. Despite this, as the section on Chinese language and Chinese characters reveals, the importance of character signs lies not in the differences between the writing systems of English and Chinese but rather in the fact that character signs, like ASL's "fingerspelled loan signs," are another example of a signed representation of a written word.

schools were founded during the Japanese occupation of the island from 1895–1945 and there was little communication between them until after World War II, when they both came under the jurisdiction of the provincial government of Taiwan. (Smith 1982, 1)

The two schools were staffed by teachers from Japan. "Teachers were sent from Tokyo and Osaka to Taipei and Tainan respectively, where they used their respective dialects of Japanese Sign Language in their classrooms" (Smith 1989, 1).

The linguistic heritage of a third Taiwanese city, Kaohsiung, is relevant here. The deaf man who established the Chiying School for deaf people in Kaohsiung in 1949 (still in existence today) was a refugee from mainland China (Smith 1976, revised 1988, 5, 30; Yau 1977, foreword; Chao, Chu, and Liu 1988, 9) and a signer of Chinese Sign Language (CSL). He preferred CSL to Taiwan's "Japanese" sign language, and so the CSL signs were taught at the school until sometime in the 1980s, when, under pressure from the government of Taiwan, the school officially switched over to TSL. Today, though there are deaf people in and around Kaohsiung who still recognize CSL, most use TSL on a daily basis.

CHINESE LANGUAGE AND CHINESE CHARACTERS

The spoken languages that we refer to as "Chinese" are actually a "family of mutually unintelligible languages" (Bloomfield 1933, 44) that, for sociolinguistic reasons, are often referred to as dialects.[4] These languages are spoken in three polities of concern here: mainland China, Taiwan, and Hong Kong. Mandarin, the language of mainland China's political capital, Beijing, boasts the greatest number of speakers and functions as a lingua franca between Chinese who speak mutually unintelligible dialects; it is also spoken in Taiwan. Southern Min (also known as Taiwanese, Hokkien, or Amoy) is spoken widely in Taiwan and in parts of the mainland. Cantonese is spoken widely in Hong Kong and parts of the mainland, including Guangzhou (Canton). Spoken Mandarin, Southern Min, and Cantonese are all mutually unintelligible.

All Chinese languages use characters as their writing system (though mainland China uses recently simplified characters, and Taiwan and

4. There is no firm linguistic distinction between "language" and "dialect." Rather, the distinction is usually a political one.

Hong Kong use older, more complex, characters). Though it is claimed that characters are mutually intelligible to all regardless of spoken dialect, this is only partly true (DeFrancis 1989, 95); some spoken words of Shanghainese and Cantonese, for example, cannot be written in Mandarin characters. All characters in this paper represent Mandarin words.

The pronunciation of Mandarin words (but not words of Shanghainese or Cantonese) might also be spelled out in Roman letters by a system known as *pinyin*. More correctly, pinyin uses both the letters of the Roman alphabet and tonal diacritics to represent the words of Mandarin: Each of the segments in the pronunciation of a character, including the tone, is represented with a (fairly) consistent phonetic symbol (or combination of symbols). Thus 中 is written "*zhōng*" [5] ('middle') in pinyin, and the *pinyin* for 台 灣 手 語 is "*tai wan shou yu*" (literally, Taiwan hand language). Knowledge of pinyin enables those who have not memorized the pronunciations of Chinese characters to pronounce them by sounding them out. Pinyin is widely used in mainland China and rarely used in Taiwan; however, because it is commonly used in the linguistic literature to transcribe Mandarin words, I use it throughout this article to name some of the TSL signs discussed.

Because Chinese characters are often misunderstood, I turn now to a brief summary of a few relevant points from DeFrancis (1984, 1989). (Interested readers should see DeFrancis's work for a fascinating and readable discussion.)

It is often claimed that Chinese characters contrast sharply with written English because characters purportedly represent ideas, and English spellings represent pronunciation of words. This "difference" between Chinese and English is illustrated by examples such as the following: In Chinese, the word *middle* is written with a character 中 that just happens to be pronounced "*zhōng*." But in English, the combination of letters in the word *middle* attempts to represent each of the phonemes in the spoken word *middle*. The argument persists that a Chinese character such as 中 could in principle have *any* pronunciation that would be grammatical in Mandarin because nothing about the character itself necessitates or even suggests the particular pronunciation "*zhōng*." To put it another way, Chinese characters cannot be "sounded out" as English words often

5. Technically, pinyin words should include a tone mark to help disambiguate them, as in "zhōng." However, I have suppressed them because, throughout the paper, either an English gloss or a Chinese character appears with the pinyin.

can be (despite the historically derived inconsistencies in the spelling system of English). To support the notion that characters represent ideas — and not pronunciations — it is often pointed out that some modern characters were originally stylized pictures of entities such as a person, the sun, and so on.

Although it is true that 1 percent of Chinese characters originally were drawings of natural objects (DeFrancis 1989, 97–101; Li and Thompson 1979, 322) and that they have been simplified and stylized throughout history, DeFrancis (1989, 119–20) points out that fairly early in their history, Chinese characters began to represent *sounds* (not pictures of things in the natural world). Therefore, DeFrancis argues strongly against assertions that Chinese has a writing system that is different from alphabetic writing systems. He claims that the written Chinese character system is trying to do the same thing that written English is trying to do: represent the sounds of their respective spoken languages (DeFrancis 1989, 119–20). Written English and written Chinese differ in how they do this: Written English tries to represent the phonemes of English, whereas written Chinese tries to represent its syllables. Written Chinese represents syllables by providing two sorts of clues in each character: a semantic character (indicates what the word generally means) and a phonetic character (indicates how the word is generally pronounced). The character that represents the semantic and the character that represents the phonetic are combined into one composite character. Most scholars now agree that the semantic (known also as the "radical") was attached to the phonetic and that the phonetic was primary (DeFrancis 1989, 105). From this description it is clear that characters represent a semantic component of a word (an "idea"), but it is equally clear that the notion that characters represent ideas alone is false. In fact, DeFrancis argues that the phonetic component to Chinese characters is far greater than introductory linguistics textbooks reveal. DeFrancis (1989, 52–53, 102–3) claims that a conservative estimate of 66 percent of characters have some phonetic usefulness, including 25 percent that reveal *exactly* how the character is pronounced. Many of the remaining characters can be considered to have phonetically useful information as a reader learns more about Chinese characters and their history.

The modern writing systems of English and Mandarin (and, for that matter, many other languages) betray inefficiencies in representing the sounds of their respective spoken languages; both are far less efficient than pinyin or Spanish, for example, and written Chinese is less efficient than written English (DeFrancis 1989, 268). But the level of relative success achieved by a given writing system notwithstanding, the important point is that all full writing systems that humans have ever invented have tried to do the same thing: represent speech, not ideas.

Turning our attention now to sign languages, discussions of two aspects of Chinese characters have appeared in the sign language literature. First, one area of psycholinguistic research mines characters for what they reveal about questions of language processing. Mounting evidence suggests that written Chinese is processed visually, unlike the processing of a language written in an alphabetic system such as English (Bellugi, Tzeng, Klima, and Fok, 1989, 148). Because sign languages cannot be processed aurally and must instead be processed visually, the Chinese writing system became interesting to sign language researchers. In an attempt to find out whether deaf signers of CSL as a first language bring an enhanced ability to the task of learning characters, deaf and hearing Chinese children were asked to watch a point light display of a person writing a pseudocharacter in the air in a darkened room with a light on the fingertip. Then they were asked to write the pseudocharacter as it would have been written on paper. The abilities of Chinese deaf children and Chinese hearing children appeared to be different: The deaf children were better at the task (Fok, Bellugi, van Hoek, and Klima 1988, 188–90). A second area of research focuses on sociolinguistic aspects of CSL in contact with Chinese script. It concludes that Chinese characters are borrowed into CSL in two ways, and it discusses some of the changes that written characters undergo as borrowings and how the characters become part of CSL by taking on the same syntactic properties as other words of the same grammatical category (Fok, Bellugi, van Hoek, and Klima 1988, 194–95).

CHARACTER SIGNS

Sign language dictionaries and other written sources published in China, Hong Kong, Taiwan, and Japan suggest the use of character signs in these polities (Chao, Chu, and Liu 1988; China Deaf and Blind Society 1960; Fok, Bellugi, van Hoek, and Klima 1988; Fu and Mei 1986; Goodstadt 1972; Nakano and Ito 1982, 1987; Osaka YMCA 1979; Republic of China Ministry of Education, Research Division of Sign Language for the Deaf 1984; Smith 1976, revised 1988; Smith and Ting 1979b). The direct information we have about character signs comes from writings about four languages: TSL, CSL, Japanese Sign Language (JSL), and Hong Kong Sign Language (HKSL). Systematic examination of all the data from all sign languages that use character signs has not been carried out. Preliminarily, however, it seems that differences exist in the way the same character is signed in different languages: For example, signers of JSL do not produce the sign that represents the character /⌐ 'person' with two 1 handshapes as do signers of TSL (see Example 17f); rather, they trace the character in the air. Smith and Ting (1979b, 1984) list the traced sign as one that is used in TSL; however, although the Kaohsiung signers certainly understand the traced character, they rarely, if ever, produce it naturally.

Character signs compose "a sign category probably unique to the Japanese and Chinese sign language families because of the use of Chinese ideographs in the writing systems of China, Korea, and Japan" (Smith 1976, revised 1988, 12). Fu and Mei (1986, 40, translation by Geraint Wong) explain that the character signs of CSL are constructed by two methods: "use the fingers of both hands to imitate the shape of either the whole or a part of a Chinese character" (see Example 1), and "writing in the air with a finger" (called "tracing" in Smith and Ting 1979b, 1984) (see Example 2). The sign language of Hong Kong (referred to as "Hong Kong" Sign Language in Fok and Bellugi [1986]) and "Chinese" Sign Language in Fok, Bellugi, van Hoek, and Klima [1988]) also possesses character signs whose formational properties are described in the same way (Fok, Bellugi, van Hoek, and Klima 1988, 195). Smith and Ting's data reveal to them that character signs in TSL are constructed in the two ways just mentioned and in two additional methods: a combination of both tracing and use of handshape (see Example 3), and use of the mouth (in addition to handshapes) to represent part or all of a character (see Example 4). These sorts of character signs are illustrated in Examples 1–4.

EXAMPLE 1: *A character sign constructed by means of handshape alone.*

WANG "king"

EXAMPLE 2: *Two character signs constructed by means of handshape and movement.*

a. CHUAN "river"   b. WAN "ten thousand"

EXAMPLE 3: *A character sign consisting of a combination of both tracing and handshape.*

MAO (a surname)

EXAMPLE 4: *A character sign constructed by use of the mouth and handshape.*

ZHONG "middle"

I do not discuss any character signs that fall into the groups represented by Examples 2b and 4. In characters that are traced strictly with the index finger (those in Example 2b), signers appear to write the character in the air just as it would be written on paper. Since this strategy is commonly used by hearing as well as deaf Chinese, these representations of characters might not be accurately described as signs in the same sense as other sorts of representations of characters. Also, because my data did not include a single token of any character sign that makes use of the mouth (Example 4), I say no more about them here. The discussion focuses entirely on character signs that use handshapes (Example 1) or handshapes and movements (Examples 2a and 3) to represent characters or parts of characters.

Data

Smith and Ting (1979b, 29) estimate that there are thirty to forty character signs in TSL.[6] Examination of my data turns up ten that recur regularly in natural signing and a few more that occur, albeit much more infrequently. The data I discuss come largely from my own field research carried out in Kaohsiung, Taiwan. Where noted, I discuss data from Smith's published and unpublished work. Smith's work is based upon his field research, largely carried out in Taipei and Tainan. The reader (and

6. Written sources and signers of JSL concur that there are some thirty character signs in JSL (Daisuke Hara, personal communication; Soya Mori, personal communication).

other researchers) would do well to remember the histories of linguistic influences upon the areas from which the data have come: Kaohsiung data and other TSL data may well differ.

All of the data were elicited by me. Consultants were never asked directly to produce character signs in isolation or in context; rather, they responded to visual stimuli (pictures of objects, comic strips, etc.) in various ways (told stories about them, used them in a sentence, explained their meaning or action, etc.). The productions of all character signs occurred naturally during such responses. In addition to their occurrence in videotaped sessions, all the character signs discussed in this article occur, to the best of my knowledge, in natural conversation among deaf Taiwanese.

Even a cursory examination of TSL's lexicon reveals that character signs are not the only signs that represent aspects of written communication. Some such signs, which seem to fall outside the normal word formation conventions of TSL, are mentioned in Smith (1976, revised 1988, 9–14). For example, one TSL sign meaning "beer" appears to have originated from the fingerspelling system used in the United States; BEER is signed as fingerspelled B-C.[7] In addition, TSL has a sign that represents letters of the Roman alphabet, curiously, *not* fingerspelled letters. The handshape in Example 5 forms the basis of this sign.

EXAMPLE 5:

"water closet"

Deaf Taiwanese point out that in Example 5, the ulnar fingers imitate the letter W, while the radial fingers form the letter C; the sign "spells out" the acronym for *water closet*. Geometric shapes such as circle, square,

7. Smith and Ting (1984, 52) explain that BEER begins with the handshape they call HU facing front, then "pulled to the right becoming the letter 'e'" (translation by Long Peng). (In ASL parlance, a fingerspelled B handshape pulls rightward, becoming a fingerspelled E handshape.) In the sign used by the Kaohsiung deaf people, however, an ASL fingerspelled B handshape clearly becomes an ASL fingerspelled C handshape. Production of a fingerspelled ASL E handshape instead is regarded as a mispronunciation.

and triangle are often signed with one or more handshapes that indicate the actual shape—*not* the Chinese character. Triangle (三 角 *san jiao*, literally, 'three angles') is signed as in Example 6. Crucially, the sign makes no reference to the character ——— *san*, as one might imagine it could.

EXAMPLE 6:

SAN JIAO "triangle"

TSL signs for mathematical symbols are often iconic depictions of the symbols themselves, crucially not the Chinese characters for the symbols. Examples are the signs meaning "multiplication," "division," "equal," and one of the signs meaning "addition."[8]

In TSL, common surnames are represented by established signs. For example, LEE is a two-handed sign in which interlocked handshapes move back and forth (Example 33), CHEN brushes upward on the nose, CHIANG indicates a moustache, and in CHENG a flat hand circles above the head. One way that deaf Taiwanese assign namesigns is by producing the established sign for a surname and adding the appropriate gender marker for the intended referent (Smith and Ting 1979b, 1–2).[9] Such "surname signs" may stand for characters, but they are not character signs because they do not attempt to represent written characters.

Finally, series of characters may be used to translate foreign terms into Mandarin (De Francis 1984, 49). For example, *Canada* is known in Man-

8. Dictionaries reveal that a one-handed iconic sign represents the mathematical symbol for division (÷) in China and Hong Kong (China Deaf and Blind Association 1960; Fu and Mei 1986; Goodstadt 1972, 200). This sign is not used by Kaohsiung consultants.

9. For a discussion about how name signs are coined in CSL (as it is signed in Guangdong [Canton], People's Republic of China), see Yau and He (1989).

darin as *jia na da*, Clinton as *ke lin dun*, and AIDS as *ai zi bing*. Signers translate these terms into TSL via Mandarin.[10] Thus, *Canada*, for example, is signed with three signs—one for each of the intended characters: JIA, NA, and DA, glossed in Smith (1976, revised 1988, 11) as "add," "take," and "big." Formal signed names such as JIA, NA, and DA are often shortened in discourse to one sign. Clearly, although the series of signs in JIA NA DA "Canada" is a TSL translation of the characters, crucially, none are character signs since none attempt to imitate the relevant characters.

FORMATION OF CHARACTER SIGNS
IN TAIWAN SIGN LANGUAGE

This article explores the measures TSL takes to represent characters and compares the signs created by those measures with native TSL signs. Though a thorough examination of *all* the signs that fall both inside and outside the set of "normal" TSL signs stands to yield more understanding as to TSL's method of word formation, I have begun this work by focusing on character signs alone.

The literature on TSL makes one major distinction between regular signs and character signs: *A character sign imitates a Chinese character (or part of a Chinese character), whereas a regular sign does not* (Smith 1976, revised 1988, 11; Smith 1989; Smith and Ting 1979b, 29; 1984). A second property of character signs is hinted at (Wayne Smith, personal communication; Deborah Chen, personal communication)—namely, a character sign must be signed a certain way by all signers, regardless of their handedness, whereas a regular sign need not be.

It seems clear that a character written on paper must be restructured in order to become a sign—an insight mentioned in Fok, Bellugi, van Hoek, and Klima (1988, 194). They claim that "as forms are borrowed . . . from Chinese script . . . to Chinese Sign Language they undergo radical change to conform to the linguistic constraints that have developed in Chinese Sign Language" (1988, 194). Then again, since character signs are iconic (in the sense that they imitate characters), one might

10. Names for foreign entities need not be translated into TSL via spoken Mandarin in this way. The Kaohsiung deaf refer to Bill Clinton with a compound sign that could be translated roughly as "white hair combed straight back."

expect their structural properties to differ from those of native signs. I argue that a close examination of TSL character signs shows that they conform to some linguistic constraints of TSL and violate others. Violations occur in the phonology of the signs. I show that character signs as a group possess the properties listed in Example 7.

EXAMPLE 7:

    a. contrastive handedness unattested in TSL except for character signs
    b. handshapes unattested in TSL except for character signs
    c. a handshape combination unattested in TSL except for character signs
    d. a point of contact unattested in TSL except for character signs

All character signs do not share all of the properties listed in Example 7; rather, each character sign must have at least one. I explain each of these properties in the subsections that follow.

Handedness in Sign Languages

Since the major articulators of any sign language are the hands, it comes as no surprise that handedness has interested researchers. It is often asserted that a signer's handedness affects the way signs are produced. The production of two sorts of signs—one-handed signs and two-handed signs with one moving hand, particularly—reveal the handedness of signers. Specifically, right-handed signers produce one-handed signs with their right hands, and left-handed signers produce them with their left hands. In two-handed signs in which one hand moves and the other does not, the moving hand is the right for right-handed signers and the left for left-handed signers. For example, a sign such as TSL YONG 'use' is correctly produced as in Example 8 or with the opposite handedness: That is, left-handed signers might produce the sign in Example 8[11] such that

11. These cases should not be confused with several brought to my attention by Susan Fischer and Richard Meier (personal communication) for ASL, in which directionality or location (*not* handedness) is contrastive: in the ASL signs EAST and LEFT, the signer must move the hand leftward, not rightward. Similarly, ASL HEART is signed on the left side of the chest (the actual location of the heart), not on the right side. In all three cases, crucially, signers can produce the sign with either hand.

the right hand acts as the base, and the left hand moves. Right-handed signers might produce the sign in Example 8 such that the left hand acts as the base, and the right hand moves.

EXAMPLE 8:

TSL YONG "use"

These differences in the pronunciation of a sign are not contrastive (Liddell and Johnson 1989; Padden and Perlmutter 1987, 338)—meaning that, pronounced either way, the signs have the same meaning, and both are judged by native signers to be pronounced correctly.

Does this characteristic of ASL hold crosslinguistically? Observation of the production of TSL native signs and character signs by right- and left-handed signers suggests that handedness overall is not contrastive in TSL, but in a few character signs, handedness is contrastive.

HANDEDNESS IN TSL SIGNS

In the subsections that follow, I examine handedness first in native signs and, second, in character signs. TSL includes native signs and character signs that are one-handed (Example 9), two-handed with alternating movement (Example 10), two-handed signs with the same movement (Example 11), and two-handed signs with one hand still and one hand moving (Example 12).

EXAMPLE 9:

LAOSHI "teacher"

EXAMPLE 10:

SUI BIAN "whatever"

EXAMPLE 11:

SHENG QI "angry"

BANG MANG "help"

In what follows, I report on my examination of the production of TSL data by two right-handed signers and one left-handed signer. I examined one hour of videotaped data per signer, collected over the course of one month. Analysis of the videotapes reveals that each signer has a clear preference for one hand to be dominant, but that there are a few discourse situations in which signers make their normally nondominant hand dominant. Therefore the list of signs produced with a dominant right hand by right-handed signers and a dominant left hand by left-handed signers is quite long. For lack of space, I include glosses of only some of the signs produced by all of the consultants.

One-Handed Native Signs

The English glosses of a selection of the TSL one-handed signs (such as those in Example 9) produced with the right hand by right-handed signers and with the left hand by left-handed signers are provided in Example 13:

EXAMPLE I3:

DON'T LIKE	IF	DEAD (one-handed version)
IS	CAN	TAIWAN
TEACHER	SKY	COLOR
BEAUTIFUL	TREE	TO BE BETTER THAN ME
LIKE	GOVERNMENT	SICK (one-handed version)
BLACK	PARENTS	NUMBERS (one-handed version)
GO	FLOWER	DON'T KNOW
STUPID	SEE	MOUSE

In the videotaped data, signers produced several of these signs in Example 13 with their nondominant hands acting as dominant in two kinds of cases. First, signers were given a sign by an off-camera questioner and asked to explain its meaning. Sometimes signers produced the signs with their nondominant hands while they were thinking of what to say, especially if they were not sure what the questioner was signing. When the signer was sure of the intended sign, the handedness shifted to his/her usual handedness. Second, the signer produced signs with the nondominant hand acting as dominant when the normally dominant hand was signing something else.

Two-Handed Native Signs

Two-handed signs of the types in Examples 10 and 11 cannot be considered because the movement of the hands leaves no way to decide which of the hands is dominant. English glosses for TSL signs that are examples of these types of signs include those in Example 14a (cf. Example 10) and 14b (cf. Example 11):

EXAMPLE 14:

a. FIRE
   BUSINESS

b. GLUE   HEARING
   DIFFERENT   EIFFEL TOWER
   NUMBERS   GO TO JAIL
   SAME   DOESN'T MATTER
   CHILD   CHANGE
   DEAF   BECOME

This section then concentrates only on signs such as that in Example 12 with one hand still and one hand moving. The English glosses of some of the TSL signs that were produced with the left hand dominant (moving) by the left-handed signer and the right hand dominant by the right-handed signers are listed in Example 15.

EXAMPLE 15:

ADD   WORK
RIGHT   1–4 YEARS
DEAD   HOW MANY YEARS
YELL AT (SOMEBODY)   INTERRUPT
ASK (SOMEBODY)   EASY
BEAT (SOMEBODY)   FINISH
NAB (SOMEBODY)   LUST AFTER

The signs listed in Examples 13 and 15 are produced by left-handed and right-handed signers in slightly different ways but clearly are intended as the same sign. The left- and right-handed versions appear to be considered correct pronunciations by both self-report and direct observation: (1) direct questioning as to the correctness of the same form with the opposite handedness almost always met with approval; (2) after having been asked about the handedness of several forms, signers sometimes provided information about its pronunciation on their own, often saying that signing with the right or left hand dominant amounted to the same thing; and (3) signers themselves seemed to prefer to sign with one hand dominant, though sometimes discourse reasons dictated that they switch handedness. The conclusions we must draw, then, are that left-handed signers are left dominant, right-handed signers are right dominant, and these differences are not contrastive in native TSL signs.

HANDEDNESS AND CHARACTER SIGNS

In this section, I discuss handedness as it relates to the character signs. Linguists and native signers alike have suspected that TSL character signs must be signed the same way by both right-handed and left-handed signers. In other words, although native signs are produced with either the right or left hand dominant, character signs ignore signers' handedness, much as both left-handed and right-handed people write the characters the same way on paper. One Kaohsiung signer perceptively remarked: If the character signs were signed "backward," they would not be understood. Careful examination reveals an interesting puzzle: The claim that handedness is contrastive is false for most character signs, but true for a few. I offer an explanation for this asymmetry.

One-Handed Character Signs

Five one-handed character signs occurred in the data: YI "one," ER "two," SAN "three," SI "four," and SHANG "above."[12] As is the case with native signs, all were produced according to signers' handedness.

12. The character signs SHANG "above" and XIA "below" occur marginally in the Kaohsiung data: SHANG occurs in Signed Mandarin expressions such as *shang ke* "go to class" and *shang tian* "up in the sky." XIA never occurred. SHANG was signed according to signers' handedness. Two signs, glossed as KUAI "fast" and MAN "slow" (in Smith and Ting) appear to be constructed from SHANG and XIA although they are not described as character signs (1979a, 113–14). Repeated instances of KUAI and MAN occur in the data by all signers; all are signed according to signers' handedness.

Two-Handed Character Signs

As with two-handed regular signs, some character signs must be excluded from our investigation since their structural properties prevent them from yielding results relevant to the question of handedness. First, two-handed character signs that exhibit the same handshape and the same movement (Example 16) would betray no difference between a right-handed and left-handed version (corresponds to Examples 14b and 11). There is no character sign whose structural properties correspond to Example 14a or Example 10.

EXAMPLE 16:

BEI "north"

Examination of character signs with two different handshapes or two different movements such as those in Examples 17a–g (which correspond to Example 12) will show whether there is any difference in the way right-handed and left-handed signers produce them.

a. GONG "labor"

b. ZHONG "middle"

c. XIAO "small"

d. GE a measure word

e. JIE "introduce"

f. REN "person"

g. XUE "blood"

An exhaustive search of the Kaohsiung data reveals that Examples 17a–e are always produced according to the signer's own handedness, suggesting that handedness is not contrastive. However, the same search turns up one additional curious fact: Examples 17f and g are produced in exactly the same way by both right- and left-handed signers, suggesting that handedness is contrastive. Could it be that handedness is contrastive in Examples 17a–e but not in Examples 17f and g?

An explanation to this puzzle suggests itself when both the character and the character sign are examined side by side. The character signs in Examples 17a–e are pictured next to the characters they represent in Examples 18a–e.

EXAMPLE 18:

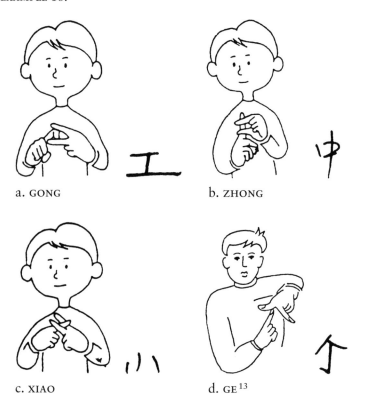

a. GONG

b. ZHONG

c. XIAO

d. GE[13]

13. Examples 17d–e and 18d–e are pronounced with a different orientation by the Kaohsiung signers.

e. JIE

None of the characters represented by the character signs in Examples 18a–e have distinctive left and right sides; that is, each character itself is symmetrical. Thus, a right-handed version of Example 18a, for example (in which the signer represents the top and bottom strokes of the character with a TSL 2 handshape [an ASL fingerspelled V handshape] on the right hand, and the downward stroke between the two with a TSL 10 handshape [an ASL fingerspelled X handshape] on the left hand) and a left-handed version (in which the same handshapes occur on the *other* hand) produce two slightly different versions of Example 18a but, crucially, still represent the character faithfully. The same is true for Examples 18b–e.

The other two characters and corresponding character signs, which did not conform to the generalization that character signs are signed according to signers' handedness, are pictured in Examples 19a and b. It is apparent that these characters are not symmetrical. If the left and right sides are switched in the written character (Example 19a), another character with a different meaning is created. In Example 19b, a noncharacter is created.

a. REN represents 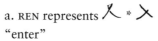   b. XUE represents _们_ * _门_
"enter"   a noncharacter

If the character signs in Examples 19a and b are to represent the characters faithfully, they must be signed the same way by right- and left-handed signers.

Summarizing, most character signs are signed according to the signer's own handedness. Only two character signs, REN and XUE, must be signed the same way by right- and left-handed signers. To my knowledge, this property of some character signs (that they must be signed the same way by all signers regardless of signers' handedness) is not shared by any native TSL signs.

Handshapes and Signs

This section discusses two observations about TSL handshapes in general and the character sign data. First, when the handshapes in any sign language are examined overall, it seems clear that some handshapes frequently recur, whereas others recur much less often. Further, it has long been noticed that some signs are iconic. Along this same line, iconicity persists at another level: Some handshapes resemble their referents, and some handshapes do not. With these observations in mind, it would seem reasonable to say that iconic handshapes would occur in character signs or other iconic signs, rather than native signs, and that noniconic handshapes would occur in native signs. But in general, this is not true. Handshapes usually occur throughout the lexicon (i.e., in both iconic and noniconic signs). For example, the handshape in Example 20 is perhaps the most common handshape in TSL, occurring in a great many native TSL signs (Ann 1993, 225). It also occurs in all traced character signs (such as THEN, ONLY THEN, PERSON [b],[14] and others) that attempt to trace either the entire character or only part of it. (Potentially, a signer could trace *any* character, that is, write it out in the air, for the benefit of an interlocutor.)

EXAMPLE 20:

Example 20 also occurs in nontraced character signs such as ZHONG "middle," WANG "king," REN "person," ZHU "main," XIAO "small," XUE "blood," and others.

Other common handshapes that occur in character signs are pictured in Example 21. A slightly less common handshape, pictured in Example 22, occurs in character signs.

EXAMPLE 21:

EXAMPLE 22:

Thus far, it seems clear that nothing suggests that the handshapes that occur in character signs are unusual.

The second observation is that a TSL handshape can almost always be associated with one or more semantic values over the set of signs in which it occurs. This observation was first made and discussed for several hand-

14. This sign, roughly the JSL character sign which means "person," was rarely if ever produced by the Kaohsiung deaf during my stays there, and it never occurred on the videotapes.

shapes in Smith (1976, revised 1988, 18–21). Consider the handshape (known in ASL as fingerspelled 1) in Example 23.

EXAMPLE 23:

Example 23 occurs in the set of TSL signs glossed in Example 24. Clearly, all of the signs in Example 24 share a semantic property: female.

EXAMPLE 24:

FEMALE	MOTHER	GRANDMOTHER
SHE	DAUGHTER	GRANDDAUGHTER
BACHELORETTE	DIVORCE	MARRIAGE

The handshape in Example 23 also occurs in signs glossed in Example 25, which all share a semantic property: bad.

EXAMPLE 25:

LOUSY   HUMBLE   GOOD OR BAD?

The handshape in Example 23 occurs in the glosses in Example 26, which all share yet another semantic property: thin.

EXAMPLE 26:

THIN   HAIR

Finally, the handshape in Example 23 occurs in the glosses in Example 27, in which no apparent shared semantic property can be discerned.

EXAMPLE 27:

PURPLE   TO BE ABLE TO

The handshape in Example 23 relates the members of different sets of signs (those in the sets of Examples 24–26). Moreover, it has an arbitrary relationship to the semantics (i.e., nothing about the handshape suggests that it must have these meanings[15]). (Example 23 also bears no relation to the character[s] for the Mandarin translation of the form.)

15. It should be noted that the handshape is used as a gesture by hearing people in many Asian countries to indicate "female," "bad," or "small."

There is one conspicuous exception to the generalizations that (1) handshapes generally occur over the whole lexicon of TSL, not just in character signs, and (2) handshapes are generally associated with meanings in at least some of the signs in which they occur. This exception concerns the handshape pictured in Example 28. Unlike all other handshapes, Example 28 occurs only in character signs and not in any native signs,[16] a point tentatively noted in Smith (1976, revised 1988, 18). Moreover, the handshape in Example 28 is not associated with any true semantic property in TSL.

EXAMPLE 28:

Example 28 does not refer to a particular size, shape, or other property of a real-life object, and so it does not function as a classifier. Nor can it be associated with a meaning or set of meanings as are other handshapes. Rather, it mimics a *written* character that names an entity in the world. Example 28 represents three strokes of a character (not always three parallel strokes, as claimed in Smith (1976, revised 1988, 18).

The English glosses for the TSL signs in Example 29 are the only signs that contain the handshape in Example 28.

EXAMPLE 29:

THREE	AFRICA	FIELD	EXIT
RIVER	CUTTLEFISH	WEDNESDAY	CANDLE
WARM SPRINGS	STATE	KING	WATER
MAIN	THIRD	TAMSUI	THIRD PLACE

It may seem that Example 29 contains subsets of semantically related signs and "stray" signs whose glosses do not betray a relation to each other; in other words, the handshape in Example 28, which recurs in the signs in Example 29, may seem similar to the case of the handshape in Example 23, which recurs in the sets of Examples 24–27. In this scenario, two sub-

16. This handshape is purported (Smith and Ting 1979, 1984) to occur in the signs CUTTLEFISH and CANDLE. The Kaohsiung informants use the four handshape in both, however.

sets of signs in Example 29 might be (1) those connected to the concept of 'three' (such as THREE, THIRD, THIRD PLACE, and WEDNESDAY [the third day of the week]) and (2) place names (such as TAMSUI, WARM SPRINGS, and AFRICA), while the rest of the signs that seem unrelated. However, a different generalization unites the entire set of signs in Example 29.

If we translate the English glosses in Example 29 into Chinese characters as in Example 30 and examine the signs for each, the generalization becomes clear.

EXAMPLE 30:

THREE	三	STATE	州
WEDNESDAY	禮拜三	EXIT	出
THIRD	第三個	RIVER	川
THIRD PLACE	第三名	KING	王
AFRICA	非	CANDLE	蜡燭
WARM SPRINGS	溫泉	CUTTLEFISH	烏賊
TAMSUI	淡水	MAIN	主
FIELD	田	WATER	水

All of the signs in Example 30 represent all or part of the character: That is, they are character signs.

The data show that Example 28 occurs in character signs but never in native signs. Example 28 could not have been borrowed from Mandarin since neither written nor spoken Mandarin is composed of any hand-shapes at all. Example 28 is an invention that represents a borrowing. This property (invented handshapes employed for character signs but not for native signs) sets the character signs apart from native signs.

In summary, the two main points of this section are, first, that the TSL lexicon contains many handshapes. In general, character signs are composed of common TSL handshapes that occur throughout the lexicon. The exception is Example 28, which occurs only in character signs. Second, in general, a TSL handshape is associated with one or several meanings in the signs in which it occurs (though that handshape may occur in signs in which it has no identifiable meaning). The exception is Example 28, which does not carry a true meaning of its own anywhere in the lexicon. Rather, it represents several strokes of a given character.

Handshape Combinations

Two-handed signs have always intrigued researchers. In ASL, two-handed signs may have one of two sorts of handshape combinations: two of the same handshape or two different handshapes. Battison (1978) relates the handshape combination in a sign with the sort of movements that occur in it. The generalizations that state these co-occurrences are known as the symmetry and dominance conditions (Battison 1978, 33–35). They are as follows:

EXAMPLE 31:

Symmetry Condition. If both hands of a sign move independently during its articulation, then both hands must be specified for the same location, the same handshape, and the same movement (whether performed simultaneously or in alternation), and the specifications for orientation must be either symmetrical or identical.

Dominance Condition. If the hands of a two-handed sign do not have the same handshape (i.e., they are different), then one hand must be passive while the active hand articulates the movement; the specification of the passive hand is restricted to a small set: A, S, B, 5, G, C, and O.

Much recent discussion in the phonology of two-handed signs considers these generalizations basic.

HANDSHAPE COMBINATIONS IN
TWO-HANDED TSL NATIVE SIGNS

TSL includes both one- and two-handed signs. A one-handed sign must use at least one of TSL's fifty-six handshapes (Smith and Ting 1984, 202). (A one-handed sign could use two handshapes if it changes handshape.) A two-handed sign can use two of the same handshape or two different handshapes. (Likewise, a two-handed sign can use more than two handshapes if the hands change shape during the sign.) For our purposes, we will leave aside the question of signs with handshape change.

Two-handed native signs in TSL can be divided into two categories:

those in which both hands have the same handshape and those in which each hand has a different handshape. Both types are numerous in the lexicon of TSL. The inventory of TSL handshapes stands at fifty-six (Smith and Ting 1984, 202). Over forty of these are attested in two-handed signs in which both hands have the same handshape.[17]

The second category of two-handed signs contains those with two different handshapes. Smith and Ting (1979a, 1984) reveal approximately 250 signs of this type. Sixty percent of these have a combination of some sort of 5 hand (if we include in this category several very similar handshapes, pictured in Example 32) and another handshape.

EXAMPLE 32:

Of the approximately 40 percent that remain, 25 percent have handshape combinations in which one of the hands assumes a handshape considered unmarked (specifically in TSL: [ASL] C, O, A, and 1/G), and the other is some other (marked) handshape. The remaining 75 percent have handshape combinations constructed from two marked handshapes. Combinations include those in Example 33:

EXAMPLE 33:

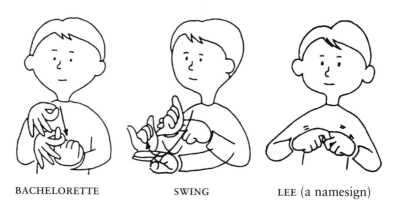

BACHELORETTE   SWING   LEE (a namesign)

17. The other sixteen occur in very few signs, none of which is two-handed. It remains to be seen whether native TSL signers would accept or coin new two-handed signs in which both hands had the same handshape (of the remaining sixteen).

Several character signs reside in this small percentage of signs, which are discussed in the next section.

HANDSHAPE COMBINATIONS IN TWO-HANDED TSL CHARACTER SIGNS

The signs pictured in Examples 34–36 imitate the characters in those illustrations.

EXAMPLE 34:

JIE represents 介

EXAMPLE 35:

GONG represents 工

EXAMPLE 36:

ZHONG represents 中

The handshape combinations in the signs in Examples 34–36 are pictured in Examples 37–39.

EXAMPLE 37:

JIE "introduce"

EXAMPLE 38:

GONG "work"

EXAMPLE 39:

ZHONG "middle"

The handshape combinations in Examples 37–39 are unattested in other TSL signs (using the Smith and Ting [1979a, 1983] glossaries as a database). Further, Examples 37 and 38 are composed of two marked hand-shapes, according to Battison (1978), and 39 is composed of one marked and one unmarked handshape.

Point of Contact and Character Signs

In two-handed signs, the hands have the option of contacting each other. If we divide the hand into general areas of potential contact, we could derive the list in Example 40. We would expect that in two-handed signs, contact between hands would occur in these areas. Moreover, since each of these possible points of contact might logically combine with all other possible points of contact, there are some thirty-six possible points of contact that we would expect the signs of TSL to fall into.

EXAMPLE 40:

volar (palm) side of the hand	contact on the fingers
	contact on the hand
dorsal side of the hand	contact on the fingers
	contact on the hand
radial side of the palm at the fingers	
ulnar side of the palm at the fingers	
tips of the fingers	
wrist	
between fingers	

My investigation of approximately 600 TSL signs shows that although some character signs have handshape combinations that are attested in native signs (i.e., REN, XUE, BEI, XIAO, GE), the two hands never contact each other in native signs the way they do in these character signs. I discuss each case separately.

EXAMPLE 41:

REN represents "person"

The character sign REN is made up of the two handshapes in Example 41, which contact each other such that the tip of one touches the volar side of the other. This handshape combination occurs in many native signs as well. However, in the signs I examined, there was no other case in which the tip of the fingers contacted the volar part of the hand with *any* hand-shape combination, including this one. The attested points of contact are listed in Example 42.

EXAMPLE 42:

radial finger to ulnar finger
radial finger to radial finger
volar finger to volar finger
volar finger to dorsal finger

The situation is similar for the character sign in Example 43. XUE is made up of two common handshapes that contact each other such that the dorsal side of the fingers on one hand touch the radial side of the fingers on the other (cf. Example 17g):

EXAMPLE 43:

XUE REPRESENTS   血   "BLOOD"

In addition, the two handshapes in Example 43 occur in four native signs, none of which have contact between the hands. The sort of contact attested here (dorsal side of fingers to radial side of fingers) was not attested for *any* handshape combination, including this one (except for XUE).

Similarly, the character sign BEI is composed of two handshapes (Example 44) that contact each other on the ulnar sides of each hand.

EXAMPLE 44:

BEI REPRESENTS   北   "NORTH"

Ulnar-ulnar contact was not attested with any handshape combination, except in the sign SHU "book." The same handshape combination occurs in twenty-one signs in TSL. Of these, thirteen have no contact, six have fingertip-fingertip contact, and two are character signs.

The character sign XIAO is made up of two handshapes (Example 45) that contact each other between the fingers.

EXAMPLE 45:

XIAO REPRESENTS　ı) \　"SMALL"

These same handshapes occur in only one other sign, and in that sign, there is no contact between them. The between-the-fingers contact in this sign occurs in several other signs as well, but there is always a 5 hand-shape involved. This is the only case in which both hands are less than a "full" hand.

Finally, the character sign GE is made up of handshapes (Example 46) that contact each other such that the fingertips touch the radial side of the finger. The same handshape combination occurs in a few native signs, but in all, there is no contact between the two handshapes.

EXAMPLE 46:

GE REPRESENTS　↑　"MEASURE WORD"

Fingertip to radial side of the finger contact does occur in several other signs with three different handshape combinations: (1) fist-pinky, (2) fist-flat O, and (3) fist-index.

In summary, the signs in this section are made up of handshape combinations that are attested in other signs, but the point of contact between the hands is rarely if ever attested between the two handshapes in a given character sign and often any other two handshapes as well.

Summary

I argued first that handedness is generally not contrastive in either native TSL signs or character signs. Thus, right- and left-handed signers produce slightly different versions of the same sign. The differences, as might be expected from the study of ASL, are not contrastive. However, there are two signs in which handedness is contrastive: Both are character signs. Second, virtually all TSL handshapes have two properties: (1) They are associated with meanings of some sort, at least in some of the signs in which they occur, and (2) they occur over the entire lexicon, including native signs and character signs. The exception is a handshape (1) that does not have a traditional meaning but stands for a written representation of a character and (2) that occurs only in TSL character signs. Third, the handshape combinations that occur in some of the character signs are unattested in other signs. Fourth, in character signs that have handshape combinations attested in other signs, the point of contact is rarely (if ever) attested between these two handshapes and often *any other handshapes* in TSL.

SIGNIFICANCE AND IMPLICATIONS

This article examines naturally occurring character signs in TSL. Even though character signs (like ASL's fingerspelled loan signs) are not best described as borrowings from written Chinese (since written Chinese possesses no handshapes to borrow), some of their properties are reminiscent of borrowings in spoken languages. For example, spoken language borrowings may be marked on various levels, a result of the fact that they have been allowed to retain their original form in the new language. Although not marked for precisely the same reason, the fact remains that character signs are marked in several ways. First, among TSL's character signs are two that have an unusual property: They must be signed the same way regardless of signers' handedness. Second, the character signs use two general strategies to represent written Chinese words: They use handshapes available in TSL (i.e., attested in other signs), and they invent new handshapes. Third, handshape combinations and points of contact between two hands in character signs differ from those attested in native signs. The phonological innovations that accommodate the forms from written Chinese cause them not to fit seamlessly into TSL: They remain somewhat outside the system in this sense.

The TSL forms from written Chinese are recent innovations, as far as we know, and time will tell whether their structural properties will change, allowing them to become more like native TSL signs. Because character signs occur in different sign languages, a full investigation of their linguistic properties would contribute enormously to a typology of devices employed by sign languages to represent words from spoken/written languages (as opposed to, for example, the ways in which one sign language borrows from another sign language). Further, a detailed investigation of many more of the morphological and syntactic properties of character signs remains to be undertaken, but anecdotal evidence suggests that on these levels, character signs are less distinguishable from native signs. For example, it is clear that JIE 'introduce' is used as a directional verb in TSL (as it is in HKSL [Fok, Bellugi, van Hoek, and Klima, 1988, 200]), that in TSL, BEI 'north' can be modified to mean 'way up north,' that TIAN 'field' can be modified to mean 'fields all over the area,' that any character sign in TSL can be indexed in space in the expected ways. Clearly, TSL and the other sign languages discussed in this article have much to offer in our quest for understanding both sociolinguistic and structural issues.

REFERENCES

Ann, J. 1993. A linguistic investigation of the relationship between physiology and handshape. Ph.D. diss., University of Arizona.

Asmah, H. O. 1987. *Malay in its sociocultural context.* Kuala Lumpur, Malaysia: Ministry of Education.

Battison, R. 1978. *Lexical borrowing in American Sign Language.* Silver Spring, Md.: Linstok Press.

Bellugi, U., O. Tzeng, E. S. Klima, and A. Fok. 1989. Dyslexia: Perspectives from sign and script. In *From reading to neurons,* ed. A. M. Galaburda, 137–72. Cambridge, Mass.: Bradford Books/MIT Press.

Bloomfield, L. 1933. *Language.* New York: Holt, Rinehart, and Winston.

Bynon, T. 1977. *Historical linguistics.* New York: Cambridge University Press.

Chao, C.-M., H.-H. Chu, and C.-C. Liu. 1988. *Taiwan natural sign language.* Taipei, Taiwan: Deaf Sign Language Research Association of the Republic of China.

China Association for the Deaf and Blind. 1960. *Long Ya Ren Shou Yu Tu* (Deaf people's manual of commonly used sign language). Shanghai: China Association for the Deaf and Blind.

Davis, J. 1989. Distinguishing language contact phenomena in ASL interpretation. In *The sociolinguistics of the Deaf community,* ed. Ceil Lucas, 85–102. New York: Academic Press.

Davis, S. 1994. Loanwords: Phonological treatment. In *The encyclopedia of language and linguistics*, vol. 4, ed. R. E. Asher, 2273–76. New York and Oxford: Pergamon Press.

De Francis, J. 1984. *The Chinese language: Fact and fantasy.* Honolulu: University of Hawaii Press.

———. 1989. *Visible speech: The oneness of writing systems.* Honolulu: University of Hawaii Press.

Fok, A., and U. Bellugi. 1986. The acquisition of visual spatial script. In *Graphonomics: Contemporary research in handwriting*, ed. H. S. R. Kao, G. P. van Galen, R. H. Hoosain. North Holland: Elsevier Science Publishers.

Fok, A., U. Bellugi, K. van Hoek, and E. Klima. 1988. The formal properties of Chinese languages in space. In *Cognitive aspects of the Chinese language*, ed. I. M. Liu, H.-C. Chen, and M. J. Chen, 187–205. Hong Kong: Asian Research Service.

Fu, Y., and C. Mei. 1986. *An introduction to sign language.* Shanghai: Xuelin Publishing Company.

Goodstadt, R. Y.-C. 1972. *Speaking with signs: A sign language manual for Hong Kong's Deaf.* Hong Kong: Government Press.

Heath, J. 1994. Borrowing. In *The encyclopedia of language and linguistics*, vol. 1, ed. R. E. Asher, 383–94. New York and Oxford: Pergamon Press.

Hock, H. H. 1986. *Principles of historical linguistics.* New York: Mouton de Gruyter.

Hodgson, K. W. 1953. *The Deaf and their problems.* London: C. A. Watts and Co. Ltd.

Li, C. N., and S. A. Thompson. 1979. Chinese dialect variations and language reform. In *Languages and their status*, ed. T. Shopen, 295–335. Cambridge, Mass.: Winthrop Publishers.

Liddell, S. K., and R. E. Johnson. 1989. American Sign Language: The phonological base. *Sign Language Studies* 64:195–277.

Lucas, C. 1989. *The Sociolinguistics of the Deaf Community.* San Diego: Academic Press.

Mohanan, T., and K. P. Mohanan. 1987. The lexical phonology of Malayalee English: Structure formation in transplanted second language systems. Stanford University.

Nakano, Y., and S. Ito. 1982. *Shuwa o Manaboo: Shakai-hen.* Tokyo: Fukumura Shuppan.

———. 1987. *Shuwa o Manaboo: Sheikatsu-hen.* Tokyo: Fukumura Shuppan.

Osaka YMCA. 1979. *Speaking with signs.* Osaka, Japan.

Padden, C. A., and D. M. Perlmutter. 1987. American Sign Language and the architecture of phonological theory. *Natural Language and Linguistic Theory* 5:335–375.

Republic of China Ministry of Education, Research Division of Sign Language for the Deaf. 1984. *Zhong Hua Min Guo Shou Yu Ge Cui Jiao Cai* (Republic of China Sign Language Song Materials).

Sandler, W. 1989. *Phonological representation of the sign: Linearity and non-linearity in American Sign Language.* Dordrecht, Holland: Foris Publications.

Smith, W. H. 1976. Rev. 1988. Taiwan Sign Language. California State University, Northridge.

———. 1982. The nature of compounding in Taiwan Sign Language. Indiana University.

———. 1989. Morphological characteristics of verbs in Taiwan Sign Language. Ph.D. diss. Indiana University.

Smith, W. H., and L.-F. Ting. 1979a. *Shou Neng Sheng Chyau: Sign language manual,* vol. 1 (Your hands can become a bridge). Taipei, Taiwan: Deaf Sign Language Research Association of the Republic of China.

———. 1979b. Unpublished English translation of *Shou Neng Sheng Chyau: Sign language manual,* vol. 1.

———. 1984. *Shou Neng Sheng Chyau: Sign language manual,* vol. 2 (Your hands can become a bridge). Taipei, Taiwan: Deaf Sign Language Research Association of the Republic of China.

Yau, S. 1977. *The Chinese signs: Lexicon of the standard sign language for the Deaf in China.* Editions Langages Croises. Kowloon, Hong Kong: Chiu Ming Publishing Co. Ltd.

Yau, S., and J. He. 1989. How Deaf children in a Chinese school get their name signs. *Sign Language Studies* 65:305–22.

Part 3 Language in Education

The Relationship of Educational Policy

to Language and Cognition in Deaf Children

Priscilla Shannon Gutierrez

Language plays a critical role in the development of cognition and communicative competence in humans. Language is required to process information, construct meaning, and participate in human interaction. Children who have limited language capabilities are disadvantaged learners. Proficiency in language is critical for facilitating communication and academic success (Daniels 1994). The underlying causes of linguistic deprivation or disadvantage often have been presumed to result from some innate problem of the child. However, a psychosociolinguistic perspective presumes instead that the deprivation or disability is social in nature (Mehan, as cited in Wertsch 1991). Children who have had limited linguistic experience within their social environment lack the cognitive tools required for academic success.

In spite of the return of manual systems of communication in the educational setting, deaf children still lag academically behind their hearing peers, much as they did 80 years ago (Strong 1991). American Sign Language (ASL), the natural language utilized by the Deaf community, has not been the language of instruction in many educational settings for deaf people. Emphasis has been placed on language learning through the use of coded forms of English. Signing Exact English (SEE) is reportedly the most widely used of these coded forms (Ramsey 1993). Educators have assumed that once a deaf child knows the coded form, this knowledge of English will facilitate literacy (Ramsey 1993). This assumption ignores the fact that many deaf children come to school linguistically and cognitively disadvantaged because their hearing parents are unable to communicate effectively with them through signed language. A small percentage of deaf children are born to deaf parents, who spontaneously sign a natural language and who can provide a sociocultural milieu that facilitates cognitive development. More than 90 percent of deaf children are born to hearing parents, and many of these parents either do not sign with them or are not fluent enough to provide spontaneous language acquisition and cognitive development (Drasgow 1993).

The acquisition of a natural signed language such as ASL and the language learning of English for deaf children in many ways parallels the experiences of other language minority students. If we define a bilingual person as one who uses two or more languages in everyday life, then a deaf person who signs ASL and uses English to communicate with the hearing majority can be considered as bilingual (Grosjean 1992). Minority languages and minority cultures, for the most part, have had only a marginal place in the educational setting. The deaf educational context is no exception.

This paper seeks to understand why so many deaf children do not succeed academically and how educational policy enhances or inhibits their cognitive development. It examines deaf educational policy at the federal, state, and local levels and the interpretation of these policies at the two sites attended by the focal student, an eight-year-old profoundly deaf boy. It investigates the sociocultural and socioeducational experiences of the focal student as they pertain to the two sites that are run by the same educational agency in conjunction with two local school districts. This paper discusses language development within a psychosociolinguistic framework, exploring the social functions of language and their relationship to cognitive development. Finally, this paper considers bilingualism within a deaf and hearing framework, investigating issues of language acquisition, language learning, and cognitive development.

REVIEW OF THE RELATED LITERATURE

Sociohistorical Background

DEAF EDUCATION (1817–1975)
The first school for deaf people, the American Asylum for the Education of the Deaf and Dumb, was founded in 1817 in Hartford, Connecticut. Over the next fifty years, two educational camps formed in the United States that espoused very distinct deaf education philosophies — manualism and oralism. The manual camp was led first by Thomas Hopkins Gallaudet, the founder of the asylum, and later by his son, Edward Miner Gallaudet, who established the National Deaf-Mute College, which subsequently became Gallaudet University. Edward Miner Gallaudet's be-

lief in the need for manual communication was strongly influenced by his experiences with his mother, Sophia, who herself was profoundly deaf and communicated through sign language. The elder Gallaudet founded the American Asylum with Laurent Clerc, a deaf man originally from France. Clerc taught for many years at the American Asylum, and, in the subsequent debate between oralists and manualists, became one of the strongest opponents of oralism. Members of the manual camp believed that many deaf children could not learn to speak or speechread well enough to use those methods as their primary means of communication (Winefield 1987).

The oralist camp was led by Alexander Graham Bell, inventor of the telephone, who believed that almost all people process language auditorally. Bell's mother, Eliza, who suffered hearing loss during her childhood, had intelligible speech. For Bell, she provided a model of a successful deaf woman who did not have to rely on manual communication. Proponents of the oralist philosophy, including educators such as Horace Mann and Samuel Gridley Howe (Winefield 1987), felt that deaf people must be prepared to live as much like hearing people as possible.

The debate between the oralist and manualist camps raged on during the last two decades of the nineteenth century. When confronted with the oralist successes of students such as Mabel Hubbard and Jeanie Lippett, Edward Miner Gallaudet attributed their success to two critical factors (Winefield 1987). One was that both girls were postlingually deaf, as was Eliza Bell. That is, all three had lost their hearing during childhood and benefited from having acquired spoken language prior to their hearing loss. The second factor was that both students came from wealthy families who could afford the best education for their daughters. Gallaudet argued that small class sizes and individual instruction, which were requirements of the oral program, were a luxury that the average family with a deaf child could not afford.

The debate reached a climax in 1880, the year the second International Congress on Education of the Deaf took place in Milan, Italy. After both proponents of the oral and the manual philosophies presented their respective cases, the convention members excluded deaf educators from voting and decided overwhelmingly to support oral education, in spite of the objections of deaf educators such as Clerc (Winefield 1987). The oralists, believing that manual communication restricted or prevented the growth of speech and language skills, utilized the convention's decision to sway deaf educational policy in the United States toward an oralist pedagogy. The decision marked the turning point in deaf education toward the exclusive use of oral methods and the exclusion of most deaf teachers and manual communication in the classroom.

Oralism persisted as the predominant method of educating deaf people during the rest of the nineteenth century and well into the twentieth century, until Total Communication reintroduced signed language back into the deaf classroom in the 1970s. During its reign as the accepted method of instruction, oralism effectively shut deaf people out of deaf education (Barnum 1984). The percentage of deaf teachers in deaf education, which was close to 50 percent in 1850, fell to 25 percent within decades and by 1960 was at 12 percent (Sacks 1989, 27).

For much of the twentieth century, deaf students attended residential schools that were run by hearing educators. During the late 1970s, a shift occurred, and deaf students began to attend programs located in regular education settings (Ramsey 1993; Schildroth and Hotto 1995). Currently, more than 75 percent of deaf children in the United States attend programs in regular public education settings whose Total Communication policies call for instruction through spoken English accompanied by some manual component (Ramsey 1993; Schildroth and Hotto 1995). And, although ASL has been utilized as the language of instruction in some classrooms, the instructional emphasis has been on SEE.

TOTAL COMMUNICATION

With recognition of ASL as a bona fide, natural language, primarily through research conducted by William Stokoe (Baker and Battison 1980), the Total Communication policies initiated in the 1970s saw the return of manual communication in the deaf classroom. In theory, Total Communication allows for a variety of methods to communicate with and teach deaf students. These include signed language, fingerspelling, written language, oral language, pantomime, and drawing. In practice, Total Communication has meant that the teacher accompanies spoken English with manual communication (Lane 1992). This simultaneous communication requires bimodal output and input on the part of both the teacher and the student. A study conducted by Strong and Charlson (1987) found that comprehension was frequently diminished as a result of the strain of simultaneous oral and manual communication. The situation was further complicated by the need to spontaneously reconcile the syntactical differences between English and ASL. Although both languages share the same lexicon, the syntactical structure of ASL differs from English and includes nonmanual grammatical markers such as eye, head, face, and body movements. The distinction between true Total Communication and simultaneous communication has been lost to educators and has resulted in very little learning in deaf children (Lane 1992).

MAINSTREAMING AND LEAST RESTRICTIVE ENVIRONMENT

Legislative attempts to remove the educational barriers that confronted students with disabilities resulted in the Education for All Handicapped Children Act (PL 94–142), which was enacted in 1975. The law guaranteed a free, appropriate education for students with disabilities and introduced the concept of Least Restrictive Environment (LRE). The legal interpretation of Least Restrictive Environment historically has meant placing disabled children in regular education classrooms with their non-disabled peers. This placement, or mainstreaming, of children with various disabilities into the regular education classroom was based on the belief that virtually all such children could benefit from a less isolated environment. The implementation of the LRE meant that a special needs child first would have to fail in the regular education setting before being placed in a special education setting, regardless of the appropriateness of that placement (Cohen 1995). Mainstreaming was also considered beneficial to regular education students who would be exposed to different kinds of people (Ramsey 1993).

Within a deaf context, this has brought about the placement of deaf students in regular education classrooms, often with a hearing teacher and hearing peers who cannot effectively communicate in signed language with the mainstreamed deaf child. By law, deaf students can be mainstreamed up to 100 percent of the school day. For those students mainstreamed into regular education classrooms, a signed language interpreter may be provided. However, interpreters are rarely employed to accompany the deaf student through the school day (Lane 1992).

Because many hearing teachers are unable to communicate with mainstreamed deaf students, the interpreter often takes on the added role of a teacher within the regular classroom. The language barrier frequently prevents any direct interaction between the hearing teacher and the deaf child. The few hearing peers and teachers who can communicate in signed language are often limited to commands or evaluations, which Ramsey (1995, 208) refers to as "caretaker-like" language (e.g., SIT, GOOD, BAD). The linguistic and social isolation the deaf child experiences in the mainstreamed setting often results in the most restrictive environment instead of the LRE that the legislature intended (Commission on Education of the Deaf 1988).

Sociocultural Background

CULTURAL BELIEFS

Legislation has assumed that the education of children with special needs is not an academic process but rather a socialization process that requires assimilation with "normal" models (Ramsey 1993, 23). If deaf children are to function like their "normal" hearing peers, then the mainstreamed classroom provides a salient opportunity for deaf children to "learn" to be like their hearing peers. Barnum (1984, 404) questioned this assumption:

> For too long we have let our desire to create "normal" children, that is seemingly hearing children, outweigh the facts of research in determining educational policy for deaf children. . . . It was decided that educating deaf people meant teaching them to speak, read, and lip-read English. . . . Where was the study group that gave credence to this theory? When does any professional field accept a hypothesis without backing and instigate its implications without reservation?

In 1988, the Commission on Education of the Deaf (p. 42) urged that "[o]utmoded educational policy be brought into line with recent scientific discoveries in linguistics."

When a dominant cultural group attributes the academic failure of any language minority student to cultural deficits that are either considered inherent in the group itself, its culture, or the result of discrimination against the group, that dominant cultural group subscribes to a cultural deficit viewpoint (Sue and Padilla 1986). An essential philosophical aspect of this deficit model is that minority language groups are incapable of acquiring the cultural competence needed for social and academic challenges. Thus, the hearing majority, embracing the cultural-deficit viewpoint, historically has considered deaf people as "deaf and dumb." In searching for an explanation as to why so many language minority students demonstrate such a significant rate of academic failure, educators have tended to decontextualize their explanations, often ignoring the dynamic relationship between sociocultural factors and academic outcomes (Cortes 1986). Freire (1970) maintained that decision-making leaders need to recognize that varying levels of knowledge exist that are based on cultural experiences and that knowledge cannot be forced upon a minority group. Freire (1993) also stated that language is not the privilege of a few but the natural right of all.

Less than 10 percent of deaf children come from deaf parents who spontaneously sign and transmit deaf culture to them (Drasgow 1993). More than 90 percent of deaf children come from hearing parents whose sociocultural experiences are entrenched in the hearing majority's cultural viewpoint of deafness as a deficiency. This negative perception has often resulted in a cultural and communication gap between nonsigning parents and their nonspeaking deaf children. The great wealth of knowledge that a hearing child learns incidentally through day-to-day sociolinguistic interactions among family members is unavailable to the deaf child whose hearing family refuses to sign with her or him, often resulting in linguistic and cognitive deficiencies (Stevens 1980). In contrast, deaf children who enter the socioeducational setting with strong ASL skills possess the linguistic and cognitive tools necessary to succeed academically. Research has shown that the academic performance of deaf children of deaf parents exceeds that of their nonsigning peers (Christensen 1989; Padden and Ramsey 1996).

CLASSROOM PRACTICES

Most deaf education programs involve a simultaneous oral and manual communication approach between the hearing teacher and the deaf child, which often results in diminished comprehension (Strong and Charlson 1987). Further adding to the problem is the fact that most hearing teachers of deaf children are not fluent in ASL. In her research in deaf classrooms, Erting (1980, 1988) found that the formal, classroom signed language used by hearing teachers was strikingly different from the signed language conversations of native deaf people. Few attempts were made by the observed hearing teachers to adjust communicative interactions to each deaf student's abilities. The sociolinguistic interactions were geared toward speech production and English language learning. It would seem that the semantic functions of language and their mediating role in cognitive development have often been either overlooked or ignored in deaf classrooms.

For many deaf children, access to a linguistic role model fluent in ASL is a critical issue in the socioeducational setting where most hearing adults are not native ASL signers. If deaf children are to be active participants in dialogue leading to linguistic, cognitive, and emotional development, Erting (1988) has suggested, at least one key adult in the deaf classroom should be fluent in ASL. Drasgow (1993) also maintained that the most competent users of ASL are deaf people themselves and that they should be included as language models in the classroom.

Although the linguistic community has accepted ASL as a natural language, the professional educational community has been slow to follow suit. For the most part, manual communication has been added to the repertoire of teaching skills instead of being utilized as the language of instruction. According to Ramsey (1993), "For all the policy attention devoted to the media of communication in deaf education, the actual functions, successes, or failures of communication in deaf education have long been 'transparent' to many practitioners. . . . Very little of what is 'taught' to deaf children is learned by them. Since . . . language is the medium which structures teaching and language, then language is a reasonable place to investigate the sources of problems."

The exclusion of ASL in deaf classrooms has contributed significantly to the academic failure of deaf children. Drasgow (1993) purported that a crucial flaw in deaf education has been the language of instruction because coded English is not a natural language that deaf children are capable of acquiring in a normal manner.

Language and Cognition within a Sociocultural Framework

The primary function of language, whether spoken or signed, is communication and social intercourse. Real communication requires both meaning and a semiotic system to convey that meaning (Vygotsky 1986). Language as a cultural artifact cannot be abstracted from the context in which it is utilized. Words are foregrounded in culturally specific associations, attitudes, and values. These cultural values are derived from the sociohistorical context in which words are used and from the activities with which they are associated (Gumperz and Hernández-Chavez 1972). The process of thinking/meaning and social situatedness are interdependent, and language is the semiotic tool that connects them (Vygotsky 1978). Language mediates human activity and is a product of the sociocultural and sociohistorical environment in which it exists.

Human cognitive functions do not appear in isolation but rather initially appear in socialized linguistic interactions that are later appropriated as internalized concepts (Vygotsky 1978). An individual's language experiences are shaped and developed within continuous interactions with other individuals. The contextual milieu in which children socialize teaches them communicative competence. This can be accomplished through a variety of mediational semiotic systems. Signed language, such as ASL, is the semiotic tool that the Deaf community employs to convey sociohistorical and sociocultural information to offspring and other members. It is the mediational tool that facilitates cognitive development in deaf children. Signed language for deaf people is the linguistic as well as the cognitive use of space (Sacks 1989).

The Zone of Proximal Development (Vygotsky 1978), or ZOPED, defines the region where cognitive development takes place within a child (Garton 1992). The ZOPED differentiates between cognitive functions that require mediation on an interpersonal, socialized level and those that can be accomplished independently on an intrapersonal level. Within any cognitive function, as the child shifts responsibility from an external sphere to an internal one, she or he progresses through a zone of potential development. Critical to progress within the ZOPED is the establishment of mutuality on the part of the learner and the more capable adult or peer. Effective mediation within the sociolinguistic interactions of the zone depends upon the degree of collaboration and the mutual understanding of the task by both participants in the interaction.

However, within the deaf child's sociolinguistic interactions with a hearing teacher or peer who does not sign, the mutuality or engagement required for cognitive development often breaks down. Communication on the social plane that is critical for cognitive development is inaccessible to deaf children surrounded by hearing families, teachers, and peers who do not utilize signed language. The normal mechanism for forming the social relationships by which learning occurs is disrupted, resulting in linguistic and cognitive deficiency (Garton 1992).

Deaf and Hearing Bilingualism

Children require a comprehensive understanding and ability in their first language before they can successfully employ the pragmatic, syntactic, and semantic components of a second language. Krashen (1981) maintained that human beings functionally acquire the syntactical structures of language through their attempts to understand messages. Language use within social interactions must be mutually comprehensible in order for both participants to construct meaning.

Successful programs for second language learners provide comprehensible input in a manner that is interesting and relevant to the student. The sociocultural experiences outside of the classroom form the basis for learning within the classroom. Successful programs employ the functional aspects of language based on those experiences to aid in language learning.

For the deaf child who has hearing parents who do not sign, there are few sociolinguistic and/or sociocultural experiences that normally form the bases for learning. The successful deaf classroom, through the use of ASL as the medium of instruction, can overcome this lack of experiences to facilitate cognitive development. However, present methods used to teach English to deaf people do not provide adequate input for understanding (Drasgow 1993). In addition, the focus on SEE and language learning in deaf classrooms inhibits access to language acquisition. American Sign Language, as a semiotic mediational tool that facilitates cognitive development, is often overlooked. As a result, many deaf students remain illiterate in English because the systematic denial of their primary signed language shuts out the most effective means for learning a second spoken language (Lane 1992).

The majority of bilingual children acquire their first language in the home from parents and family members. However, deaf children of hearing parents who do not sign acquire their knowledge of ASL in residential schools or deaf education programs from either Deaf peers or adults. This has often occurred outside the classroom milieu, where the instructional emphasis has been on language learning. However, in spite of the change in location of language acquisition, the issues remain the same: Effective communication within social interactions forms the basis of language competence and cognitive development, and competence in a natural, primary language must be acquired before it can be attained in a second language. The Commission on Education of the Deaf (1988) recommended that the Department of Education take positive action to encourage bilingual practices that would enhance the quality of education received by deaf children. And Supalla (1992) stated that the right of deaf children to have access to a language they can acquire and develop competence in has never been adequately addressed by policymakers.

As Ramsey (1993) and Grosjean (1992) have noted, bilingualism, when considered within the context of deafness, demonstrates some peculiar features. Deaf bilingualism is not a transitional situation, much as it is for other language minority groups in the socioeducational setting. Because of the inability to process language auditorally, the deaf child will remain bilingual for her or his entire life. Certain skills in the second language (i.e., speaking) may never be fully learned by deaf individuals, with the result that English language production is usually confined to print functions.

However, goals for Deaf bilingual students remain the same as for other language minorities. The primary goal is academic achievement at a level comparable to that of hearing peers. Another goal is fluency in English (at least in its written form) while developing proficiency in ASL. Still a third goal is cognitive development through the semiotic medium of primary signed language (Strong 1991).

Summary of the Review of Literature

In spite of the return of manual communication in deaf classrooms, as well as the enactment of legislation intended to protect the educational rights of children with special needs, the academic achievement of deaf students still lags behind that of their hearing peers. Simultaneous oral and manual communication, under the guise of Total Communication, is the dominant pedagogical practice in deaf classrooms, and instructional emphasis has been on language learning through coded English. In addition, the mainstreaming of deaf students into regular education settings, under the title of Least Restrictive Environment, has routinely been practiced, regardless of the appropriateness of such placement.

Cognitive development in young children is directly related to their sociocultural and sociolinguistic experiences outside the educational setting. Many deaf children with hearing parents who do not sign enter school with cognitive and linguistic deficiencies that they struggle to overcome in the classroom. Moreover, most hearing teachers of the deaf are not fluent in ASL and cannot provide enough comprehensible input to facilitate cognitive development. Furthermore, the emphasis on SEE inhibits the acquisition of a natural signed language that could be accessed for language learning. These cognitive and linguistic deficiencies can be traced to the lack of a mutual semiotic system to convey meaning, both outside of and within the deaf classroom.

DESIGN AND METHODOLOGY

Overview

The research for this paper was guided by four factors: (1) the various documents related to deaf educational policy, (2) the focal student's socio-educational experiences within the context of language use and cognitive development at both sites included in the study, (3) the expertise and expectations of the teachers and administrators who work either in or within a supervisory capacity for both sites, and (4) the effect of the implementation of deaf educational policy on student outcomes in language and learning. Data collection included an analysis of policy documents, mainstreaming practices at each site, interviews with the teachers and administrators responsible for implementation of the programs at each site, and classroom observations of language use in socioeducational interactions among peers, teachers, and interpreters.

Educational Policy

FEDERAL LEVEL

Within the numerous educational codes and regulations at the federal level, three major pieces of legislation form the impetus for guidance and implementation of educational policy specifically with regard to the deaf and hard of hearing. The first of these, the Education for All Handicapped Children Act (PL 94–142), was enacted in 1975. This act guarantees a free, appropriate education (FAPE) to all special needs students. The act requires local educational agencies, such as school districts and counties, to formulate an individualized education plan (IEP) for each special needs student that outlines specific goals and objectives for the student. The IEP must identify the particular services that will be offered, the provider of these services, and an assessment of each student's current educational level. In formulating the IEP, districts and counties are expected to address the Least Restrictive Environment (LRE) when considering placement of the special needs student.

In 1990, the Education for All Handicapped Children Act was amended as PL 101–476, or the Individuals with Disabilities Education Act (IDEA), which constitutes the second major piece of legislation affecting deaf and hard of hearing students. This amendment, when addressing the LRE, "denotes a clear preference by Congress for inclusion of handicapped children in classes with other children" and "imposes affirmative obligations on school districts to consider placing disabled children in regular classroom settings, with the use of supplementary aids and services, before exploring other alternative placements" (Individuals with Disabilities Education Act of 1990, note 45). The IDEA stressed the importance of developing social and communication skills between disabled and nondisabled peers as an educational goal.

However, in 1992, Secretary of Education Lamar Alexander issued a Deaf Students Education Services Policy Guidance, which attempted to address the sociolinguistic concerns expressed in the report issued by the Commission on Education of the Deaf (1988). Recognizing that "[c]ommunication is the area most hampered between a deaf child and his or her hearing peers and teachers," the policy guidance stated that "[a]ny setting, including a regular classroom, that prevents a child who is deaf from receiving an appropriate education that meets his or her needs . . . is not the LRE for that individual child" (Fed. Reg. 49275, 1992). The policy guidance further recommended that when formulating an IEP for a deaf student, the local educational agency must take into consideration the communication needs of that student. This policy guidance marked the first time that the federal government recognized that the FAPE should take precedence in determining the LRE for a deaf student.

The third major piece of legislation that guides policy for deaf and hard of hearing people is the Americans with Disabilities Act of 1990 (ADA). The purpose of the ADA, or PL 101–336, is to "establish clear and comprehensive prohibition of discrimination on the basis of disability" (Americans with Disabilities Act of 1990). The ADA requires that people with disabilities who receive services provided by public agencies, including educational agencies, will "gain the same result, benefit or reach same level of achievement provided to others" and that "communications with the disabled are as effective as communications with others" (Americans with Disabilities Act of 1990). The ADA further requires that all benefits and services provided to the disabled be equal to those afforded to the nondisabled.

A fourth example of federal legislation that addresses the education of language minority students but that historically has excluded native users of ASL is the Bilingual Education Act of 1968 (BEA). This act attempted to address the needs of students with limited English proficiency whose access to the core curriculum was denied because of the language barrier. The BEA (1968) defined individuals with limited English proficiency as native users of a language other than English or as those who come from an environment where another language either is dominant or has had a significant impact on their level of English proficiency; and who have insufficient ability in speaking, reading, writing, or understanding English to learn successfully in classrooms where English is the language of instruction. The small number of native ASL users (i.e., deaf children born to deaf parents) has been considered as insufficient to be included in the act's definition of limited English proficiency; furthermore, the act was never intended to include ASL (Strong 1991).

STATE LEVEL

The California Educational Code includes deaf and hard of hearing children as part of their low-incidence, special education population. This targets disabilities that have an incidence rate of less than 1 percent of the total statewide enrollment in kindergarten through twelfth grade. As of 1992, there were more than 20,000 students who fell into this category (California Assembly Resolution 55 of 1992). Other examples of low-incidence handicaps include people who are deaf-blind and the orthopedically challenged.

Legislation guiding educational policy at the state level mirrors many of the federal laws related to special education. The California State Education Code (§56345) requires the development of an IEP that includes the student's present level of academic performance, annual goals, specific special educational instruction, and the extent of participation in regular education programs. With regard to LRE, the California State Education Code (§56364.1) states that "[e]ach public agency shall ensure that each individual with exceptional needs participates in those activities with nondisabled peers to the maximum extent appropriate." However, the code does require that equal opportunity for communication access be considered when formulating a deaf student's IEP.

In 1994, the California Assembly passed the Deaf and Hard of Hearing Education Rights Bill (AB 1836), which recognized that the communication needs of deaf students must be central in determining their LRE. The language of the bill was incorporated into the California Education Code, which states that "[d]eafness involves the most basic of human needs—the ability to communicate" (§56000.5).

LOCAL LEVEL: DESERT VIEW COUNTY

Desert View County (all names at the local level have been changed), along with several other local school districts in the area, constitutes the

Special Education Local Plan Area (SELPA), which acts as the local governing board for all special education programs within a specific area. Some of the main responsibilities of a given SELPA are to determine the number of personnel at each site, determine student caseloads and class sizes, and disburse the state's funds to local education agencies within the SELPA's jurisdiction.

In their policy handbook, the Desert View County Board of Education recognizes that all students with exceptional needs have a right to appropriate individual instruction and that the primary responsibility of the board is to apply its resources to establish programs that provide for the optimal development of each student. The policy handbook indicates that students' LRE must be appropriate to their individual needs and that the LRE should enable them to achieve their potential for independence as well as promote acceptance and understanding between the handicapped and the nonhandicapped student.

LOCAL LEVEL: POPPY HILL SCHOOL DISTRICT

The Poppy Hill School District lies within part of the local SELPA. Panguitch Elementary School, one of the sites for this study, is part of this district. In its policy handbook, the school district board indicates that each individual with exceptional needs has a right to a free, appropriate education that meets her or his individual needs. The policy handbook further considers one of the primary purposes of education to be the provision of quality programs that assist students in becoming effective citizens and that each student in the Poppy Hill School District is entitled to opportunities for optimal development.

LOCAL LEVEL: ARROYO SECO SCHOOL DISTRICT

The Arroyo Seco School District also falls within the local SELPA. Vista del Lago School, the second site for this study, is part of this district. The board policy expresses a commitment to provide students with a quality education that emphasizes dignity and provides opportunities for them to achieve their fullest potential.

The Arroyo Seco board policy states that exceptional needs students should be educated in the LRE, which may include placement within a regular education classroom. Prior to a student's placement in a regular education classroom, the mainstream teacher is expected to receive copies of the student's IEP, as well as participate in a planning meeting. In addition, the board policy indicates that the placement of exceptional needs

TABLE 1. *Summary of Educational Policy*

	Federal Level	State Level	Local Level
Language use	IDEA provides no clear guidelines for use of ASL or English. Mandates an IEP to meet educational needs. ADA and 1992 policy guidance addressed communication needs of deaf people.	State code does not address language use. Mandates formulation of an IEP. Code requires equal opportunity for communication access.	Board policy does not address language use. Emphasizes optimal development of each disabled student.
Mainstreaming	LRE mandates inclusion in regular education classrooms to develop social and communication skills.	Follows federal mandate for LRE to include disabled children in regular education classrooms to maximum extent possible.	Follows federal and state mandates for LRE. Calls for planning meetings prior to placement.
Bilingualism	ASL not considered one of the languages covered by BEA for educating language minority students; does not address Deaf bilingualism.	Follows federal mandates for educating language minority students; does not address Deaf bilingualism.	Follows federal and state mandates for educating language minority students; does not address Deaf bilingualism.

IDEA = Individuals with Disabilities Education Act
IEP = Individualized Education Plan
LRE = Least Restrictive Environment

students in the regular classroom should be appropriate for the regular education teacher and peers in the program.

Description of the Focal Student

The subject of this study, Ruben, is an eight-year-old male who was diagnosed with a severe hearing loss (i.e., a hearing threshold of 70–90 decibels) at one year of age. At present, Ruben's hearing loss has increased to a profound level (i.e., a hearing threshold of greater than 90 decibels). His latest audiogram indicates a threshold of 115–120 decibels in both ears.

Both of the subject's parents and his three older female half-siblings are hearing. Ruben's mother, who is also the researcher in this study, is the most fluent signer within the family unit. Upon learning of Ruben's hearing loss when her son was one year old, the mother began to communicate in signed language, utilizing signs self-taught from a book. The mother subsequently has taken classes in ASL at the college level. Furthermore, Ruben's mother has developed contacts within the local Deaf community. Both she and Ruben attend monthly Deaf events together. Ruben has frequently spent time with Deaf families or has had Deaf visitors to his home in order to facilitate language acquisition and participate in Deaf culture.

Ruben's father and half-siblings are limited in their signing ability. Much of their communicative interactions with the subject are within Ramsey's (1993) caretaker domain. Few interactions involve complete ASL or English signed sentences. This language barrier between Ruben and his family members has resulted in the development of an interpreter role for the mother on behalf of the other family members. They are frequently unable to understand Ruben's sociolinguistic interactions with them and are unable to communicate effectively with him.

Ruben attended kindergarten and first grade through the deaf and hard of hearing (DHH) program offered by Desert View County at several sites within the Poppy Hill school district. He then attended second and third grade at a single site within the Arroyo Seco school district, which is also part of the Desert View County program.

Site Selection

The sites selected for this study were both DHH programs run by Desert View County in conjunction with the Poppy Hill and Arroyo Seco school districts. Because of the dual county-district nature of the DHH program, each of the sites was supervised by a district principal and a county principal. Both districts are located within the geographical boundaries of Desert View County and together have the largest student populations within the jurisdiction of the local SELPA.

Both sites were selected for this study because Ruben attended the DHH program in both districts. Ruben is a resident of Poppy Hill and initially attended the DHH program at various sites within that district's boundaries. During the course of the study, he was transferred, at the mother's request, to the DHH program at the site within the Arroyo Seco school district.

Site Description: Panguitch Elementary School

Panguitch Elementary School, whose district-appointed principal was Mr. O'Hara, was a regular education campus within the Poppy Hill school district and served 760 students in kindergarten through sixth grade. Panguitch also housed a primary-level and a middle-level DHH classroom, as well as a third special-education class. During the course of the study, Ruben was a first-grade student in the primary-level DHH classroom with Mrs. Burke, a hearing teacher employed by Desert View County. All of the adults in the program were hearing with the exception of one aide, Mrs. Randolph, who had been deafened later in life. There were a total of nine students in the classroom with Mrs. Burke.

During the time Ruben attended the DHH program at Panguitch, the school building was under construction. All student classrooms during construction were housed in temporary trailers located on site. These trailers were separated from the main building under construction by a continuous safety fence. Just prior to the end of the school year, construction was completed. Poppy Hill School District indicated that an alternative learning program would be moved into the vacated trailers and that the safety fence would remain to separate the two schools.

However, underprojection of enrollment at Panguitch resulted in insufficient classroom space for all of the students in the main building. Parents of the students in the DHH program were informed by the district that the DHH students would remain in the trailers. Parents objected strongly to this decision, and an initial compromise was reached, wherein the primary-level DHH classroom would move into the main building. However, Mrs. Burke, the primary-level DHH teacher, upon moving into a classroom in the main building, was informed by Mr. O'Hara, the principal, that she could not occupy a full classroom. Part of the DHH classroom was partitioned off, and the DHH program was allowed to remain in approximately one-third of the room. The remaining section of the partitioned classroom was initially utilized for band practice. Numerous complaints by Mrs. Burke, however, resulted in the termination of band practice and the placement of a kindergarten class on the other side of the partition.

Language Use and Development: Panguitch Elementary School

Mrs. Burke, the hearing teacher in the primary-level DHH classroom, has had over thirty years experience in special education. When she first began teaching deaf students in the 1960s, an oralist philosophy dictated classroom practices. When interviewed, she expressed her frustration at the lack of communication and the difficulty teaching her students while they were forced to "sit on their hands." She was relieved when the shift to Total Communication in the 1970s allowed her deaf students to use manual communication. When Mrs. Burke was forced to rely solely on oral communication, she stated that her students "struggled because they were not getting the concepts."

Mrs. Burke's main resources for learning signed language were various books that she purchased over the years. She has had no formal training in signed language. Mrs. Burke indicated that she frequently had to rely upon her interpreters to help her with ASL vocabulary to communicate with students. However, she did not consider this an obstacle in her interactions with students, nor did she feel this diminished cognitive development, stating that, "It's communication as long as I can communicate." When questioned about language and policy, Mrs. Burke indicated that the official Desert View County policy put an emphasis on SEE, although she frequently had to rely on ASL to convey concepts. Nonetheless, when teaching reading, Mrs. Burke felt that "a straight English approach" was called for and that she expected students to "be on target, grade level . . . as close to the hearing child as possible."

During informal classroom observations, Mrs. Burke had to ask her aides and interpreters to clarify concepts or help her with specific signs. The aides and interpreters in the classroom were certificated in ASL through the local educational agency, but the signed language of classroom functions resembled the syntactic form of English, using some ASL signs. Most signs utilized in the classroom were SEE signs as opposed to actual ASL signs (e.g., putting two B hands together to sign the word *bus* rather than fingerspelling B-U-S, which is how the word is expressed in ASL).

Mrs. Burke's philosophy on language use and policy were somewhat in contrast to statements made by her principal, Mrs. Wynne, during an interview. Mrs. Wynne was employed by Desert View county as the principal of all special education programs housed within Poppy Hill School District campuses. Mrs. Wynne expressed her belief in the need to acquire

ASL for cognitive development, stating that "ASL, for all intents and purposes is the native language of the deaf." She stated that her belief in ASL as a native language of Deaf people stemmed from ASL classes she had previously taken.

When questioned about language policy and use in Mrs. Burke's classroom, Mrs. Wynne insisted that no SEE was used in the primary-level classroom and that the Total Communication approach utilized in Desert View County programs focused on deaf children's need for ASL to communicate and learn. When questioned about the need for ASL language models in the classroom, Mrs. Wynne stated that the hearing interpreters were proficient enough in ASL to provide correct language models. She did not feel that there was a need to bring any additional deaf adults into the program, citing the fact that Mrs. Randolph, an aide in Mrs. Burke's classroom, was a Deaf adult.

Neither administrator at the Poppy Hill School District level, when interviewed, knew which language was in use in the DHH classroom at Panguitch or what the official language policy was. Mr. Connor, the assistant superintendent of Poppy Hill School District, stated that he had been under the impression that ASL was the language of instruction but realized "that may not be the case." And Mr. O'Hara, the principal of Panguitch, stated, "There is a whole lot I need to know . . . but I trust the county's expertise."

MAINSTREAMING PRACTICES:
PANGUITCH ELEMENTARY SCHOOL

While Ruben attended first grade at Panguitch, he was, at the mother's request, mainstreamed into a regular education classroom, along with two other DHH students, for approximately 75 percent of his school day. The mother cited low-level expectations and practices within the DHH classroom as the reason for the request. Mainstreamed subjects included mathematics, science, and physical education. Ruben and the two other DHH students mainstreamed with him ate lunch and went to recess with their hearing peers. The DHH students at Panguitch were unable to mainstream for language arts because of the phonics-based program in practice at the site.

When questioned about mainstreaming the DHH students, Principal O'Hara stated that he "hoped that the deaf students would learn to read the literature that the other students are responsible for." He also expressed the hope that the DHH students would interact with and be accepted by the other students on the campus because "academic problems are linked to low self-esteem." Mr. O'Hara indicated that through future adaptations, the DHH students could be fully included for language arts instruction.

Informal observations in the mainstreamed classroom revealed that the hearing teacher was virtually unable to communicate directly with the DHH students and had to rely exclusively on the interpreter who accompanied them for any communicative interactions, as well as for all academic instruction. Ruben and his deaf peers were closely grouped in the front of the mainstreamed classroom. Social interactions with hearing peers was also limited within the classroom but increased somewhat on the playground, where the hearing students made efforts to include Ruben and the other DHH students in their play activities.

While in the mainstreamed classroom, Ruben frequently had trouble attending to tasks and would become disruptive. Often he was sent back to the DHH classroom because of his behavior. Toward the end of Ruben's year at Panguitch, he spent less time in the mainstreamed classroom.

DEAF AND HEARING BILINGUALISM:
PANGUITCH ELEMENTARY SCHOOL

During the interviews conducted with Mrs. Burke and Mrs. Wynne, both were questioned about bilingual theory and language minority students. Mrs. Burke, the DHH teacher, stated that "I'm not real familiar with those kinds of ideas." Mrs. Wynne, the DHH principal, responded with a question: "Is that the immersion program?" When prompted with the names of several of the leading theorists in bilingual education (e.g., Krashen and Cummins), Mrs. Burke indicated that she was unfamiliar with them, but Mrs. Wynne mentioned that she had heard their names.

In discussing the possible application of bilingual education theory to a Deaf context, Mrs. Wynne maintained that "[i]t's just like English immersion for the Hispanic kids who come from Mexico. . . . [I]t's ASL immersion and the survival is in the communication." During an interview, Mr. Connor, the assistant superintendent for Poppy Hill, stated that he was familiar with bilingual theory and would like to learn more about applying the theory to deaf programs. And Mr. O'Hara, the principal of Panguitch Elementary School, who at one time taught in a migrant education program, stated that language minority students must be taught the core curriculum in their native language and that, with regard to deaf students, he "would assume that the theory would be the same."

Vista del Lago School was a regular education campus within the Arroyo Seco School District, serving 1,047 students in kindergarten through sixth grade. The DHH students were housed in a classroom in the school building in proximity to the other primary-level classrooms. Because only one DHH class had been established by Desert View County at Vista del Lago, the grade levels within the single DHH classroom ranged from preschool through sixth grade. This class had been established by Desert View County to handle the overflow from the DHH program in Poppy Hill. There were a total of nine students in the DHH classroom while Ruben was in second grade and a total of twelve students while Ruben was in third grade.

The teacher in this DHH classroom, Mrs. Thomas, was Deaf. One of the aides who worked in the classroom was hard of hearing. The remaining aides and interpreters who worked with Mrs. Thomas were hearing. These aides were certificated in ASL through the local educational agency.

LANGUAGE USE AND DEVELOPMENT: VISTA DEL LAGO SCHOOL
Mrs. Thomas, the Deaf teacher in the DHH classroom at Vista del Lago, has a master's degree in deaf education. She was raised in a hearing family who used an oralist approach with her. She subsequently learned ASL in the student dormitories while attending a state school for deaf children. The program at the state school espoused an oralist philosophy, and students were prohibited from using any form of manual communication, including gestures. Mrs. Thomas recalled having to write 500 times, "I will not use my hands to talk" and having to wear a sign that stated, "I am a monkey because I use my hands." She is fluent in both English and ASL and, in fact, also teaches ASL courses at the local college.

When questioned about which language was used for instruction in her DHH classroom, Mrs. Thomas indicated that ASL was the primary language used but that SEE was employed to teach English grammar during reading and writing. However, she stated that she "goes back to ASL to get the concept across" and that "[k]ids need to have a basic language to begin with, so ASL is what I use." Expressing her belief in the need to use a natural language with children for cognitive development, Mrs. Thomas asserted that "SEE is a code for English and not a natural language." She also stressed the importance of Deaf adults in the classroom to provide correct language models because so many deaf children come to school without any kind of a language base.

When discussing language policy in Desert View County, Mrs. Thomas indicated frustration with the lack of a cohesive, official policy. Upon being hired with Desert View, she was told to "[u]se what's best for the kids." This lack of a clearly defined language policy has resulted in differing classroom practices that Mrs. Thomas felt confused the students. She reported that students who have moved frequently between the programs at Poppy Hill and Arroyo Seco school districts have "kept moving back and forth between ASL and signed English" and contended that this "messes up the child's sense of language." Mrs. Thomas also expressed feelings of isolation with regard to curriculum and staff development, citing the fact that professional development at both sites was often conducted separately.

Informal classroom observations revealed that Mrs. Thomas used ASL signs exclusively in her communicative interactions with students; however, the syntactic structure of much of the classroom academic functions more closely resembled English. Mrs. Thomas appeared to adapt her linguistic registers to specific classroom functions. In story-retelling activities, the register included ASL classifiers to express action. During reading lessons, the register utilized kept classifiers to a minimum and focused more on signing English word order. However, Mrs. Thomas frequently attempted to develop a metalinguistic sense in her students to help them understand the relationship between ASL and English, as well as the appropriate time to use each language. In addition, during literacy activities, Mrs. Thomas often demonstrated how two or more English words can be represented by a sole ASL sign. Interviews and additional observations revealed that fingerspelling activities in both spelling and pragmatic functions played an important part of day-to-day interactions. Mrs. Thomas stated that, because fingerspelling represented such a strong component of ASL, she felt that it was important for students to have daily opportunities to practice it.

When discussing language use, Mrs. Gardner, the Desert View principal responsible for the DHH program at Vista del Lago, indicated that language development in deaf children was critical because their limited sign experience "presents a cognitive deficit in terms of language experience." She reported that ASL was the language that was used in the DHH program but that English structure was also taught. During an interview, Mr. James, liaison for the DHH program in the Arroyo Seco school district, stated that a primary goal of the program was to "develop equal proficiency with ASL as a communicative tool . . . and . . . reading and writing in English." Mr. James also expressed his belief that ASL was the primary language of instruction in the DHH classroom.

MAINSTREAM PRACTICES: VISTA DEL LAGO SCHOOL

After transferring to Vista del Lago, Ruben spent approximately 80 percent of his school day in the DHH classroom with Mrs. Thomas. He was mainstreamed into a regular education classroom with an interpreter for the subject of mathematics. The hearing teacher in this mainstreamed classroom had limited signing ability but benefited from four years of experience working with Mrs. Thomas and the deaf students in the program. Reports from the mainstreamed teacher and the interpreter who accompanied Ruben indicated that, although he was below grade level (at a first-grade level), he demonstrated sufficient effort and was making progress. Also, he presented no behavior problems in this mainstreamed classroom. Moreover, the interpreter, in a conversation with Ruben's mother, stated that the hearing teacher made efforts to include Ruben in her lessons, frequently calling on him for the answer to a question.

Informal observations revealed that outside the mainstreamed classroom, Ruben had little interaction with hearing peers from the regular education class. During recess time, he tended to socialize with his deaf peers. Ruben appeared not to have developed any friendships with other hearing students at Vista del Lago. Apart from recess time and the mainstreamed regular-education classroom, Ruben's only other contact with hearing peers was at lunchtime. Social interaction in the cafeteria was limited, however, because Ruben and his deaf peers sat at a separate table with Mrs. Thomas and/or the other aides from the DHH classroom.

DEAF AND HEARING BILINGUALISM: VISTA DEL LAGO SCHOOL

Mrs. Thomas, during her interview and subsequent conversations, remarked that she had some knowledge of bilingual theory and its application to the deaf population. While working in another district with a large "language minority population," she had received in-service training in bilingual education theory but had not attended any such formal training on Deaf bilingualism. Her philosophy on Deaf bilingualism stemmed from her own experiences as a Deaf person as well as from coursework for her master's degree.

When discussing classroom practices with regard to English and ASL, Mrs. Thomas stated that "It's bilingual for sure" and that "students needed to have a base in a natural first language before they could transfer the concepts into coded English." She also indicated that her students "must understand that they are using two different languages . . . how each one works and when to use it."

During an interview, Mrs. Gardner stated that, although Desert View County had conducted in-service training on bilingual theory, it related only to non–English-speaking students and not "specifically to ASL as a primary language" but that "I have a sense of language . . . in terms of language acquisition." However, because of her experience as an oralist teacher, Mrs. Gardner expressed concern over the assumption that deaf children "will not speak and so . . . they will use a sign language." When questioned about Deaf and hearing bilingualism, Mr. James, from Arroyo Seco school district, stated that the agreement with Desert View County with regard to the DHH program was to establish "campuses that were user-friendly to a bilingual development." He also discussed the difference between ASL and English, stating that "[g]rammar in English and ASL are about as different as night and day" but that deaf students needed to learn the crossover between the two languages in order to be successful.

Analysis and Discussion

This study investigated deaf educational policy and the translation of that policy into pedagogical practices at the two sites selected for this study. These pedagogical practices were then examined to show how they related to the socioeducational experiences of the focal student, a profoundly deaf eight-year-old male.

During the course of the study, the focal student, Ruben, attended first grade at a DHH program run by Desert View County at a regular-education campus within the Poppy Hill school district. The teacher for this DHH program, Mrs. Burke, was a hearing adult with no formal, signed language training. While at this campus, Ruben, accompanied by an interpreter, was mainstreamed for the majority of his day in a regular

TABLE 2. *Summary of Classroom Practices*

Educational Practice	Panguitch Elementary School	Vista del Lago Elementary School
Language use	Classroom practices focused on SEE. Teacher not trained in ASL. Little or no finger-spelling in evidence. Language utilized in the classroom followed English word order using SEE signs.	Classroom practices focused on both ASL and SEE. Teacher fluent in both ASL and English. Daily finger-spelling in evidence. Language utilized in the classroom depended on context and included both ASL and English word order using ASL signs.
Mainstreaming	Focal student mainstreamed for 80 percent of the day. Regular education teacher not trained in signed language. Interpreter accompanied focal student and had dual role of interpreter and teacher. Little or no communication with hearing peers.	Focal student mainstreamed for 20 percent of the day. Regular educational teacher not trained in signed language. Interpreter accompanied focal student and had dual role of interpreter and teacher. Little or no communication with hearing peers.
Bilingualism	Teacher not familiar with either hearing or Deaf bilingualism. Administrators had varying knowledge of hearing bilingualism. Only two administrators had any knowledge of Deaf bilingualism. Classroom practices focused on English language development.	Teacher familiar with both hearing and Deaf bilingualism. Administrators had varying knowledge of hearing and Deaf bilingualism. Classroom practices based on a bilingual education framework.

classroom. The focal student then attended second and third grade at the Desert View DHH program housed at a second regular-education site in the Arroyo Seco school district. Ruben has been mainstreamed at this campus for approximately 20 percent of his school day. The teacher for this second DHH program, Mrs. Thomas, was a Deaf adult fluent in both ASL and English.

With regard to language policy and practices at both sites, data revealed little or no guidance for language use within the various legal documents examined as well as at the local policy level. None of the documents analyzed stated which language—ASL, oral, or signed English—was preferable nor did they address which language facilitated cognitive development in deaf children. The Poppy Hill and Arroyo Seco school district policies both professed a general goal to realize the potential of all students but failed to specifically address the role language plays in cognitive development, especially with regard to deaf students.

Although both program sites included in this study were run by Desert View County, the pedagogical practices in place at the two sites varied tremendously and were more of a reflection of personal philosophies and beliefs as opposed to a uniform language policy dictated by the district educational agency. At the local level, teachers were directed to "do what's best for the kids," without any guidance as to what "best" meant. Deaf students who moved between the two sites were exposed to and expected to adapt to varying language practices within the classrooms, regardless of their developmental or chronological ages or their prior sociolinguistic experiences. Little or no discussion among the various constituents of the program took place, and that which did was limited to budget and personnel issues taken up at the SELPA level. Professional development often was separate for the teachers in both programs. Furthermore, professional development conducted by either the Poppy Hill or the Arroyo Seco school districts virtually never included the DHH teachers, in spite of their being housed on campus and in spite of their students being mainstreamed into district classes.

This profound lack of discussion as well as the lack of a concrete, uniform language policy has produced a DHH program that is not cohesive and which vacillates between ASL, a natural language, and SEE, a coded form of English, depending upon teachers' beliefs and experiences. Although both the hearing teacher and the Deaf teacher in the DHH program recognized sociocultural and sociolinguistic experiences as the bases for cognitive development, this translated into very different philosophies and classroom practices. The resultant socioeducational milieu confused deaf students, who oftentimes lacked the sociolinguistic or metalinguistic savvy to successfully adapt to the differing pedagogical practices. Language and cognitive development were diminished and thereby limited student potential, regardless of the intent of local board policy.

The Total Communication philosophy that dominated pedagogical practices in Mrs. Burke's classroom emphasized oral English accompanied by coded English. The practices were based on Mrs. Burke's experiences as a hearing person as well as a prior oralist teacher for deaf students. Mrs. Burke's lack of training in ASL and the absence of any native ASL signers in her classroom prevented deaf students' access to a sociolinguistic and/or sociocultural role model. Moreover, Mrs. Burke's inability to sign fluently with her students presented a linguistic barrier that she did not seem aware of and one that did not facilitate the mutuality and engagement the literature suggests is required for cognitive development. None of the administrators responsible for the program in Desert View County or the Poppy Hill School District seemed to have a clear idea as to which language was in use in Mrs. Burke's classroom.

Mrs. Thomas's pedagogical practices emphasized ASL as a cognitive tool and the recognition of SEE as a coded form of English used for literary functions. As a Deaf adult, Mrs. Thomas was both a sociolinguistic and a sociocultural role model for her deaf students. Her fluency in both ASL and English enabled her to teach her deaf students the pragmatic functions of both languages. No linguistic barrier was evident, and it would appear from the data that Mrs. Thomas's sociolinguistic interactions were cognitively more facilitative than Mrs. Burke's interactions.

Also, the administrators at both the Desert View County and the Arroyo Seco school district responsible for the DHH program at Vista del Lago School seemed to be more knowledgeable about actual language use with the DHH classroom than the administrators responsible for the program at the Panguitch School.

With regard to mainstreaming, data indicated an intent from the various constituents at the local level to comply with the legal requirements for LRE set forth by the legislature. At both sites, the focal student spent part of his day mainstreamed into a regular education classroom. However, as the literature suggests, such mainstreaming situations are often characterized by a lack of adaptation (i.e., the mainstreamed teachers' inability to communicate in signed language) and a lack of social relationships with hearing peers. Given Ruben's difficulty when mainstreamed for the majority of his school day, it would appear that, although the intent of the legislature was to protect the civil rights of the student with a disability, the mainstreamed classroom context often results in the most restrictive environment for the deaf student.

Data presented in reference to Deaf and hearing bilingualism indicated that, although ASL is not considered one of the languages included in the Bilingual Education Act of 1968, pedagogical practices that emphasize bilingualism may be beneficial to deaf students. The literature suggests that a foundation in a natural language is a prerequisite to learning a second language and that comprehensible input, regardless of the modality of the language, provides a semiotic tool that facilitates mutuality and cognitive development. Mrs. Thomas, the Deaf teacher, was familiar with issues of Deaf bilingualism and made it a point to develop metalinguistic skills in her deaf students when addressing the form and functions of ASL and English. In contrast, Mrs. Burke, the hearing teacher, was not familiar with either hearing or Deaf bilingualism. Furthermore, she was also unfamiliar with the pragmatic functions of both languages in spite of her need to utilize ASL during reading lessons when her deaf students could not comprehend the material in English.

Recommendations

The results of this study suggest a need for a cohesive, multilevel, deaf educational policy that is grounded in scientific sociolinguistic research and facilitates cognitive development in deaf children. The findings also indicate a need to address the concept of Least Restrictive Environment as it relates specifically to deaf students. Communicative and cognitive access should form the bases for defining the LRE for deaf students in order to prevent the sociolinguistic and socioeducational isolation that so many deaf children suffer from in mainstreamed classrooms. Finally, the results of this study indicate that a bilingual framework that addresses the issues of language acquisition and language learning and how they relate to cognitive development in deaf children should be more thoroughly investigated and perhaps piloted on a larger scale within deaf education.

LEGAL RESOURCES

Americans with Disabilities Act of 1990, 42 U.S.C. § 12117. (ADA Handbook. Washington, D.C.: U.S. Government Printing Office, 1991.)

Assembly Concurrent Resolution 55, California Assembly and Senate, Resolution, chapter 30, (Legislative Counsel's Digest, 1992).

Bilingual Education Act of 1968, 20 U.S.C.A. § 3282 (West, 1994).

Deaf and Hard of Hearing Rights Bill, AB 1836, California § 56–364.1 (1994).

Deaf Students Education Services Policy Guidance, 57, Federal Register 49275 (1992).

Individuals with Disabilities Education Act of 1990, 20 U.S.C.A. § 1400 Notes (West, 1994).

REFERENCES

Baker, C., and R. Battison, eds. 1980. *Sign language and the Deaf community.*
Silver Spring, Md.: National Association of the Deaf.

Barnum, M. 1984. In support of bilingual/bicultural education for deaf
children. *American Annals of the Deaf* 129(5):404–8.

Christensen, K. M. 1989. ASL/ESL: A bilingual approach to education of
children who are deaf. *Teaching English to Deaf and Second Language
Learners* (winter):9–14.

Cohen, O. P. 1995. Perspectives on the full inclusion movement in the education
of deaf children. In *Inclusion? Defining quality education for Deaf and hard
of hearing students,* ed. B. D. Snider. Washington, D.C.: College for
Continuing Education, Gallaudet University.

Commission on Education of the Deaf. 1988. Toward equality: Education of
the Deaf. A report to the President and the Congress of the United States.
Washington, D.C.: U.S. Government Printing Office.

Cortes, C. E. 1986. The education of language minority students: A contextual
interaction model. *Beyond language: Social and cultural factors in schooling
language minority students.* Los Angeles: Evaluation, Dissemination, and
Assessment Center, California State University at Los Angeles.

Daniels, M. 1994. Words more powerful than sounds. *Sign Language Studies*
82:155–67.

Drasgow, E. 1993. Bilingual/bicultural deaf education: An overview. *Sign
Language Studies* 80:243–65.

Erting, C. 1980. Sign language and communication between adults and
children. In *Sign language and the Deaf community,* ed. C. Baker and R.
Battison, 159–76. Silver Spring, Md.: National Association of the Deaf.

———. 1988. Acquiring linguistic and social identity: Interactions of deaf
children with a hearing teacher and a deaf adult. In *Language, learning and
deafness,* ed. M. Strong, 192–219. Cambridge: Cambridge University Press.

Freire, P. 1970. *Pedagogy of the oppressed.* Trans. M. Bergman-Ramos. New
York: Continuum.

Garton, A. F. 1992. *Social interaction and the development of language and
cognition.* Hillsdale, N.J.: Lawrence Erlbaum Associates.

Grosjean, F. 1992. The bilingual and bicultural person in the hearing and the
deaf world. *Sign Language Studies* 77:307–20.

Gumperz, J. J., and E. Hernández-Chavez. 1972. Bilingualism, bidialectism,
and classroom interaction. In *Functions of language in the classroom,*
ed. C. Cazden, V. P. John, and D. Hymes, 84–110. Prospect Heights, Ill.:
Waveland Press.

Krashen, S. D. 1981. Bilingual education and second language acquisition theory. In *Schooling and language minority students: A theoretical framework*. Los Angeles: Evaluation, Dissemination, and Assessment Center, California State University at Los Angeles.

Lane, H. 1992. *The mask of benevolence: Disabling the Deaf community*. New York: Vintage Press.

Padden, C., and C. Ramsey. 1996. Deaf students as readers and writers: A mixed mode research approach. Final report. San Diego: Research Center in Language and Literacy, University of California, San Diego.

Ramsey, C. 1993. A description of classroom discourse and literacy learning among deaf elementary students in a mainstreaming program. Ph.D. diss., University of California, Berkeley.

——. 1995. Integration, ideology and studenthood for deaf children. In *Inclusion? Defining quality education for Deaf and hard of hearing students*, ed. B. D. Snider, 205–13. Washington, D.C.: College for Continuing Education, Gallaudet University.

——. 1997. *Deaf children in public schools: Placement, context, and consequences*. Sociolinguistics in Deaf Communities, vol. 3. Washington, D.C.: Gallaudet University Press.

Sacks, O. 1989. *Seeing voices: A journey into the world of the Deaf*. New York: Harper Collins.

Schildroth, A. N., and S. A. Hotto. 1995. Deaf students and full inclusion: Who wants to be excluded? In *Inclusion? Defining quality education for Deaf and hard of hearing students*, ed. B. D. Snider, 173–94. Washington, D.C.: College for Continuing Education, Gallaudet University.

Stevens, R. 1980. Education in schools for deaf children. In *Sign language and the Deaf community*, ed. C. Baker and R. Battison, 177–92. Silver Spring, Md.: National Association of the Deaf.

Stinson, M. S., and I. W. Leigh. 1995. Inclusion and the psychosocial development of Deaf children and youths. In *Inclusion? Defining quality education for Deaf and hard of hearing students*, ed. B. D. Snider, 153–62. Washington, D.C.: College for Continuing Education, Gallaudet University.

Strong, M. 1988. A bilingual approach to the education of young deaf children: ASL and English. In *Language, learning and deafness*, ed. M. Strong, 113–29. Cambridge: Cambridge University Press.

——. 1991. Working within the bilingual education act: Why deaf children should not be excluded. In *Bilingual considerations in the education of Deaf students: ASL and English*, ed. Juanita Cebe, 106–22. Washington, D.C.: College for Continuing Education, Gallaudet University.

Strong, M., and E. S. Charlson. 1987. Simultaneous communication: Are teachers attempting an impossible task? *American Annals of the Deaf* 132(4):376–82.

Sue, S., and A. Padilla. 1986. Ethnic minority issues in the United States: Challenges for the educational system. In *Beyond language: Social and cultural factors in school language minority students,* 25–72. Los Angeles: Evaluation, Dissemination, and Assessment Center, California State University at Los Angeles.

Supalla, S. 1992. Equal educational opportunity: The deaf version. In *A free hand: Enfranchising the education of Deaf children,* ed. M. Walworth, D. F. Moores, and T. J. O'Rourke, 170–81. Silver Spring, Md.: T. J. Publishers.

Vygotsky, L. S. 1978. Mind in society: The development of higher psychological processes, ed. M. Cole, V. John-Steiner, S. Scribner, and E. Souberman. Cambridge: Harvard University Press.

———. 1986. *Thought and language.* Ed. and trans. A. Kozuhn. Cambridge, Mass.: MIT Press.

Wertsh, J. 1991. *Voices of the mind: A Sociocultural Approach to Mediated Action.* Cambridge: Harvard University Press.

Winefield, R. 1987. *Never the twain shall meet. Bell, Gallaudet, and the communications debate.* Washington, D.C.: Gallaudet University Press.

Part 4 Discourse Analysis

Conversational Repairs in ASL

Valerie L. Dively

Studies on spoken language conversations indicate that natural languages contain mechanisms called *repairs*. Repairs are used for handling breakdowns in the conversation but also come into play when a speaker is monitoring and adjusting his or her own utterances. In fact, speakers in conversations are more likely to repair their own utterances than addressees repair the other speakers' utterances (Moerman 1977; Schegloff, Jefferson, and Sacks 1977; Schiffrin 1987). Ethnographic interviews with two Native Deaf informants[1] are used as the sociolinguistic fieldwork that provided data for this paper's preliminary investigation of conversational repairs in American Sign Language (ASL). A comparison of conversational repairs in ASL, a visual-spatial language, and English, an aural-vocal language, also is included. This study provides new insights regarding the structure of ASL and fluent Deaf ASL signers' capabilities in communicating with one another in ASL.[2]

ETHNOGRAPHIC INTERVIEWS

The data consist of two videotaped and transcribed ASL ethnographic interviews. One full-blooded Hopi Deaf female informant, one full-blooded Akimel O' odham (formerly known as Pima) Deaf male informant[3] and myself, the investigator, as the mixed-blooded Deaf female ethnographer were the participants in the interviews for this study on the organization of conversational repairs in ASL. With ASL as our primary

1. In this paper, the term *Native* refers to indigenous peoples in the Americas (Native Americans and indigenous peoples of the North American Arctic).

2. Funding for this research was provided through the Small Grants Fund, Gallaudet University, Washington, D.C.

3. I want to give special thanks to the informants for their participation in this study. In this paper, the informants' names have been changed to keep their identities confidential.

language, the informants and I all are fluent ASL signers. The informants were in their twenties, and I was my thirties during the time the interviews were conducted.

Informants

The Native Deaf informants both were born and raised in hearing Native families on a federally recognized reservation. They attended the same state residential school for Deaf children—the Arizona School for the Deaf and Blind in Tucson, Arizona—during all of their precollege school years. They graduated from the school and both live in the same major Arizona city.

Most of Holly's (the Hopi informant) immediate family members were bilinguals. Hopi was spoken as their primary language, and English was spoken as their second language. These family members spoke Hopi at home and with other Hopi people whereas they spoke English at school and with non-Hopi people. One of Holly's siblings was a trilingual, fluent in Hopi, English, and ASL. This sibling also was a certified ASL interpreter. Holly was three years old when her parents decided to send her to live with a hearing Euro-American couple[4] in Tucson, Arizona, while Holly attended the residential school during her preschool and elementary school years. This hearing couple was proficient at ASL and a *signed language contact variety.*[5]

Most of Art's (the Akimel O' odham informant) immediate family members used English as their primary language, whereas a few members of his immediate family used a Native language as their primary language. Art believed their Native language was the language of the Akimel O' odham people. Most of his relatives outside his immediate family spoke in this same Native language. Art had a difficult time communicating with his relatives because they had not learned a signed language, and he could not communicate well in either spoken or written English or in his relatives' Native language. Art stated that he wished he had a hearing relative or knew a hearing Native person with ASL skills so he could communi-

4. *Euro-American* in this study refers to white people with European heritages who live in the Americas.

5. Signed language contact variety in this paper refers to a form of signed language used in language contact settings in a Deaf community (e.g., a signed system that is a mixture of two languages' features, such as English and ASL features [Lucas and Valli 1989, 1992]).

cate in ASL with his relatives. He feels that bringing a Euro-American ASL interpreter home is not an option because his relatives would not be comfortable communicating with one another and with him in the presence of a non-Native person. Art had one distant Akimel O' odham Deaf relative whose primary language was ASL. I did not ask Art how often he sees this Deaf relative. Art stated that this Deaf relative preferred to live on his own reservation and that this relative did not interact much with Deaf people outside the reservation.

Table 1 contains general information on the informants' (a) Native tribe and/or nation, (b) residency, (c) onset of deafness, (d) relatives' use of visual-spatial communication systems, and (e) age when they first acquired ASL.

Ethnographer

I was born deaf and raised in Michigan in a hearing Euro-American family with an older Deaf brother. I attended a state residential school for the deaf—the Michigan School for the Deaf in Flint, Michigan—during all of my elementary and secondary school years. I spent my preschool years at an oral-educational day program in the same city. All of my immediate hearing family members, whose primary language is U.S. English, used home signs and gestures when my Deaf brother and I were very young. The hearing family members later acquired ASL and a signed language contact variety when I was approximately seven years old. They mainly use a signed language contact variety for signed interactions. My Deaf brother's primary language is ASL. I first acquired ASL from him when I was approximately four years old.

As a half-blooded German-American with several other Euro-American heritages and a Native heritage, my father's appearance is that of a Native. In my father's family circles, the name of the Native heritage is not exactly known. My mother is a half-blooded Norwegian-American with several other Euro-American heritages. I am Norwegian in appearance. I have lived in the Washington, D.C., metropolitan area since 1978.

Interviews

This paper's two ethnographic interviews were adopted from an ethnographic study I conducted on Native Deaf peoples in United States (Dively 1996). Ethnography is the study and systematic recording of human cultures by an anthropologist conducting fieldwork, such as observing people

TABLE 1. *Informants*

Informants	Native Tribe and/or Nation, and Residency	Onset of Deafness	Relatives' Use of Visual-Spatial Communication	Age When First Acquired ASL
Art	Akimel O' odham; born and raised on the Gila River reservation in Arizona; currently lives in a major Arizona city	probably born deaf	A few immediate family members use home signs[1] and gestures;[2] one distant Deaf relative uses ASL	age 4 when first attended state residential school for deaf children
Holly	Hopi; born and raised on the Hopi reservation in Arizona; currently lives in a major Arizona city	born hearing; became deaf at the age of 2½	one hearing sibling is a certified ASL interpreter; other immediate family members use home signs and gestures	age 3 when first attended state residential school for deaf children

1. Home signs are visual-spatial communicative items standardized within family circles, not within a community. Home signs occur in families with Deaf, hard of hearing, and deafened members. Characteristics of home signs are: larger signing space, repeated signs, eye gazes dependent on environmental items, and a limited number of distinct handshapes (Frishberg 1987).

2. Gestures are nonstandard visual-spatial communicative items that occur among hearing people's interactions, among Deaf/hard of hearing/deafened people's interactions, and in hearing people and Deaf/hard of hearing people's interactions (Klima and Bellugi 1979).

of a cultural group and their ways of life, learning a new language, asking those people questions, observing ceremonies, and interviewing informants (Spradley 1979). I also adopt another part of the definition of anthropology to fully describe the nature of my ethnographic study, which is similar to Megan Biesele's (a U.S. social anthropologist) fieldwork with Ju/'hoan people, commonly known as Bushmen, in Namibia. With her extended field participation and linguistic fluency in the Ju/'hoan community, Biesele provided Ju/'hoan people opportunities to speak for themselves about their community and ways of life in her scholarly works (Biesele 1993).

Because Art and Holly both lived in the same city, the ethnographic interviews were conducted on a one-to-one informal basis in a convenient setting in Tucson, Arizona. Art was interviewed in a conference room in the Community Outreach Program of the Deaf, in Tucson on April 19, 1994. Holly was interviewed in a conference room in the Arizona School for the Deaf and Blind in Tucson on April 20, 1994. Art, Holly, and I had never met until the interviews.

After introductions and informal discussion, I gave each informant room to share their various Native Deaf experiences. We discussed family life, schooling, and Deaf and hearing communities. The total amount of time involved in the study's two videotaped and transcribed ethnographic interviews is nearly 63 minutes. The interview with Art is approximately 23 minutes in length, whereas that with Holly is approximately 40 minutes long.

TRANSCRIPTION CONVENTIONS

Several transcription conventions need to be described here before the ASL utterances in this study can be observed, analyzed, and discussed. The symbol *rh* refers to right-handed manual signs, and the symbol *lh* refers to left-handed manual signs. The symbol *H* refers to Holly, the Hopi Deaf female informant, and the symbol *A* refers to Art, the Akimel O' odham Deaf male informant. The symbol *V* refers to me, the mixed-blooded Deaf female ethnographer. Holly, Art, and I all used our right hands as our main (dominant) hand. Numbers that accompany the symbols H and A refer to each excerpt that came from the study's ASL ethnographic interviews. English translations of these excerpts are also provided in italics and follow each excerpt in this paper. The lowercase letter *o*, which accompanies H, A, or V, represents a speaker's overlapped utterances.

My system for transcribing is primarily based on Liddell and Johnson's (1989) autosegmental phonology model, along with my two main observations regarding ASL morphology. The first observation is that there are many ASL-independent lexical items (or free morphemes) produced without the use of hands. These independent lexical items are called *nonhanded signs* (Dively 1996). The second observation is that fluent ASL signers are capable of producing two independent lexical items at the same time in an ASL utterance.

Nonhanded signs are produced without the use of a hand and function as full lexical items, such as **OH-I-SEE** and **UNSURE**. Most ASL nonhanded signs consist of three parameters: head with or without other nonmanual features, head movement, and head orientation. Head movement and head orientation tend to be tied together in nonhanded signs. In this paper, non-bold English glosses in small capital letters represent ASL manual signs, whereas bold English glosses in small capital letters represent ASL nonhanded signs. The nonhanded signs **OH-I-SEE, YES, NO,** and **I-WRONG** and one manual sign, WELL, which appear in this paper merit a description regarding their phonological aspects and function in an ASL utterance.

The two nonhanded signs, **OH-I-SEE** and **YES,** which frequently appear in this paper's transcribed ASL utterances, need to be differentiated here. The nonhanded sign **OH-I-SEE** is synonymous in meaning to the manual sign OH-I-SEE. **OH-I-SEE** is produced with either a quick/slow up-and-down head movement or a soft/slow nodding movement to convey meanings of "oh," "I understand," or "oh, I see." The nonhanded sign, **YES,** is synonymous in meaning to the manual sign YES. **YES** is produced with a standardized head nodding movement to indicate "yes" or "yes, I understand."

The nonhanded sign **I-WRONG** has at least two variations; this sign is produced with either a brief headshake or the head moving to left or right and then returning to the neutral place. The semantics and phonological features of this nonhanded sign are clearly distinguished from the nonhanded sign **NO,** which is synonymous in meaning to the manual sign #NO++. (For further information on nonhanded signs, see Dively 1996.)

The manual sign WELL consists of at least two different definitions. The first definition refers to a predicate with a meaning of "it was no use" or "I could not do anything" (for example, see A5). The second definition refers to a particle whose meaning is similar to the English particle *well* (for example, see A2 and A3).

Based on an autosegmental phonological description of lexical items, ASL has four categories of independent lexical items: left-handed one-handed manual signs, right-handed one-handed manual signs, two-handed manual signs, and nonhanded signs. ASL signers can produce two one-handed signs at the same time: one left-handed one-handed sign and one right-handed one-handed signs (see H4). They can also produce one one-handed sign—either a left-handed one-handed sign or a right-handed one-handed sign—and one nonhanded sign at the same time (see A1 and H1). They can also produce one two-handed manual sign and one nonhanded sign at the same time (see H1).

In other words, if ASL signers were speaking a spoken language, they would need two mouths, as it were, to utter two separate words at once, because left-handed one-handed signs, right-handed one-handed signs, two-handed manual signs, and nonhanded signs each contain a different internal structure. This study's ethnographic interviews indicate that the informants most frequently produce one sign; they next most frequently produce one manual sign—either a one-handed sign or a two-handed sign—and a nonhanded sign concurrently. They least frequently produce a left-handed one-handed sign and a right-handed one-handed sign at the same time. More research is needed in this area.

Two examples of a two-layered staff of signs with the transcription conventions described above are found in A1 below.

A1

		rhet

A   MAYBE SPEAK DIFFERENT Qwg (pause)   NATIVE

                                                          neg-q

Vo   OH-I-SEE DON'T-KNOW

Arh   UNSURE.......

Arh   SPEAK DIFFERENT.

lh   PRO.1

Vo   OH-I-SEE

                                                   q

Vo   POSS.3-rt PRO.3-rt. NATIVE SPEAK NATIVE PRO.3-rt.

Arh   UNSURE con't ....

lh   DON'T-KNOW POSS.3-lf++.

Vo   DON'T-KNOW OH-I-SEE.

A   *They [the hearing Akimel O' odham relatives] may speak*

A   *in a different language.(pause) They speak   in a Native*

Vo   *I see.*

A   *I'm not sure..*

A   *language, a different language.*   *I do not know*

Vo   *I see....*

Vo   *You do not know what Native language they speak in?*

A   *I'm not sure.........*

A   *know [the name of] their Native language.*

Vo   *I see.............*

Vo   *[You] do not know [the language]. Yes, I understand.*

The first example of a two-layered staff of signs, produced by Art, contained an upper-layered staff of the nonhanded sign, UNSURE, and a lower layered staff of the

UNSURE..............................

sentence of left-handed manual signs: PRO.1 don't-know POSS.3-lf. Another example of a two-layered staff of signs, produced by me, was an overlap consisting of an upper-layered staff of the nonhanded sign OH-I-SEE and a lower-layered staff of the manual sign DON'T-KNOW: OH-I-SEE....... DON'T-KNOW. Both examples indicated there are two sets of completed sentences produced at the same time: an upper-layered staff of a nonhanded sign functioning as a complete sentence and a lower-layered staff of a manual sign or signs functioning as a complete sentence. A1 also contained several overlapped utterances, all produced by me.

SELF-REPAIRS AND OTHER-REPAIRS

Following Schegloff, Jefferson, and Sacks (1977) (henceforth referred to as S, J, and S), a conversational repair refers to either the repairing or monitoring of utterances in conversations. One phenomenon S, J, and S address is that repairs can occur regardless of whether a *trouble source* has occurred. Trouble source refers to an apparent error that can be corrected in conversations. For example, misspelled names, unclear sentences, and ungrammatical utterances are frequent trouble sources in English and ASL. Trouble sources in conversations can be corrected or go unrepaired.

S, J, and S call repairs produced by speakers *self-repairs,* and they call repairs produced by addressees *other-repairs.* Consistent with S, J, and S, repairs in this study occur on the basis of the speakers' and addressees' use of both language and communication. For example, the first sentence of H2 indicated that Holly realizes that she had selected an improper choice for the sign KID. This repair was related to language use or grammatical aspects. Repairs related to communication use or communication skills are also found in H2. For example, in H2 I did not clarify what I meant when I commented to Holly that there were many Native deaf students at her deaf residential school. H2 will be discussed in detail later in this paper.

The following is a description of self-repairs and other-repairs based on S, J, and S, with examples found in H1, from the study's ASL ethnographic interviews.

Self-Initiated Repairs

This type of repair usually refers to lexical items, utterances, and non-lexical items produced by a speaker to signal the repairing or monitoring of his or her own utterances, with or without a trouble source having occurred. For example, both Holly and Art, in the study's ASL ethnographic interviews, had used the nonhanded sign I-WRONG as a self-initiated repair to signal that a previous utterance contained incorrect information. The symbol *si* is used to identify self-initiated repairs in this paper's transcribed ASL utterances.

Self-Completed Repairs

This type of repair usually refers to lexical items and utterances produced by a speaker for completing a self-repair, with or without repairing a trouble source. For example, both Holly and Art had each completed a self-initiated repair by replacing the previous utterance, containing incorrect information, with another utterance that contained correct information. The replaced utterance functioned as a self-completed repair. The symbol *sc* is used to identify self-completed repairs in this paper's transcribed ASL utterances.

Other-Initiated Repairs

This type of repair usually refers to lexical items, utterances, and non-lexical items produced by an addressee to signal his or her repairing or monitoring of a speaker's utterances, with or without a trouble source having occurred. For example, an addressee asked a speaker a question for clarification because the speaker's previous utterances did not contain clear information on one aspect of the company's procedure in purchasing another company. This question functioned as an other-initiated repair. The symbol *oi* is used to identify other-initiated repairs in this paper's transcribed ASL utterances.

Other-Completed Repairs

This type of repair usually refers to lexical items and utterances produced by an addressee for completing either a self-initiated repair or an other-initiated repair, with or without repairing a trouble source. For example, an addressee replaced the speaker's utterance containing incorrect information with an utterance that contained correct information. The replaced utterance functioned as an other-completed repair. The symbol *oc* is used to identify other-completed repairs in this paper's transcribed ASL utterances.

H1 below provides ASL examples of a self-initiated repair, an other-initiated repair, and two other-completed repairs.

H1

```
                                        ___oc___
                          _____cond_____
H    HOME PRO.3-rt........ THEN SPEAK-rt #HOPI-rt LANGUAGE-rt.

                          ____oi____
                          ____q_____
Vo   PRO.2 HOME    YES.    YES.                YES++.
H                    t       NOT-LIKE.
H    PRO.3-lf SCHOOL ENGLISH. REQUIRED.
Vo                         YES++.

                   _____q__
V    YES++. REQUIRED SELF.3-rt "school" #HOPI #OR

                   __q cont.__
V    GOVERMENT REQUIRED.
Ho                 GOVERNMENT

                                      ___brow raised___
H    GOVERNMENT ESTABLISH SCHOOL FOR      PRO.3-lf....

                   _____q_____
Vo                 U......S. [U.S.]           OH-I-SEE.

                   _____si_____
     head and eye gaze to rh
H    UNSURE...........................
H    B-I-A.          B...                    YES++.

                                        ___oc___
Vo               OH-I-SEE B-I-A YES++.
```

H	At home............................ *they speak in the Hopi*
Vo	*Your home? Yes, I now understand.* Yes. Yes,
H	*I do not like it.*
H	*language. In school, they speak English as it is required.*
Vo	*yes.* Yes, I understand.
V	*Yes, I understand. The school requires students to speak*
V	*[English]? Or Hopi people require this or the government*
V	*requires this?*
Ho	*The government.*
H	*The government had established a school...................*
Vo	Is [this government] U.S. [federal
Vo	government]?
H	*for [Hopi people].... [That's the government agency,]*
Vo	I see.
H	*I am not sure [how to spell].*
H	*BIA. B...* Yes, that's the one.
Vo	Oh, I see, BIA, yes.

There were one self-initiated repair, one other-initiated repair, and two other-completed repairs, plus two repaired trouble sources and one unrepaired trouble source in H1. The first trouble source was Holly's lack of clarification in regard to which home she was referring to when she signed the first utterance in H1 as she used a determiner PRO.3-rt. Normally, signers would say HOME PRO.3 or use a topicalized sentence such as HOME PRO.3 to indicate that the home is theirs. Here, Holly used a conditional sentence, and her previous utterances did not provide adequate information about which home she was referring to. I thus asked Holly an overlapped ASL question for clarification about whose home she was alluding to. This overlapped question functioned as an other-initiated repair. Holly responded to my question by prolonging the use of the manual sign PRO.3-rt to indicate this home was indeed hers, including Hopi people living on the Hopi reservation. I then confirmed that I understood the meaning of prolonged use of the manual sign by signing a non-handed sign YES, also in an overlapped ASL utterance. The prolonged use of the manual sign PRO.3-rt functioned here as an other-completed repair as Holly acted as an addressee, not as a speaker, when she responded and completed the other-initiated repair (my overlapped question for clarification).

The second trouble source was my improper choice of a sign in the first overlapped sentence in H1: PRO.2. The correct choice would be POSS.2. This trouble source was not repaired but had no effect on further conversations between Holly and me, as Holly understood exactly what I meant.

The third trouble source was Holly's not being sure of the spelling of the agency's full name, U.S. Bureau of Indian Affairs (BIA). To signal this trouble source, Holly used head movement and eye-gazing toward her fingerspelling and the two-layered staff of signs: upper-layered staff of a nonhanded sign—UNSURE—and lower-layered staff of the two manual signs—fingerspelled sign B-I-A and incomplete fingerspelled B. This phenomenon frequently occurs in ASL discourse when signers signal their uncertainty of the right fingerspelling. They do this by using nonhanded signs such as UNSURE and DON'T-KNOW along with eye-gazing at the hand that produced the fingerspelled signs. Holly used this same tactic in H2, where it functioned as a self-initiated repair. This repair also served as a word-search repair. (A description of word-search repairs will be given in the following section.) When Holly began to fingerspell the name a second time, she ceased fingerspelling as I confirmed that I knew exactly which government agency she was referring to. This was represented in an overlapped utterance by my fingerspelling the agency's initialized name, BIA, and by my indicating that there was no need for fingerspelling the full name of the agency. This overlapped utterance functioned as an other-completed repair in spite of the fact that this utterance did not contain a fingerspelled sign of the full name of the agency but a fingerspelled sign of the agency's acronym. From my personal observations, ASL signers often do not bother with producing a completed fingerspelled sign of a full or initialized name if it has been comprehended. ASL signers tend to cease fingerspelling in the middle of a completed fingerspelled sign if the involved parties know which lexical item(s) they are referring to. I view this phenomenon as *part self-completed repairs* or *part other-completed repairs,* depending on who—speaker or addressee—produced the repair. Hence, my observation here is that the last overlapped utterance in H1 functioned as a part other-completed repair that, completed the self-initiated repair. This other-completed repair also corrected the third trouble source.

The S, J, and S study does not include a description and discussion of the three types of utterances I observed that function as unique forms of conversational repairs. The first type is an unrepaired trouble source that takes place when neither the speaker nor the addressee is aware of the existence of the trouble source. For example, the English speaker may say, "I went to Giant grocery store," not realizing that he or she really meant to say, "I went to Safeway grocery store." Since *Giant* is the name of a grocery store, the addressee has no way of knowing the speaker really meant to say *Safeway* instead.

The second type not mentioned in the S, J, and S study is a repair raised by addressees outside their direct conversations with speakers—for example, when friends talked to one another about aspects of a speaker's lecture that did not make sense to them because the speaker had used imperfect English. These persons did not directly provide the speaker with input on the lecture. Also, the S, J, and S study does not discuss a third type of repair raised by speakers outside their direct conversations with addressees. For example, if a speaker completed her lecture and later realized that she needed to repair certain utterances with trouble sources in her lecture, she might later explain the repairs to her friends. In other words, this speaker would repair the trouble sources if she had the opportunity to do so. This paper's ASL ethnographic interviews do not contain the three types of repairs just described, but they are mentioned to give the reader a broad view of different types of repairs.

REPLACEMENT REPAIRS AND WORD-SEARCH REPAIRS

S, J, and S also mentioned two other types of repairs produced by both speakers and addressees in conversations: replacement repairs and word-search repairs. Their description of these two types follows, with examples from the study's ASL ethnographic interviews.

Replacement Repairs

This type of repair usually refers to lexical items produced by speakers and addressees that replace a lexical item or items with or without a trouble source having occurred. For example, see A2.

A2

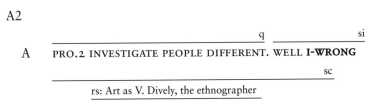

		q

A SO-CALL PRO.1-ASK-PRO.2-lf; alt.   OTHER

Vo   **YES++**

       ___sc cont.___

       ___q cont.___

A PEOPLE NATIVE.

A *Do you do an investigation on different people? Well, no, I*

A *mean, do you interview various Native people?*

Vo   *Yes, yes.*

The manual sign WELL and the nonhanded sign I-WRONG were used here by Art as a self-initiated repair to signal the need for a repair. Art then replaced the question, produced prior to the signs WELL and I-WRONG, with another question containing more detailed information regarding my interviews with people—Native people, not people in general—who were interviewed. This replaced question functioned as a replacement repair as well as a self-completed repair since Art himself repaired and completed the self-initiated repair in the previous dialog excerpt. This replacement thus functioned as two different types of repairs occurring at the same time: self-completed and replacement repair. These three repairs occurred without an apparent trouble source having occurred, as Art was rephrasing his question regarding my interviews in order to obtain clarification.

Word-Search Repairs

This type of repair usually refers to lexical and nonlexical items produced by speakers and addressees that signal a repair in which (1) a person tries to recall information or (2) a person searches for the right choice of lexical items. These repairs take place with or without a trouble source having occurred. Studies of spoken language conversations as well as this study's ethnographic interviews indicate that word-search repairs occur more frequently than replacement repairs. For example, see A3.

A3

		si	
	cs head and gaze down to rt		sc

A PAST++. (pause)   WELL-lh 2-WEEK-PAST FINISH

     ___sc cont.___

A 2-WEEK-PAST.

Vo OH-I-SEE.

A   [*The powwow*] *recently occurred. Hmmm, well, it actually*
A   *occurred 2 weeks ago.*
Vo   *Oh, I see.*

Nonmanual features, head movement, eye gaze downward to the right, and the manual sign WELL were used by Art as both a self-initiated repair and a word-search repair to recall the date of a particular powwow. The utterance, produced by Art to follow the manual sign WELL and non-manual features, contained information about the date of the powwow and thus completed the self-initiated repair. This utterance thus functioned as a self-completed repair. These three repairs took place without the trouble source having occurred.

CONVERSATIONAL REPAIRS IN ENGLISH AND ASL

The following utterances are adopted from the S, J, and S 1977 study, and this study's ethnographic interviews provided for analysis and discussion of replacement repairs and word-search repairs in U.S. English and ASL conversations. In this paper, numbers that accompany the symbol SJS refer to excerpts of transcribed spoken English utterances adapted from the S, J, and S study.

Replacement Repairs in English

SJS1 contains an example of replacement repair in English.

SJS1

Roger: We're just workin on a different thing, the same thing.

The speaker here signaled a self-initiated repair by replacing the noun phrase "a different thing" with another noun phrase, "the same thing." The replaced noun phrase functioned as a replacement repair because it replaced the previous incorrect noun phrase with correct information. Since the new noun phrase contained correct information and completed the self-initiated repair, this phrase also functioned as a self-completed repair. The replacement thus functioned as three different types of repairs occurring at the same time: self-initiated, self-completed, and replacement repair. These repairs occurred with a trouble source having taken place (the noun phrase with incorrect information). This trouble source was repaired with correct information.

SJS2 contains another example of replacement repair in English.

SJS2

Louise: Isn't it next week we're outta school?
Roger: Yeah next week. No // not next week, // the week after.

The utterance with a negation ("No // not next week" [// signifies a pause]) was used by Roger as a self-initiated repair to signal that his previous utterance, "Yeah next week," contained a trouble source: an incorrect date. Roger repaired this trouble source by replacing it with another utterance containing the correct date. Since the replaced utterance contained the correct date, this utterance functioned as both a self-completed repair and a replacement repair. Like SJS1, this replacement noun phrase functioned as three different types of repairs occurring at the same time: self-initiated, self-completed, and replacement repair. These repairs took place with a trouble source having occurred (the utterance with a wrong date). This trouble source was repaired with the correct date.

Replacement Repairs in ASL

H2 below contains several replacement repairs in ASL.

H2

		t		si and sc
H	POSS.1 GOAL TEACH KID CHILDREN			
Vo			**OH-I-SEE.**	
V	**YES** OH-I-SEE GOOD **YES**. NEED NATIVE DEAF TEACH. MANY			

		q
V	NATIVE HERE-[ASDB]. RIGHT.	
Ho	**YES.**	

	oi
H	**NOT-THINK-SO.**

	neq-q		neg-q
V	HERE-[ASDB]. NATIVE DEAF FEW. NOT MANY **NO++**.....		

		oi
Ho		**NO SEEM^NOT NO**. NO++.................
Vrh	**YES++**...**YES** HERE HEAR PRO.1 AROUND 50 NATIVE	
lh	HERE-lh-[ASDB]................	
Ho	...**YES** HERE-[ASDB].	

V   HERE. DEAF SMALL SO-CALL.

                                                    oc
                                         si and sc
              rhet   nod
H   YES. HERE STUDENT YES HAVE NATIVE SMALL MANY YES.
Vo   YES++.

                      oc con't
                   t   neg
H   BUT TEACH^AGENT NONE-lh.

                                  t   neg
V   OH-I-SEE. RIGHT++-to H. TEACH^AGENT-rt NONE-2h-rt.
Ho   YES.   YES.
V   BUT STUDENT PRO.3-pl-front RESIDENTIAL-SCHOOL
Ho   YES.   YES++..........
Ho   YES.

                   nod-q
V   NATIVE DEAF YES++.
Ho   YES++.
H   *I hope to teach [deaf] kids, children.*
Vo   *Oh.*
V   *Yes, I understand. That's great. [The deaf educational*
V   *programs/schools] do need Native Deaf teachers. There*
V   *are many Natives (I referred to Native Deaf students) [here*
V   *at the Arizona School for the Deaf and Blind]? Correct?*
Ho   *Yes.*
H   *No, I do not think [that there are any]. (Holly referred to*
     Native Deaf teachers here).
V   *There aren't any (I still referred to Native Deaf students*
V   *here) here [at the school]? Few Native deaf (I still referred*
Ho   *No, it does not seem that there*
V   *to students here) [here at the school]?*
Ho   *are any Native Deaf (Holly still referred to teachers).*
V   *Not many [here at the school]? Okay yes. Oh, ok, I've*
Ho   *No, no........................... Yes, [there aren't any Native*
V   *heard that there are approximately 50 Native [Deaf]*
Ho   *Here [at the school; a left-handed one-handed sign]*
Ho   *Deaf] (Holly still referred to teachers).*

V	*students here. Are there few [or decrease in numbers of*
V	*Native] Deaf [students here at the school]?*
H	*Yes, there are few, many Native students here [at the*
Vo	*Yes, yes.*
H	*school]. But there is not one [Native deaf] teacher here.*
V	*Oh, I understand now. You indeed are right as there aren't*
Ho	*Yes.*
V	*any Native Deaf teachers [here at the school]. But there*
Ho	*Yes.*
V	*are Native deaf students here at the residential school,*
Ho	*Yes, yes....*
Ho	*Yes.*
Ho	*Yes.*
V	*correct? Yes, yes?*
Ho	*Yes, yes.*

H2 contained three repaired trouble sources, three replacement repairs, two self-initiated repairs, two self-completed repairs, two other-initiated repairs, and one other-completed repair. The first trouble source was that Holly made an improper choice of sign, KID, in the first utterance in H2. She immediately repaired what she felt was a trouble source by replacing the manual sign KID with another manual sign, CHILDREN. This replacement functions as both a self-initiated repair and a replacement repair. Since the replacement sign CHILDREN was what she considered a proper choice of sign, the replacement completed the self-initiated repair and thus functioned as a self-completed repair. Thus this replacement functioned as three different types of repairs occurring simultaneously: self-initiated, self-completed, and replacement repair.

The second trouble source in H2 referred to Holly's using a manual sign with incorrect information, SMALL. Holly immediately repaired this trouble source by replacing the sign SMALL with another manual sign, MANY. Like the first repaired trouble source in H2, this replacement also functioned as three different types of repairs occurring at the same time: self-initiated, self-completed, and replacement repair. This second trouble source probably occurred in Holly's unintentional adoption of the same sign, SMALL, from my previous question regarding the number of Native deaf students.

The third trouble source was my asking Holly an incomplete or vague question regarding the number of Native Deaf students at her deaf residential school. I did not mention students in this question. Hence, Holly thought I was still talking about Native Deaf teachers and explained that there were not any Native Deaf teachers at the school. There was no need to mention teachers in several repeated statements, based on the content of the previous conversations on her career goals as a teacher. This trouble source was not immediately repaired because Holly provided two other-initiated repairs to my statements that contained apparently incorrect information about the number of Native Deaf teachers. I continued to discuss the number of Native Deaf students without any mention of the word *students*. Inwardly I believed that Holly knew that there were many Native Deaf students. I simply did not recognize the third trouble source in my repeated statements regarding the number of Native Deaf students at the school. Eventually, however, Holly detected this trouble source. She repaired it and completed the two other-initiated repairs by providing a long other-completed repair that contained two sentences. The first referred to the fact that there are indeed many Native Deaf students at the school, and the second referred to the fact that there are no Native Deaf teachers at the school. This other-completed repair also functioned as a replacement repair since Holly replaced my previous unclear statements on Native Deaf students and her previous statements on Native Deaf teachers with two clear statements on the number of both Native Deaf students and Native Deaf teachers at her school.

H3 below contains another example of replacement repair in ASL.

H3

Hrh PRO.1 FROM {full fingerspelled name of a place} NATIVE
lh   PRO.3-lf
Vo   **YES.**
V   **YES.**
H   H-O-P-I R-RESERVE. PRO.3-lf POSS.3-2h++-lf TOWN

		si
H	Eng. mouthing of "village"	Eng. mouthing of "village"
	TOWN	V-I

	si cont		sc
H	**I-WRONG** TOWN {full fingerspelled name of a village}.		

H   **YES++......**
H   THAT WHERE PRO.1 LIVE PRO.3-lf.

	q
Vo BE-RAISED......	

H	I [came] from the {name of a section} on the Hopi
Vo	Yes.
V	Yes.
H	reservation. My home village's name is vi [incompletely
H	fingerspelled English word "village"], no, my home
H	village's name is {full fingerspelled the name of the
H	village}.
H	Yes, yes.
H	That's where I used to live...........................
Vo	[That's where] you grew up?

H3 contained one repaired trouble source, one self-initiated repair, and one self-completed repair. The trouble source here was Holly's selection of a wrong fingerspelled sign since she was supposed to fingerspell the name of her Hopi home village,[6] not the word *village*. Holly instantly acknowledged this trouble source and began to repair it by ceasing to fingerspell in the middle of the fingerspelled sign V-I-L-L-A-G-E. She followed this with the nonhanded sign **I-WRONG**. This set of the incomplete fingerspelled sign and the nonhanded sign **I-WRONG** functioned as a self-initiated repair. Holly then replaced the incomplete fingerspelled sign with another fingerspelled sign—the name of her home village (replacement repair). This also functioned as a self-completed repair because it contained a correct choice of sign that Holly herself produced.

Here is an interesting observation regarding the structure of ASL and ASL signers' capabilities in communicating with one another. With her production of a two-layered staff of signs:

YES++......

....PRO.3-lf, Holly was able to respond to my last overlapped question with the use of the nonhanded sign **YES** while she was still talking during her last utterance, which was not a response to the overlapped question. Hence, Holly was producing two completely separate utterances at the same time. This was possible due to the two utterances' separate internal structures: one utterance consisting of a nonhanded sign and another utterance consisting of manual signs.

H4 illustrates another example of replacement repair in ASL.

6. The brackets in this paper refer to lexical items, such as names of a Native hometown or village, which are not transcribed in order to keep the informants' identities confidential.

	t

H POSS.1-body to rt MOTHER-body to rt THINK PRO.1 CAN
H BECOME HEARING. LATER CAN++.
Vo OH-I-SEE.

_____ si and sc

Hrh PRO.1.. SO-CALL
lh WAIT-A-MINUTE-hs-5-body to lf
Hrh M-I-R-A-C-L-E-S. PRO.1.. YES.
lh WAIT-A-MINUTE-hs-5-body to lf.

_____ q

Vo YES. PRAY++............................
H *My mother thought I would become hearing at a later time*
H *as she believed such a miracle would occur.*
H *I...*
H *I then said to her, "Hey, wait a*
Vo *Yes, I understand. Yes, did [your mother]*
H *I cont...........................*
H *minute!........................" Yes.*
Vo *pray [for this miracle]?*

In previous references to her mother, Holly used a right spatial locus to locate her mother as the referent. She continued to use the same location during the first utterance in H4. Holly later replaced the right spatial locus with a left spatial locus when locating her mother as the referent. This replacement probably occurred due to Holly's preference for the dominant (right) hand for utterances consisting of right-handed signs, while she used her nondominant (left) hand for producing utterances that consisted of left-handed signs. The latter utterances, consisting of left-handed signs, were Holly's response to her mother's desire to heal her deafness. The replaced location functioned as three different types of repairs occurring at the same time: self-initiated, self-completed, and replacement repair. These occurred without a trouble source having occurred.

Word-Search Repairs in English

SJS3 contains an example of word-search repair in English.

SJS3

Clacia: B't, a—another one theh wentuh school with me wa:s a girl na:med uh, (0.7 second) W't th' hell wz er name. Karen. Right. Karen.

In SJS3, the speaker used "uh," a pause (0.7 seconds), and the utterance "W't th' hell wz er name" to signal that she was trying to recall some information (the girl's name). This signal functioned both as a self-initiated and a word-search repair. The speaker completed the self-initiated repair by producing utterances with the girl's first name (self-completed repair) that followed the utterance "W't th' hell wz er name." These repairs occurred without a trouble source having occurred.

SJS4 contains another example of word-search repair in English.

SJS4

Olive: Yihknow Mary uh::::: (0.3 second) oh:: what was it. Uh:: Tho:mpson.

In SJS4, the prolonged use of "uh," "oh," a pause (0.3 seconds), and the utterance "what was it" were used by the speaker to signal that she was trying to recall some information (Mary's last name). Like SJS3, this signal functioned both as a self-initiated and a word-search repair. The speaker completed the self-initiated repair by uttering Mary's last name, "Thompson." These repairs took place without a trouble source having occurred.

Word-Search Repairs in ASL

A4 contains an example of word-search repair in ASL.

A4

$$\overline{\hspace{5cm}\text{si}}$$

$$\overline{\text{head and gaze down and then to rt}}$$

A   OH-I-SEE. PRO.1 BORN IN TRY-TO-REMEMBER-fingers wg

$$\overline{\hspace{7cm}\text{sc}}$$

A   {full fingerspelled name of his hometown on the Gila River

$$\overline{\text{sc cont}}$$

reservation}.

V   YES.

A   ARIZONA.

A   *I understand. I was born in, hmmm, {the name of his home town on the Gila River reservation}.*

V   *Yes.*

A   *[This town is in] Arizona.*

Art used the manual sign TRY-TO-REMEMBER and two nonmanual features—head movement and eye-gazing—to signal that he was recalling
some information (the spelling of his hometown's Native name). This set
of the manual sign and the nonmanual features functioned both as a self-
initiated and a word-search repair. The utterance following the manual
sign TRY-TO-REMEMBER along with the nonmanual features contained the
needed information (fingerspelled name of the town). This utterance thus
functions as a self-completed repair. These three repairs occurred without
a trouble source having occurred.

H5 contains other examples of word-search repairs in ASL.

H5

			si
	neg	gaze to lf^down~	
Hrh	ONLY-ONE.....................N-A-V-A-J-O-lf~fingerspelled		
lh	PRO.3-pl; lf to rt.........................PRO.3-lf^		
Vo		**YES.**	

		si cont.	si and sc
		head and gaze to rt	head and gaze to rh
Hrh	sign O is prolonged and then a pause	P-I-M-A-rt,	
lh	PRO-3-rt..		
H	AREA++-in several spatial loci; rt to lf-[other deaf students		
H	of different Native heritages].		
Vo	**YES++............**		
H	*They...*		
H	*I'm only one [Hopi Deaf student at my school]. There are*		
H	*They cont...*		
H	*Navajo [deaf students].......... (pause) Pima [deaf students],*		
Vo	*Yes.*		
H	*and other [deaf students of different Native heritages].*		
Vo	*Yes, yes............*		

H5 contained two self-initiated, one self-completed, and two word-
search repairs. These occurred without a trouble source. The first self-
initiated repair occurred when Holly used the two nonmanual features,
head movement and eye-gazing. She began by turning her head and gaze
toward a left spatial locus; next she turned her head and gazed downward
and ended with both head movement and eye-gazing toward a right spatial
locus. These were accompanied by a prolonged use of the last handshape
(O) of the fingerspelled sign N-A-V-A-J-O and the manual sign PRO.3-rt to

signal that she was recalling some information (names of Native deaf students' tribes and/or nations). This set of nonlexical items functioned as two repairs occurring at the same time: a self-initiated repair (the first of two) and a word-search repair (the first of two).

It may appear that the fingerspelled sign N-A-V-A-J-O functioned as a self-completed repair, but this was not the case. An analysis of H5 indicated that Holly was not thinking of Navajo people as she signed the full fingerspelled sign N-A-V-A-J-O in a quick and confident manner. Holly here appeared to think of other Native deaf students' Native tribes and/or nations' names other than Navajo (also called Dine') nation while she produced this fingerspelled sign. The fingerspelled sign, N-A-V-A-J-O, therefore appears not to function as a self-completed repair.

Like the first self-initiated repair described above, the second one occurred when Holly used the other nonmanual features, head movement and eye-gazing toward her right-handed fingerspelled sign P-I-M-A to signal that she was recalling some information (names of other Native deaf students' tribes and/or nations). An analysis of these nonmanual features and the utterance following them, AREA++, indicated Holly indeed was recalling this information during her production of the fingerspelled sign P-I-M-A. This analysis also indicated that Holly completed the first self-initiated repair, not the second one, by producing the fingerspelled sign P-I-M-A (self-completed repair). The second self-initiated repair was not completely repaired by either Holly or me in the following utterances; hence there was no repair to complete this (second) self-initiated repair. For example, following these nonmanual features and the fingerspelled sign, P-I-M-A, Holly used the manual AREA++ to indicate there were other deaf students of Native heritages. At this point Holly ceased to recall the names of other deaf students' Native heritages. The second self-initiated repair also functioned as a word-search repair (the second of two in H5) as Holly was searching for names of other deaf students' Native heritages while producing the second fingerspelled sign (P-I-M-A).

Mixture of Replacement Repairs and Word-Search Repairs in English and ASL

Often a mixture of a replacement repair and a word-search repair occurs within an utterance. The following is an example of such phenomena found in U.S. English conversations.

SJS5

C: C'n you tell me (one second pause) D'you have any records...of whether you—whether you—who you sent—Oh(hh) shit.

G: What'd you say?

C: I'm having the worst trouble talking.

SJS5 contained one unrepaired trouble source, one self-initiated repair, one other-initiated repair, one word-search repair, and two replacement repairs. The trouble source in SJS5 was the speaker's (C) inability to produce a complete and clear question. The speaker used a word-search repair, a self-initiated repair, and two replacement repairs in utterances prior to the addressee's attempt to repair the trouble source. The lengthy repair consisted of a one-second pause, a brief pause following the word *records,* the repetition of an incomplete phrase, "whether you," and the prolonged use of the last phonological item, "Oh." In addition, there were also incomplete utterances and the use of a swearword.

The first of the two replacement repairs occurred when the speaker replaced the first question in SJS5 with another (incomplete) question, "D'you have any records . . . of whether you—." The second replacement repair occurred when the speaker continued to repair the trouble source and replaced the phrase "whether you—" with another (incomplete) question: "who you sent—." The set of two replacement repairs and the word-search repair functioned as a self-initiated repair, inasmuch as the speaker continued to attempt to repair the trouble source in the utterances beginning with the one-second pause and ending with the swearword in the utterances.

The addressee's (G) response indicated he or she did not understand what the speaker (C) was trying to say. This response functioned as an other-initiated repair. Since there was no indication of the speaker's or the addressee's completion of the two initiated repairs in SJS5 (the self-initiated and the other-initiated repair), there was no completed repair. Neither was there a self- or an other-completed repair. The speaker's utterance "I'm having the worst trouble talking," which occurred after the addressee's response, confirmed this observation as the speaker was unable to complete or had not yet completed the initiated repairs. Hence, the trouble source, the speaker's inability to produce a complete and clear question, was not repaired.

A5 contains an example of a mixture of a replacement repair and a word-search repair in ASL conversations.

		si
	cond	gaze to lf

A MANY #IF GET-TOGETHER DO-EVENTS FRIEND-not fully

Vo   YES   NO YES++.

si cont.		sc

A produced FRIEND CL:5wg-2h "people coming to".

Vo   YES.   YES.

                          neg DISAPPOINTED

A BUT NOTHING. WELL.

Vo   YES++.

A *If many [Native deaf people] show up at an event, [my]*

Vo   *Yes, no,*

A *fri- friends [Native Deaf] would come. But we do not have*

Vo *Yes, yes.*   *Yes.*   *Yes.*

A   *I'm disappointed.*

A *[any such events like that here]. Oh well.*

Vo   *Yes, yes.*

Art's first production of the manual sign FRIEND was incomplete. At the same time, Art used the nonmanual feature, eye-gazing, to look toward a left spatial locus. This indicated the presence of a word-search repair, as Art was either trying to figure out how to express his thoughts in ASL utterances or attempting to recall information. This set of nonlexical items also functioned as a self-initiated repair. He then replaced the incomplete production of the sign FRIEND with the completed production of that sign, which functioned as a replacement repair. The word-search and replacement repairs just described occurred within the same utterance, the conditional sentence in A5. The utterance with the replaced sign, FRIEND, functions as a self-completed repair as Art completed the self-initiated repair. There was no indication of any further repairs being made on the self-initiated repair. All the repairs in A5 occurred without a trouble source having occurred.

H6 contains another example of a mixture of a replacement and a word-search repair in ASL.

H6

		si
	neg	gaze up

H NO #NO++. AT-FIRST not completely produced with a pause;

	si cont.
	gaze up cont.

H   then completely produced with pause afterward

	sc

H   PRO.1 BORN HEARING LATER UNTIL AGE^3

si	sc

H   I-WRONG 2^½ BECOME DEAF.

H   *No, I, at f – irst, (pause) was born hearing until the age of*

H   *three, no, [when I was] two and a half years old, I became*

H   *deaf.*

H6 contained one repaired trouble source, two self-initiated repairs, two self-completed repairs, one word-search repair, and one replacement repair. The word-search repair occurred when Holly used the nonmanual feature, eye-gazing upward, along with the prolonged use of the incomplete manual sign AT-FIRST to signal that she was trying to recall some information (her onset of deafness). This word-search repair also functioned as a self-initiated repair (the first of two in H6). She then completed this self-initiated repair by following up with manual signs, beginning with the completion of the sign AT-FIRST and ending with the compound manual sign AGE^3. This set of following manual signs functioned as a self-completed repair (the first of two in H6). These occurred without a trouble source having occurred.

Holly instantly acknowledged her production of an incorrect age, the sign AGE^3. By using the nonhanded sign I-WRONG as a self-initiated repair (the second one in H6), she signaled a trouble source or a need for repair. Holly then repaired the trouble source, the incorrect age, by replacing the sign AGE^3 with the compound manual sign 2^½. This replacement functioned both as a replacement repair and a self-completed repair (the second of two self-completed repairs in H6). Both the word-search repair and the replacement repair just described occurred in one utterance.

UNREPAIRED TROUBLE SOURCES IN ENGLISH AND ASL

This section presents examples of utterances adopted from S, J, and S's study and this paper's research for a discussion of various kinds of repairs in U.S. English and ASL conversations. SJS6 contains an unrepaired trouble source in English.

SJS6

> Avon Lady: And for ninety-nine cents uh especially in, Rapture, and the Au Coeur, which is the newest fragrances, uh that is a very good value.
> Customer: Uh huh.

The trouble source above is the ungrammatical addition of the suffix -*s*, a bound morpheme that indicates plurality in nouns, to the singular noun *fragrance*. The speaker, the "Avon Lady," was referring to a new fragrance, not to two or more new fragrances. This trouble source was not repaired by either the speaker or the addressee (the customer).

A6 contains an unrepaired trouble source in ASL.

A6

<pre>
                        t
Arh A-P-A-C-H-E DIFFERENT   SO-CALL CRUEL
lh   POSS.3-lf++.

                                                nod-q
Vo   YES.   YES.   YES.   DIFFERENT.
A   POSS.3-lf. SO-CALL #APACHE POSS.3-rt.
Vo   OH-I-SEE YES.   YES.
A   #NAVAJO-body to lf FRIENDLY YES.
V   YES.

          t
     head and gaze down   head and gaze to rh
A   POSS.1++   P-I-M-A   YES FRIENDLY.
Vo   YES.
A   si
A   gaze up   sc   DIFFERENT
A   H-O-P-I YES FRIENDLY. PRO.3-pl; rt to lf ONE-lf
Vo   YES.   OH-I-SEE
Arh A-P-A-C-H-E DIFFERENT
lh   POSS.3-lf.
Vo   OH-I-SEE cont..............
</pre>

A   *Apache people are different [from other Native peoples*
Vo   *Yes*   *Yes, yes.*
A   *regarding their physical features, not personalities].*
A   *They [appear to be] so called mean people.*
Vo   *I understand.*   *They are different [from*
Vo   *other Native peoples]? Yes, I understand.*

A	*That's what Apaches [appear different from other Native*
Vo	*Yes.*
A	*peoples]. Navajo people (also called as Dine') [appear to*
A	*be] friendly people.*
V	*Yes.*
A	*My [people,] Pima people (also called as Akimel O'*
A	*odham), [also appear to be] friendly people. Hmmm.*
A	*Hopi people [also appear to be] friendly people.*
Vo	*Yes.*
A	*[They are] different.*
A	*Apache people [appear to] have the most distinct*
Vo	*I see..*
A	*[physical features of Native peoples in Arizona].*

Art used a left spatial locus twice, a left-handed sign POSS.3-lf signed twice, in his signing space for a location fixing for Apache people. He then used a right spatial locus for these people with the right-handed sign POSS.3-rt and used the left spatial locus for Dine' people with the right-handed lexicalized fingerspelled sign NAVAJO-body to lf. He later used the left spatial locus for Apache people with a right-handed sign ONE-lf and a left-handed POSS.3-lf in the last ASL utterance in A6. These utterances indicate that Art intended to use a left spatial locus as a location for Apache people and a right spatial locus as a location for Dine' people. He thus used incorrect location fixings for Apache people and Dine' people by placing the former group in a right spatial locus and the latter in a left spatial locus. This trouble source was not repaired by either the speaker (Art) or the addressee (me). This trouble source probably occurred due to Art's use of a right-handed sign, POSS.3-rt, for referring to Apache people. In addition, the problem may have occurred because ASL signers tend to use a right spatial locus when they sign right-handed pronouns such as PRO.3 and POSS.3 for establishing a location (unless they have established a position in a nonright spatial locus in previous utterances). Furthermore, the difficulty may be due in part to an inclination to establish a location in a nonright spatial locus where the referent is. Because of this tendency, it may be that Art did not realize he used the wrong spatial loci to refer to Apache people and Dine' people.

Art used the nonmanual features—head turning and gazing—as repairs for recalling information. These repairs occurred without a trouble source having occurred. This phenomenon occurred frequently in the study's ethnographic interviews.

CONCLUSIONS AND IMPLICATIONS OF DATA

This study's findings on ASL conversational repairs indicate a consistency with the English and Thai studies regarding self-repairs, other-repairs, replacement repairs, and word-search repairs. Like English and Thai speakers, signers in this study's ASL ethnographic interviews are more likely to participate in their own repairs, either by initiating or completing it. Following is the summary of findings from the ASL ethnographic interviews:

Self-initiated repairs occur more frequently than other-initiated repairs.
Repairs take place with a trouble source having occurred. [H1, H2, H3, H6]
Repairs take place without a trouble source having occurred. [A2, A3, A4, A5, A6, H4, H5, H6]
Unrepaired trouble sources occur. [A6, H1]

Several observations may be unique to the ASL repair system and possibly to other natural signed language repair systems. Nonhanded signs are frequently used by ASL signers for producing a two-layered staff of utterances with or without a repair (see A1 and H1). To the best of my knowledge, there is no literature that indicates that English and other spoken languages have the capacity to produce a two-layered staff of utterances containing a repair in their repair systems. However, one could argue that some English gestures function as lexical items or manual signs, for example, THUMB-UP, THUMB-DOWN, FINE (index finger touching thumb with other fingers up), and SO-SO (Dively 1996). If this is the case, it is then possible that there can exist a two-layered staff of utterances in a spoken English interaction. Further research on nonmanual and manual linguistic features and two-layered staffs of utterances in spoken languages and signed languages is needed.

As a visual-spatial language, ASL contains mechanisms for repairing or monitoring utterances with the use of space (see H4). The structure of space in ASL is significantly different from that of English, which, as an aural-vocal language, contains no multidimensional structure such as the space found in ASL and other natural signed languages. Hence, English does not have reason to use mechanisms for repairing or monitoring utterances regarding the use of space.

ASL appears to have some lexical items such as I-WRONG and TRY-TO-REMEMBER (see A2 and A5) that function solely as repair signs. These two signs appear not to function as nonrepair signs. Lexical items functioning solely as repair words appear to be nonexistent in English discourse; however, more research is needed here. Like English lexical items such as *no* and *well*, ASL has signs that can function either as nonrepair or repair signs, for example, UNSURE and WELL (see A1, A3, A5, and H1).

Nonmanual features such as eye-gazing and head turns are frequently used by signers for repairing or monitoring utterances in ASL discourse (see A3 and H5). However, these features have more than one function in ASL discourse. Baker's study (1977) on ASL conversations and Mather's studies (1987, 1996) on interactions between Deaf teachers and Deaf students indicate that eye-gazing frequently is used by signers as an initiation regulator to elicit the addressee's attention in ASL discourse. A slight simultaneous forward movement of both the head and torso function as part of syntactic markers such as yes-no questions and Wh-questions in ASL (Baker 1976a, 1976b; Baker and Cokely 1980; Bellugi and Fischer 1972; Liddell 1980). Head tilt and eye gaze function as nonmanual expressions of syntactic agreement, marking agreement within determiner and inflectional projections in ASL (Bahan 1996). Again, to the best of my knowledge, there is no literature to indicate that English has such features in its repair system. Based on my personal observations, I would surmise that English speakers do use eye-gazing and head turns for repairing or monitoring utterances in a spoken English interaction; however, further investigation is needed.

As with English speakers, prolonged use of one phonological aspect of a lexical item, repetition of a lexical item, pausing, and incomplete productions of a lexical item are frequently used by ASL signers for repairing or monitoring (see A5, H3, H5, and H6). ASL signers also often correct or repair one another's signing to help each other produce more proper or acceptable ASL utterances. ASL signers also ask for clarification regarding a particular sign, as there are several signed systems and regional signs across Deaf communities in the United States. Such behaviors appear in this paper's ethnographic interviews. In fact, nearly all of these behaviors are related to the use of regional signs, as I had never been in Arizona before.

The repair of one another's ungrammatical ASL utterances does not appear in the ASL ethnographic interviews. That is to be expected as the informants and I had never met prior to the interviews. These behaviors tend to occur more frequently among friends, relatives, and ASL instructors or interpreter educators regarding their students' signed interactions. An investigation into signers' repairs for one another in the production of acceptable ASL utterances and/or single signs is among the priorities in forthcoming studies on the ASL repair system. It is likely that such studies contribute further insights into ASL as a language.

Studies on conversational repairs also contribute to an understanding of what the norm is for production of utterances during an interaction. Findings from these studies can, for instance, apply to language proficiency evaluations and interpretation performance evaluations. Evaluators can review these studies in order to provide a better evaluation of one's language proficiency or interpretation performance by taking into account the use of repairs as part of an acceptable norm for the production of utterances. These evaluators will need to determine which repairs are part of an acceptable norm and which are not, as a person with limited language skills or interpretation skills may overuse pauses and repetition/correction of a lexical item.

REFERENCES

Bahan, B. 1996. Nonmanual realization of agreement in American Sign Language. Ph.D. diss., Boston University.

Baker, C. 1976a. Eye-openers in ASL. In *California Linguistics Association Conference Proceedings*, 1–3. San Diego: San Diego State University.

———. 1976b. What's not on the other hand in American Sign Language. In *Papers from the twelfth regional meeting of the Chicago Linguistic Society*, ed. S. Mufwene and S. Steever, 24–32. Chicago: Chicago Linguistic Society.

———. 1977. Regulators and turn-taking in American Sign Language discourse. In *On the other hand: New perspectives on American Sign Language*, ed. L. Friedman, 215–41. New York: Academic Press.

Baker, C., and D. Cokely. 1980. *American Sign Language: A teacher's resource text on grammar and culture*. Silver Spring, Md.: T. J. Publishers.

Bellugi, U., and S. D. Fischer. 1972. A comparison of sign language and spoken language: Rate and grammatical mechanisms. *Cognition* 1 (3):173–200.

Biesele, M. 1993. The Bushmen of today. In *Talking about people: Readings in contemporary cultural anthropology,* ed. W. A. Haviland and R. J. Gordon, 289–95. Mountain View, Calif.: Mayfield Publishing Company.

Dively, V. 1996. Native Deaf peoples in the U.S. and American Sign Language nonhand signs. Ph.D. diss., Union Institute, Cincinnati, Ohio.

Frishberg, N. 1987. Home signs. In *Gallaudet encyclopedia of Deaf people and deafness,* ed. J. V. Van Cleve, 3:128–31. New York: McGraw-Hill.

Klima, E., and U. Bellugi. 1979. *The signs of language.* Cambridge, Mass.: Harvard University Press.

Liddell, S. K. 1980. *American Sign Language syntax.* The Hague: Mouton.

Liddell, S. K., and R. E. Johnson. 1989. American Sign Language: The phonological base. *Sign Language Studies* 64:195–278.

Lucas, C., and C. Valli. 1989. Language contact in the American Deaf community. In *The sociolinguistics of the Deaf community,* ed. C. Lucas, 11–40. San Diego: Academic Press.

———. 1992. *Language contact in the American Deaf community.* San Diego: Academic Press.

Mather, S. M. 1987. Eye gaze and communication in a deaf classroom. *Sign Language Studies* 54:11–30.

———. 1996. Initiation in visually constructed dialogue: Reading books with three- to eight-year-old students who are deaf and hard of hearing. In *Multicultural aspects of sociolinguistics in Deaf communities,* ed. C. Lucas, 109–31. Washington, D.C.: Gallaudet University Press.

Moerman, M. 1977. The preference for self-correction in a Thai conversational corpus. *Language* 53:872–82.

Schegloff, E. A., G. Jefferson, and H. Sacks. 1977. The preference for self-correction in the organization of repair in conversation. *Language* 53:361–82.

Schiffrin. D. 1987. *Discourse markers.* Cambridge: Cambridge University Press.

Spradley, J. 1979. *The ethnographic interview.* Orlando, Fla.: Holt, Rinehart and Winston.

Eye Gaze and Pronominal Reference in

American Sign Language

Melanie Metzger

For many years linguists have focused on the role of the hands in the phonology and syntax of signed languages. More recently, researchers have focused on other aspects of signed languages, including meaningful forms conveyed by body movements, head tilts, and eyebrow, cheek, and mouth movements. These aspects of signed languages, appropriately labeled nonmanual signals, appear to function at times as grammatical markers such as negatives (Baker 1976a; Baker and Cokely 1980; Bellugi and Fischer 1972; Dively 1996; Liddell 1980; Stokoe 1960); topicalizers (Baker and Cokely 1980; Fischer 1975; Friedman 1976; Liddell 1978, 1980); and adverbs (Bahan 1996; Baker 1976a, 1976b; Coulter 1978; Liddell 1980). They even carry a variety of discourse functions both intralingually (Engberg-Pedersen 1995; Metzger 1995; Pizzuto, Giuranna, and Gambino 1990; Roy 1989; Wallin 1987; Winston 1993) and as a result of contact between a signed and a spoken language (Boyes Braem 1984; Davis 1989; Lucas and Valli 1989, 1992; Schermer 1990; Vogt-Svendson 1984; Winston 1989).

Because signed languages have numerous potential articulators serving a variety of functions, perhaps simultaneously, many areas are ripe for investigation. For example, some researchers have concentrated on pronominal reference in signed languages such as American Sign Language (ASL), while others have examined nonmanual signals, such as eye gaze. One area still open to research is the study of pronouns as they coincide with or are replaceable by eye gaze. The quantitative analysis of eye-gaze direction and its relationship to pronominal reference in ASL narrative discourse is the focus of this paper.

Previous research has established that eye gaze functions in a variety of ways in ASL. Overall, there is some basic agreement in the literature regarding functions of eye gaze, which has been found to regulate turn taking, mark constituent boundaries in conversational ASL discourse (Baker 1976a, 1976b, 1977; Baker and Padden 1978), and indicate constituent boundaries in ASL narrative discourse (Bahan and Supalla 1995). In addition, Bellugi and Fischer (1972), Friedman (1975), Baker (1976a), Bendixen (1976), Lillo-Martin and Klima (1990), and Meier (1990) all discuss the role of eye gaze in role playing and direct quotation in ASL. Bellugi and Fischer (1972) and Bendixen (1976) distinguish between the noncontact eye gaze of a nonnarrator "character" and the eye contact maintained during the narration of a story. In addition, Meier (1990) suggests that a narrator may sustain eye gaze at a location associated with a character in the narrative without gazing at the addressee, even though no direct quotation occurs.

Fischer (1975) discusses the gaze used by nonnarrator characters within a narrative or quoted conversation. Baker (1976a) points out that, although eye gaze in direct quotes is *from* the referent (the person making the quote), in pronominal reference eye gaze is *toward* the referent. Further, Lillo-Martin and Klima (1990) support this notion by suggesting that eye gaze is one signifier of changes in frame-of-reference. In another discussion of eye gaze shifting in its reference, Bahan (1996) proposes that eye gaze marks object agreement syntactically, except when articulatory obstacles occur. An articulatory obstacle might be first-person reference, since the eyes cannot gaze inward toward the signer.

Baker (1976a, 1976b), Baker and Cokely (1980), Bellugi and Fischer (1972), Bendixen (1976), Liddell (1980), Lillo-Martin and Klima (1990), Meier (1990), and Padden (1990) also discuss the role of eye gaze in pronominal reference. Baker (1976a, 1976b), Bendixen (1976), and Baker and Cokely (1980) examine the occurrence of eye gaze as pronominal reference with or without the manual sign. Bendixen (1976) suggests that a combination of eye gaze and lexical reference is used only for emphasis. In contrast, Baker (1976a) and Baker and Cokely (1980) discuss the secretive or discreet quality of pronominal reference without a manual component. Bahan refers to the use of eye gaze without a manual index as a "whisper" register (1996, 270). Although the interpretations of gaze-only reference differ somewhat, researchers seem to agree that eye gaze alone can serve a referential function.

Some researchers discuss the manual index and eye gaze as providing complementary information. For example, Bellugi and Fischer (1972) and Baker and Cokely (1980) indicate that eye gaze serves to distinguish person reference in ASL. Lillo-Martin and Klima (1990), Meier (1990), and Padden (1990) appear not to support that notion, at least not grammatically, since Padden refers to eye gaze as a pragmatic feature of pronominal reference (1990, 120). Meier maintains that eye gaze is not a crucial part of deictic pronominal reference by indicating that first-person reference can co-occur with a gaze to the addressee, "[t]hus, gaze at the addressee not only is a property of signs that refer to the addressee but is also a frequent property of first-person pointing signs that refer to the signer. . . . [G]aze does not appear to be a necessary accompaniment of deictic reference to one's addressee" (1990, 186).

Some studies disagree with regard to whether eye gaze functions deictically with pronominal reference in ASL. For example, while Meier suggests that gaze is not a necessary part of deictic pronominal reference, Baker (1976a), Baker and Cokely (1980), and Bahan (1996) contend that eye gaze alone can function referentially. As Meier (1990) points out, manual pronouns can be both deictic (they identify people spatially and temporally [Lyons 1977]) and anaphoric (they can refer to entities previously established in the discourse [see also Levinson 1983]). Therefore, the question remains whether eye gaze, with or without manual pronouns, conveys deictic pronominal reference in ASL. The current study is an empirical examination of the relationship between eye gaze and pronominal reference in five ASL narratives.

METHODOLOGY

In order to conduct an empirical analysis of eye gaze and deictic reference in ASL, the data include five videotaped sociolinguistic interviews ranging in length from 30 seconds to 4 minutes and yielding a total of 8 minutes and 27 seconds of data for the analysis. These narratives were signed by four different informants, all white college students (both graduate and undergraduate; three males, one female) and native ASL signers. The interviews include a variety of narrative genres, ranging from personal experience narratives to the description of a Garfield comic strip.

All interviews included two informants, both native signers. An outside consultant (a native Deaf signer and a trained linguist) judged that all samples represented ASL and assisted in transcribing and coding the data. This study conforms to the conventions for transcribing ASL manual signs via English glosses and, where applicable, includes additional articulations such as body position, head placement, mouth, cheek, and eyebrow movements, and eye gaze. A description of the transcription conventions appears in Appendix A.

All occurrences of manual pronominal deictic reference, including both the G handshape and its variations, were compared and analyzed with respect to eye gaze. Each occurrence was tabulated with regard for direction of eye gaze as it co-occurred with manual reference. This information was then analyzed in terms of specific person reference. For example, the total number of first-person-singular references was tabulated and divided into categories based on direction of gaze. The analysis of these data yields an interesting finding regarding the direction of eye gaze co-occurring with first-person pronouns.

DATA ANALYSIS

The total number of occurrences of manual pronominal reference is seventy-six (see Table 1). Of these, forty-four are first-person singular, two are first-person singular possessive, and one is first-person plural. There are nine occurrences of second-person singular, and no occurrences of second-person possessive or plural pronouns. The data contain sixteen occurrences of third-person singular, four occurrences of third-person plural, and no occurrences of third-person possessive.

Of the forty-four first-person-singular pronouns, four tokens co-occur with eye gaze to the addressee, three co-occur with eye gaze directed at an imagined addressee within a role-playing sequence, and twenty-three co-

TABLE 1. *Number of Pronominal Occurrences*

Reference	To Signer	To Addressee	To Other	Total
Singular	44	9	16	69
Plural	1	0	4	5
Possessive	2	0	0	2
Total	47	9	20	76

TABLE 2. *Distribution of Eye Gaze in Singular Pronominal Reference*

Gaze Direction	To Present Addressee		To Imagined Addressee		To Non-addressee Referent		Non-directed Gaze		Eyes Closed		Gaze Not Visible	
(N)	n	%	n	%	n	%	n	%	n	%	n	%
Reference to signer (44)	4	9	3	7	0	—	23	52	0	—	14	3.
Reference to addressee (9)	6	67	1	11	0	—	0	—	0	—	2	2.
Reference to other (16)	11	69	0	—	1	6	0	—	1	6	3	1

occur with eye gaze apparently not directed at any referent. These gazes range from left or right of the addressee to up- or downward gazes and thus will be labeled as nonspecific gazes. There are fourteen tokens that involve eye gaze that is not clearly visible on the videotape.

Only two tokens of second-person-singular reference involve eye gaze that is not clearly visible. In one token, eye gaze is directed toward an imagined addressee within a role-playing sequence, and six of the nine tokens co-occur with eye gaze directed at the addressee.

Eye gaze toward the addressee also co-occurs with eleven of the sixteen tokens of third-person-singular manual pronominal reference. For one token, eye gaze is directed toward the referent; for another token, eyes are closed for emphasis; and eye gaze is not distinguishable for three tokens. Of the third-person-plural tokens, three are not clearly distinguishable, and one is directed at the imaginary addressee within a role-playing sequence. For an analysis of first, second, and third-person-singular pronouns on the basis of gaze direction, see Table 2.

First-person singular occurs most frequently—in just over half the tokens—with nonspecific gaze. In example 1, the signer is relating a personal experience about two friends who had regularly threatened to fight each other for almost ten years. The signer is describing the fact that these friends have carried a grudge against one another since their days as classmates at a school for deaf children.

EXAMPLE 1

to side of A	gaze left	gaze to addressee

PRO.1   LOOK-AT-THEM TALK NO A-C-T HIT NOTHING TALK

And I looked at my two friends, but they were all talk and no action.

In this example, the signer clearly gazes in the direction of the referents during the verb LOOK-AT but gazes toward neither the referents nor the addressee during the production of the first-person pronoun. As a single example, one could argue that any number of factors contribute to the nonspecific gaze that co-occurs with the first-person pronoun. What is striking, however, is that 52 percent of the first-person pronouns in the data occurred with a nonspecific gaze, including gazes that are off-center, downward, and to the right or left when no referent has been established in that direction.

Of the forty-four gazes that co-occur with first-person singular, three are actually the result of role-playing sequences and are directed toward the imagined addressee. In the following example, the signer is recounting a personal experience about a card game. In the narrative, an unknown card player has just come up to the players and asked if they know someone named Baker. The signer is constructing the actions of the card-player named Baker. Notice that the signer maintains his gaze toward the imagined addressee during the first-person singular:

EXAMPLE 2

to A gaze forward to up left	lower lip extended, gaze up left

MAN CL:4 (cards in hand) LOOK-UP THAT (raise hand) THAT PRO.1
So one of the guys at the table says, "Yeah, I'm Baker, that's me."

In Example 2, the signer has maintained the eye gaze attributed to the character in the story, Baker. The fact that eye gaze and pronominal reference seem to function differently within role-playing sequences may be due to other pragmatic functions of eye gaze in such circumstances. For instance, eye gaze may be functioning deictically to indicate the relationships between imagined interlocutors (Leow 1984; see also Roy 1989; Liddell 1990, 1995; Winston 1991, 1992; Lillo-Martin 1995; Metzger 1995; van Hoek 1996 for recent discussion of the role-playing feature of ASL discourse). Research regarding the use of eye gaze in ASL role-playing sequences is a rich area for further study.

Only four of the forty-four gazes that co-occur with first-person singular are directed at the addressee, and this may represent an overlap with other eye-gaze functions, such as constituent boundaries. Nevertheless, it is worth noting that first-person reference can co-occur with the addressee gaze, since Meier (1990) suggests that this is evidence against the deictic nature of eye gaze. Also remarkable is how infrequently this occurred, perhaps indicating that gaze to an addressee with first-person reference is not necessarily preferred but, as Bahan (1996) suggests, can be affected by "articulatory obstacles." An intriguing area for further examination would be the identification of eye-gaze functions that take precedence and the circumstances in which they occur. The data here also support the notion that eye gaze co-occurring with first-person reference carries a deictic function. This is because nonspecific gazes that are not directed deictically toward other referents occur more frequently with the first-person reference (and because it is not possible to actually gaze inward at oneself). This is an additional area that warrants further research with a larger corpus of data.

The data also seem to provide very strong evidence of the importance of gaze direction in reference to addressees. For second-person reference, the only gaze not directed at the present addressee occurs within role-playing sequences and is directed at the imagined addressee. The relatively low occurrence of second-person pronouns in the data is significant. Nevertheless, eye gaze toward the addressee co-occurs with second-person reference consistently. Interestingly, the majority of eye gazes co-occurring with third-person-singular pronouns are also directed toward the addressee. In addition, although first-person-singular possessive pronouns are rare in the data, co-occurring gaze appears to be directed at the addressee.

In the data examined here, use of eye gaze is evidently nonspecific with first-person singular but directed toward the addressee for non-first-person pronouns. This, too, is an area that deserves further investigation, since it has been proposed that ASL pronouns do not have a person distinction (Lillo-Martin and Klima 1990), based on the analysis of the manual pronoun. Lillo-Martin and Klima argue that manual pronouns can point in a potentially infinite number of directions and that there is only one pronoun in ASL whose direction is determined by pairing the sign with a discourse referent. Conversely, Meier (1990) cites the lexicalized ASL sign OUR, which, unlike the plural first-person sign glossed as WE, does not change form based on the presence or absence of referents. Meier also points out that the pronoun referring to first person in ASL can be used to refer to someone other than the signer when the signer is taking the role of another character, for example. Because there are differing proposals regarding the status of person distinction in ASL, it is interesting to note the presence of eye-gaze distinctions between first and non-first-person pronominal reference in these data. This could support Meier's (1990) claim that ASL has first and non-first-person categories.

Although the use of eye gaze alone for pronominal reference is beyond the scope of this paper, one should note that these findings indicate the potential existence of a pronominal form not yet discussed. The existence of nonspecific eye gaze with first-person pronominal reference suggests the possibility that nonspecific eye gaze alone could carry the first-person reference. Evidence of this exists in the following example, a narrative in which the signer talks about the growth of her personal identity over time:

EXAMPLE 3

to A down	to addressee	right

NOW KNOW ABOUT LESBIAN PRO.1

Now that I'm aware of the existence of a Lesbian lifestyle . . .

In this utterance the signer does not sign a first-person pronominal subject. In ASL this is not uncommon, and evidence of the dropped subject is the subject pronoun copy at the end of this utterance. However, during the execution of the verb *know,* the signer's gaze shifts downward in the same manner as nonspecific eye gaze that co-occurs with the first-person pronouns in the data. This suggests that nonspecific eye gaze co-occurs with verb forms in utterance-initial positions as an indicator of first-person-singular pronominal reference in ASL. Future research in this area could have a significant impact on the understanding of the dropped pronoun in ASL.

CONCLUSION

Eye gaze plays a meaningful role in pronominal reference in the ASL narratives analyzed in this study. Eye gaze that co-occurs with pronominal reference differs for first person and non-first person. That is, the gaze that co-occurs with non-first-person reference is most often directed toward the addressee and is, therefore, not particularly deictic in nature. However, a large percentage of the gazes that co-occur with first-person reference are not directed at the addressee. Although eye gaze cannot easily be deictically directed at oneself, the nonspecific gazes seen in these data are clearly not pointing at other referents. This may be interpreted as a deictic quality of the eye gaze associated with first-person reference.

The fact that nonspecific eye gaze also occurred without the manual first-person pronoun raises some interesting questions. First, gaze alone for deictic reference has been described in the literature as a form of register variation in ASL. For non-first-person reference, gaze alone has been described as conveying a secretive or whispering quality (Baker 1976a; Baker and Cokely 1980; Bahan 1996). Because signers have the option of using the manual sign only, the manual sign with eye gaze, or eye gaze alone, further examination of the significance of such choices is warranted. Specifically, it would be useful to determine the nature of the variation when the signer refers to self, the addressee, or others.

In addition to the question of variation, the presence of nonspecific gaze co-occurring with the verb is an additional area for exploration. Determining how eye gaze co-occurring with specific verb types will be a difficult task, considering the many functions associated with eye gaze and the verb system in ASL (see Bahan 1996). Thus, further research regarding the multiple functions of eye gaze and their interaction within narrative discourse is warranted. For example, one could focus on how pronominal eye gaze interacts with the types of gazes that mark constituent boundaries in ASL discourse. Such a study might measure not only the direction of gaze, as addressed in this paper, but also the relative duration of eye gazes performing specific functions. A systematic analysis of eye gaze within a larger corpus of narratives would be useful and might also provide information regarding which eye gaze functions become secondary and which become the "articulatory obstacles" referred to by Bahan (1996).

REFERENCES

Bahan, B. 1996. Nonmanual realization of agreement in American Sign Language. Ph.D. diss., Boston University.

Bahan, B., and S. Supalla. 1995. Line segmentation and narrative structure: A study of eye gaze behavior in American Sign Language. In *Language, gesture, and space,* ed. K. Emmorey and J. Reilly, 171–94. Hillsdale, N.J.: Lawrence Erlbaum Associates.

Baker, C. 1976a. Eye-openers in ASL. In *California Linguistics Association Conference Proceedings,* 1–13. San Diego: San Diego State University.

———. 1976b. What's not on the other hand in American Sign Language. In *Papers from the twelfth regional meeting of the Chicago Linguistic Society,* ed. S. S. Mufwene, 24–32. Chicago: Chicago Linguistic Society.

———. 1977. Regulators and turn-taking in American Sign Language discourse. In *On the other hand: New perspectives on American Sign Language,* ed. L. Friedman, 215–36. New York: Academic Press.

Baker, C., and C. Padden. 1978. Focusing on the nonmanual components of American Sign Language. In *Understanding language through sign language research*, ed. P. Siple, 59–90. New York: Academic Press.

Baker, C., and D. Cokely. 1980. *American Sign Language: A teacher's resource text on grammar and culture.* Washington, D.C.: Gallaudet University Press.

Bellugi, U., and S. Fischer. 1972. A comparison of signed and spoken language. *Cognition* 1:173–200.

Bendixen, B. 1976. Eye behaviors functioning in American Sign Language. Manuscript, Salk Institute for Biological Studies, San Diego, Calif.

Boyes Braem, P. 1984. Studying Swiss German sign dialects. In *Recent research on European sign languages*, ed. F. Loncke, P. Boyes Braem, and Y. Lebrun, 93–103. Lisse, Netherlands: Swets and Zeitlinger B. V.

Bridges, B., and M. Metzger. 1996. *DEAF TEND YOUR: Nonmanual signals in American Sign Language.* Silver Spring, Md.: Calliope Press.

Coulter, G. 1978. Raised eyebrows and wrinkled noses: The grammatical function of facial expression in relative clauses and related constructions. In *Proceedings of the Second National Symposium on Sign Language Research and Teaching*, ed. F. Caccamise and D. Hicks, 65–74. Silver Spring, Md.: National Association of the Deaf.

Davis, J. 1989. Distinguishing language contact phenomena in ASL interpretation. In *The sociolinguistics of the Deaf community*, ed. C. Lucas, 85–102. San Diego: Academic Press.

Dively, V. 1996. Native Deaf people in the U.S. and American Sign Language: Nonhand signs. Ph.D. diss., Union Institute. Cincinnati, Ohio.

Engberg-Pedersen, E. 1995. Point of view expressed through shifters. In *Language, gesture, and space*, ed. K. Emmorey and J. Reilly, 133–54. Hillsdale, N.J.: Lawrence Erlbaum Associates.

Fischer, S. 1975. Influences on word order change in American Sign Language. In *Word order and word order change*, ed. C. Li, 1–25. Austin: University of Texas Press.

Friedman, L. 1975. On the semantics of space, time, and person reference in the American Sign Language. *Language* 51:940–61.

———. 1976. The manifestation of subject, object, and topic in American Sign Language. In *Subject and topic*, ed. C. Li, 125–48. Austin: University of Texas Press.

Leow, R. 1984. Roles and reference in American Sign Language: A developmental perspective. Ph.D. diss., University of Minnesota.

Levinson, S. 1983. *Pragmatics.* Cambridge: Cambridge University Press.

Liddell, S. 1978. Nonmanual signals and relative clauses in American Sign Language. In *Understanding language through sign language research*, ed. P. Siple, 59–90. New York: Academic Press.

———. 1980. *American Sign Language syntax.* The Hague: Mouton.

————. 1990. Four functions of a locus: Re-examining the structure of space in ASL. In *Sign language research: Theoretical issues,* ed. C. Lucas, 176–98. Washington, D.C.: Gallaudet University Press.

————. 1995. Real, surrogate, and token space: Grammatical consequences in ASL. In *Language, gesture, and space,* ed. K. Emmorey and J. Reilly, 19–41. Hillsdale, N.J.: Lawrence Erlbaum Associates.

Lillo-Martin, D. 1995. The point of view predicate in American Sign Language. In *Language, gesture, and space,* ed. K. Emmorey and J. Reilly, 155–70. Hillsdale, N.J.: Lawrence Erlbaum Associates.

Lillo-Martin, D., and E. Klima. 1990. Pointing out differences: ASL pronouns in syntactic theory. In *Theoretical issues in sign language research,* vol. 1, ed. S. Fischer and P. Siple, 191–210. Chicago: University of Chicago Press.

Lucas, C., and C. Valli. 1989. Language contact in the American Deaf community. In *The sociolinguistics of the Deaf community,* ed. C. Lucas, 11–40. San Diego: Academic Press.

————, 1992. *Language contact in the American Deaf community.* San Diego: Academic Press.

Lyons, J. 1977. Deixis and anaphora. In *The development of conversation and discourse,* ed. T. Myers. Edinburgh: Edinburgh University Press.

Meier, R. 1990. Person deixis in American Sign Language. In *Theoretical issues in sign language research,* vol.1, ed. S. Fischer and P. Siple, 175–90. Chicago: University of Chicago Press.

Metzger, M. 1995. Constructed dialogue and constructed action in American Sign Language. In *Sociolinguistics in Deaf communities,* ed. C. Lucas, 255–71. Washington, D.C.: Gallaudet University Press.

Padden, C. 1990. The relation between space and grammar in ASL verb morphology. In *Sign language research: Theoretical issues,* ed. C. Lucas, 118–32. Washington, D.C.: Gallaudet University Press.

Pizzuto, E., E. Giuranna, and G. Gambino. 1990. Manual and nonmanual morphology in Italian Sign Language: Grammatical constraints and discourse processes. In *Sign language research: Theoretical issues,* ed. C. Lucas, 83–102. Washington, D.C.: Gallaudet University Press.

Roy, C. B. 1989. Features of discourse in an American Sign Language lecture. In *The sociolinguistics of the Deaf community,* ed. C. Lucas, 231–251. San Diego: Academic Press.

Schermer, G. 1990. *In search of a language. Influences from spoken Dutch on the sign language of the Netherlands.* Delft: Eburon Publ.

Stokoe, W. C. 1960. Sign language structure: An outline of the visual communication system of the American Deaf. *Studies in linguistics, occasional papers,* vol. 8. Buffalo, N.Y.: State University of New York. Rev. ed. Silver Spring, Md.: Linstok Press, 1978.

van Hoek, K. 1996. Conceptual locations for reference in American Sign Language. In *Spaces, worlds, and grammar*, ed. G. Fauconnier and E. Sweetser, 334–50. Chicago: University of Chicago Press.

Vogt-Svendson, M. 1984. Word pictures in Norwegian Sign Language: A preliminary analysis. Working papers in linguistics, no. 2. Trondheim, Norway: University of Trondheim. 112–41.

Wallin, L. 1987. Nonmanual anaphoric reference in Swedish sign language. Supplement for *Forskning om Teckensprak*, Videogram 2 (Research on sign language, Video Report 2). Stockholm: Institute of Linguistics, University of Stockholm.

Winston, E. A. 1989. Transliteration: What's the message? In *The sociolinguistics of the Deaf community*, ed. C. Lucas, 147–64. San Diego: Academic Press.

———. 1991. Spatial referencing and cohesion in an American Sign Language text. *Sign Language Studies* 73:397–410.

———. 1992. Space and involvement in an American Sign Language lecture. In *Expanding horizons: Proceedings of the twelfth national convention of the Registry of Interpreters for the Deaf*, ed. J. Plant-Moeller, 93–105. Silver Spring, Md.: RID Publications.

———. 1993. Spatial mapping in comparative discourse frames in an American Sign Language lecture. Ph.D. diss., Georgetown University, Washington, D.C.

Transcription Conventions

Symbol	Example	Use
Capital letters	ME	English gloss for a specific manual sign
Hyphen	LOOK-AT	Used when more than one English word is required to represent the ASL sign
CL: with #	CL:1	Represents a classifier predicate; the number or letter represents the handshape, as in the fist with index finger extended (represented by the I in this example)
PRO #	PRO. 1	Represents pronominal reference; the number following the colon represents person (in this case, first person)
Plus signs	+++	Repetition of a sign
(Actions)	(cards in hand)	Indicates visual/spatial information
Gaze direction	gaze to A	Indicates gaze direction; "A" refers to addressee

Spatial Mapping and Involvement

in ASL Storytelling

Susan Mather and Elizabeth A. Winston

Spatial mapping is an essential ASL discourse feature and is used by fluent signers throughout discourse. Signers use space and spatial structuring in ASL to help the audience process the flow of information they are watching, structuring it into coherent and cohesive chunks of language. By using space both referentially and prosodically, signers can structure, or map, concepts in the signing space, evoking conceptual referents in the mind of the audience. Utterance boundaries can be marked in space. No specific entity needs to be mapped in the signing space; the utterance boundary can be recognized by the shifting of the signing space from one area to another. Referential mapping produces visual patterns in space, as in the juxtaposition of referential spaces in comparatives or the diagonal movement backward and forward on temporal maps. Prosodic use of space also produces visual patterns, from basic movements from point A to point B that bound utterances to the more rhythmic, flowing patterns of poetry and literature in ASL. Space in ASL serves as a foundation for linguistic and conceptual structures of ASL messages. Signers choose to use spatial strategies in order to render a message meaningful.

Fluent ASL signing is often noted for the fluid beauty of the signs and the visual patterns and structures. Nonfluent signing often lacks the fluidity and visual spatial patterns that make ASL a coherent language. Much ASL research has focused on isolated, often invented, linguistic structures, ignoring the use of the language in context. Thus, the spatial visual patterns that connect and make the language coherent have been overlooked.

This study was supported by the Office of Special Education and Rehabilitative Services (OSERS), U.S. Department of Education, CFDA 84.023N, Gallaudet University, Washington, D.C.: Visual Involvement in Literacy: Reading and Discussing Books with Three- to Eight-Year-Old Students who are Deaf and Hard of Hearing, with Dr. Susan Mather as principal investigator.

This study is one part of a three-year research grant investigating visual involvement strategies in literacy in Deaf and hard of hearing children between the ages of three and eight years old. The larger project is studying the use of a variety of ASL involvement strategies by signers who are reading to students from books. The signers have varying degrees of fluency in ASL and English and are working with several different classroom styles and populations—from small classrooms at residential schools with all Deaf and hard of hearing students to large classrooms in public schools that are "reversed mainstreamed," with hearing students joining Deaf and hard of hearing children for the reading sessions. All the children in the study are between the ages of three and eight years old.

This paper focuses on a very small portion of the data collected. Specifically, it investigates the use of spatial patterns, both referential and prosodic, in the storytelling strategies of teachers who are translating a written English story to a signed mode for Deaf and hard of hearing children. Actually, this investigation is narrowed even further because a review of the data revealed that only one of the signers used spatial patterning throughout the storytelling.[1]

Because this is a translation, it is necessary to understand both the involvement strategies of written English stories that are meant to be read aloud and the nature of involvement strategies of ASL visual structures that are intended to portray the stories. Writers use rhyme and rhythm to structure a story for the audience, involving them in developing their understanding of the story as well as surrounding them in the pleasurable sound patterns of the language. In the same way, signers use space and spatial mapping in ASL to help the audience process the flow of information they are watching, structuring it into coherent and cohesive chunks of meaning. The use of spatial structuring is one essential feature of discourse structuring and is used by fluent ASL signers throughout discourse. Anyone attempting to produce an effective message in ASL must

1. This signer is the only one considered to be a fluent ASL signer. Since one objective of the overall research project is to analyze effective strategies used in translating English to ASL, this signer was chosen as the specific focus of this portion of the research. Spatial strategies used by the other signers in translating this story are referred to when they occur at different points in the story, but these are rare. Nonfluent ASL signers use spatial mapping rarely, inconsistently, and at the lexical and syntactic level rather than at the discourse level, thus neglecting to provide their audiences with an essential linguistic feature needed for appropriately processing the story for both content and enjoyment.

incorporate its underlying spatial structures; anyone attempting to produce a translation from one language to the other must consider these underlying structures and linguistic patterns in order to achieve an effective, meaningful translation.

THEORETICAL FRAMEWORK

Target Language: Functions of Space in ASL

REFERENTIAL SPATIAL MAPPING

Referential spatial mapping is the process of pointing to areas of the signing space in order to evoke conceptual referents in the watchers' minds. Most research on the use of space in ASL has focused on the strategies of spatial referencing, that is, the use of space for referring to entities introduced in the discourse. Padden (1990), Meier (1990), Van Hoek (1988, 1989) and Liddell (1990) have analyzed a variety of grammatical features of spatial referencing at the morphological and syntactic levels.

At the discourse level, Van Hoek (1989) discusses repeated referential mapping and the phenomena of locus shifting and locus sharing across larger segments of discourse. Van Hoek, Norman, and O'Grady analyze the development of spatial cohesion in ASL narratives in children. Metzger (1995) analyzes the use of spatial mapping in constructed action in narratives, and Metzger and Liddell (1995) expand that research. Locker-McKee (1992) discusses the use of space in the establishment of footing in ASL. Winston (1993) analyzes the use of spatial mapping as a powerful strategy for structuring ASL discourse. Signers use spatial mapping to reflect their mental representation of discourse structure to the audience, expecting that the audience will use the spatial maps to build their own mental representations of the discourse and arrive at an understanding of the text that is similar to that of the signer. When repeated, it is a powerful tool at the discourse level, especially when it is repeated in order to structure the text. Winston (1993, 1995) analyzes the mapping of comparatives in an ASL lecture. An example of these mappings is the comparison of the art and science of ASL poetry. In this example, the signer mapped one concept, the art of ASL poetry, on one side of the signing space and another, the science of ASL poetry, on the other side, then proceeded to compare his understanding of the two. These spatial mappings provided structures that allowed the audience to participate in the creation of meaning by requiring them to interpret spatial referents previously established.

Spatial mapping is a salient characteristic of comparative frames; it marks the topic by adding spatial dimensions to linear, sequential text, making it more salient to the audience. Such marking provides the signer with powerful cues with which to guide the audience in their interpretation of the meaning of the signed production. Watchers perceiving the introduction of spatial mapping into discourse will note the salience of the spatially mapped chunk of text as being important to the overall coherence of the presentation. As such, spatial mapping is a powerful marker for ASL discourse structure. (Winston 1995, 109)

In addition, spatial mapping allowed the audience to predict the point of the comparison, finding that old or given information was mapped on the nondominant side first, followed by the mapping of the new information in the comparison on the dominant side second. The signer used a variety of pointing strategies to point to the map, including shifting of body stance, head pointings, hand dominance shifting, and signing in the space as well as the more customary pointing with an index handshape. The signer mapped abstract entities in the comparisons, not being restricted to mapping only physical entities and relationships.

VISUAL PATTERNS: RHYTHM AND RHYME

A second function of spatial mapping is prosodic. The spatial maps discussed in the preceding section are all referential; they are maps that allow the audience to interpret references to entities established in the discourse. However, use of space in ASL also functions in phrasing and chunking utterances and ideas in ASL. Signers shift their location in space between utterances, using the shift to mark utterance boundaries. The locations to and from which they move are not necessarily locations that map entities but are simply locations that are different from where they were before, indicating a shift in topic, a new thought or utterance, or a shift of frame. Thus space functions to differentiate one chunk from another and can create visual patterns familiar to the audience. These patterns involve the audience, making the texts more visually accessible and, at times, such as in poetry and storytelling, more pleasurable.

Rhythm and rhyme patterns in ASL have not yet been analyzed in great depth, but a growing body of research clearly demonstrates that both rhyme and rhythm occur in ASL and are achieved through visual strategies. Boundary markers for narrative are analyzed by Bahan and Supalla (1995), who find that eye gaze is an important feature of boundary marking in ASL. Wilbur (1994) analyzes eye blink as a boundary marker in ASL. In ongoing research, Boyes Braem (1995) is analyzing the shifting of signers' bodies for marking discourse chunks. Valli's research (1993) on rhyme and meter in ASL poetry is a seminal work on this topic. He identifies several features of ASL that effectively produce rhymes and rhythm in ASL poetry. These include eye gaze, body shift, head shift, use of handshapes, and use of movement path contours. All of these features shape the space, affecting the visual impact created by the signer and involving the watcher in the rhythms and rhymes of ASL.

Valli's description of visual patterns in ASL poetry is valuable to this study for its work on spatial patterns, especially because he compares the patterns of rhythm and rhyme created through ASL strategies in a child's poem and in one created for adults. As becomes clear in the teachers' storytelling translations in this study, only one teacher consistently uses ASL rhythm and rhyme strategies to tell the story to the children (although all do use some of the rhymes and rhythms of ASL in smaller segments of text). These strategies are not only ASL strategies; rather, Valli identifies them as "children's" devices that make the discourse linguistically simpler and easier for children to comprehend, memorize, and produce.

SPATIAL PATTERNS AS INVOLVEMENT STRATEGIES

Interlocutors interact through a variety of strategies, many of which are linguistic. In linguistic terms, involvement strategies are those that speakers use to "reflect and simultaneously create interpersonal involvement" (Tannen 1989, 1). This involvement is achieved when the speaker encourages the audience to take an active role in creating the meaning of the discourse. Tannen (1984, 1989) describes two categories of involvement strategies. One involves the audience in understanding the content of the message, using constructed dialogue, imagery and detail, ellipsis, and lexical choice. The audience is asked to create a mental representation of the story, visualizing the people and events by interpreting the words of the speaker. The second category encourages the audience to experience the patterns of the language, an aesthetic pleasure that allows the audience to enjoy the experience of the text. Such devices include rhyme, rhythm, intonation, and repetition to enhance the audience's enjoyment and processing of the text.

Involvement strategies in ASL include all of these methods. Roy (1989) discusses the use of constructed dialogue in ASL as an example of an involvement strategy; Zimmer (1989) views constructed dialogue as an involvement strategy that adds the imagery and detail of characters—their "voices"—to discourse (Schiffrin 1994). In an earlier study, Mather (1989) compares the use of space by both a hearing and a Deaf teacher in making a story more interesting for Deaf children. Metzger, in her investigation of constructed action (1995), discusses spatial referencing as an involvement strategy. In discussions of the functions of spatial referencing in discourse frames such as comparatives, performatives, and temporals, Winston (1991, 1993, 1995) describes these spatial patterns as involvement strategies, claiming that space and its functions in ASL are very powerful means for shaping the structure of discourse and eliciting involvement in the audience. She analyzes the use of space in three ASL involvement strategies: comparisons, performatives (constructed dialogue and action), and time maps. Each of these relies heavily (although not entirely) on the use of referential spatial mapping to involve the audience in sense making and in the visual patterns of the texts. As Winston (1992) states:

Comparisons use space to involve the watcher by placing items in space and allowing the watcher to make comparisons, and thus sense, of the placements; performatives use space to create scenes and personal involvement in the same way that constructed dialogue does in other languages; time mapping uses space to involve the watcher in events in time, as well as in the passage of time itself, through the use of imagery and detail.

Use of space and spatial mapping in ASL comparatives is a powerful discourse mechanism that involves the audience in both the creation of meaning and the visual patterns molded by the signer.

The Source Language: Written English Stories

WRITING CHILDREN'S STORIES IN ENGLISH

Written stories, especially children's books, are composed with the effect of the spoken word in mind. Thus rhyme and rhythm are part of the author's goal in the original composition. Authors put time and effort into composing the stories to carefully combine both words and sounds. Even though readers may not know the author's exact intention, they have a general understanding of English sound and rhythm patterns that are more or less effectively conveyed when the story is read aloud. Thus it is possible for native English speakers to read aloud with little preparation and still provide at least some of the sound and rhythm patterns of the story. Children's stories are designed to evoke both the emotional and cognitive involvement of the children, using features that rhyme and create a musical rhythm. These qualities add to the enjoyment children experience by the repetition of established rhymes and rhythms (Johnstone 1994).

READING THE STORY ALOUD:
THE READER'S FRAME

Fluent English speakers approach the task of reading aloud as one of taking the words and repeating them, adding intonation and rhythm to their speech. They have little difficulty in reproducing the rhymes and rhythms of the story. With little preparation, they are able to reproduce the effect wanted by the author—the combination of both form and content—to involve the children in the storytelling event.

Translation: From Source to Target

The task of "reading" is altered significantly when the "reader" is asked to translate an English-based story to another language such as ASL. Translation, changing a message from one language to another, means that the form of the message must be changed. For text that is more propositional, more content-dependent, this is not such a problem, for translation deals with the transformation very well. However, when the text is form-dependent (e.g., in text such as poetry, jokes, rhymes, and rhythms), the translator faces a dilemma. The rhythms, rhymes, and poetic features of the source language rarely coincide with the rhymes, rhythms, and poetic features of the target language. For example, in the original English story, the words *squeak, creak, hiss,* and *swish* are used extensively in the rhyme structure. In ASL, there are no specific signs for these words, making rhyme difficult. In order to produce a dynamically equivalent translation, the reader/translator will have to balance the form of the message in the target language with the content. The form of the resulting translation, if it is dynamic, will have the content of the message, with poetic forms and features that balance those of the source. (These forms will not be identical; rather, they will strive to produce the same effect of pleasure and comprehension in the target language as was created by the source language text.) In the case of a children's story that is dependent on both form and content to achieve the author's intent, a translation that accomplishes the same goal can be attained only by someone who is fluent in the target language and has spent some time and effort in preparing the translation's form.

The translation requires the same effort and time spent on meshing the rhyme and rhythm patterns of the target language before the dual goals of sense and pattern can be achieved. Without this time and effort, the translation is little more than a string of words without the author's intended rhyme or rhythm. The story loses its attraction, especially when the audience is children and the goal is primarily the combination of sound and sense. Unless the reader/translator provides the appropriate rhythm and rhyme strategies in the target language, involvement is lost. Thus, a "reader" simply transcoding the words without the patterns provides neither an effective nor a successful "reading" for the audience. Such a translation provides no dynamically equivalent text (Nida 1964; Hatim and Mason 1990).

As discussed earlier, one of the major linguistic structures of ASL at the discourse level is the use of space. It helps the audience interpret the signer's intentions and re-create the meaning of the text in their own minds. This paper focuses specifically on the use of this feature in the signed telling of the story, *Too Much Noise*. In the telling, only one teacher consistently used space for discourse chunking and prosodic marking throughout the reading of the story. This was the first teacher described, Ms. Daniels, who is regarded as a noted signer and storyteller in the ASL community. Others occasionally used space for referential mapping, but this was infrequent and often inconsistent and was applied at the lexical or syntactic level rather than the discourse level. This paper focuses on the effective use of discourse space and mapping in the storytelling of the one teacher who produced a dynamic equivalent of the story for her audience.[2]

2. This is in contrast to all the others, who use the book to show pictures rather than describe the animals. Since this is the point of having the pictures, it is not inappropriate. Nevertheless, it seems to break up the flow of the story for the other storytellers and the students. Reading aloud to hearing children, the teacher can often read and show the story at the same time, not having to take a great break between reading and showing. And they can talk while showing the pictures, saying things like, "Do you see the sheep?" or "Have you seen a sheep before?" They are able to keep the students' attention with both the visual and auditory channels. For signing, the teachers place the book in their laps while reading, their hands in neutral space. When they want to show the pictures, they

DISCUSSION

Data Collection

BOOK SELECTION

Two English stories were chosen for the larger project: *Too Much Noise*, by Ann McGovern, and *Five Chinese Brothers*, by Claire Bishop. These books were selected based on the following criteria: They contain involvement strategies (dialogue, repetition, imagery, and details) to encourage the production of imagery and detail involvement by the teachers, and they are generally popular, which encourages a successful book-reading event for everyone. The analysis in this project is limited to the reading/translation of the story *Too Much Noise*.

TEACHERS' BACKGROUND, THEIR SCHOOLS, AND THEIR STYLE OF READING *Too Much Noise*

Five teachers were involved in the larger project. Although only one rendition of the signed text, that of Ms. Daniels,[3] is analyzed for spatial

_____

have to stop, turn the book around, and show it, then turn it back around, put it down, and start signing again. Although none of these movements requires a great deal of time individually, the overall effect is that there is a great deal of time when nothing is happening. In addition, when reading directly from the book, the teachers lose all eye contact during the telling, the time when they need to be monitoring for understanding in the children. They receive no cues from the children about what they are understanding unless one of them becomes restless or disruptive. This was the case during the readings of the four other teachers. The teachers were interrupted by children and had to consistently regain their attention. Only Ms. Daniels kept their attention throughout the entire event without interruption.

Ms. Daniels avoided the problem by not reading from the book. Rather, she read it through, then translated the story into ASL. Because she does not have to stop for interruptions, she is able to monitor, adding information when she spots puzzlement in the children. She also is the only teacher who stands, giving herself the full range of movement and space to create the most visual impact. Whereas all the students can see her easily, the other signers seem to have a problem with the students not being able to see. By using signs rather than the pictures to describe the events, Ms. Daniels does not have long periods of waiting with little or no eye contact with the children.

3. Any names used to refer to the participants in the study are fictitious and have been assigned to preserve the participants' identities.

usage, the data from the other stories are referred to when appropriate. Although the other four readers did not use space as a basic structure, they did use some of the prosodic features such as ASL rhyme and rhythm that help to create the visual impact of ASL. Therefore, we refer to their renditions to illustrate points in the analysis and discussion. The following sections describe each teacher's signing skill, classroom setting, and approach to the translation task.

Two teachers work in a residential school setting; one is hearing and one is Deaf. They both tend to use ASL with their students. The Deaf teacher, Ms. Daniels, is also a well-known storyteller. Videotapes of her storytelling are sold nationwide by a company that specializes in videotapes and books of signed stories in ASL. Ms. Daniels had a group of six students who were six to eight years old. Her style of book reading is to read the whole book first and retell the story in ASL without the English text.

The second teacher (we will not assign names to the remaining four teachers) is hearing and a well-known person in the community for her involvement with people who are Deaf and hard of hearing. She also is a certified sign language interpreter. She had a group of six students who were four to six years old. Utilizing a somewhat different style of reading, she read each page first before signing the story.

The third teacher works in a self-contained classroom in a public school setting. This setting and teacher were chosen because of strong recommendations from the community and colleagues of the teachers. A certified sign language interpreter, she can switch from ASL to Manually Coded English (MCE)[4] effectively and effortlessly. She used both ASL and MCE with her group of six students ranging from three to five years old. In this task she read the story directly from the book, simultaneously producing a transcoded version of English signing on her hands.

The fourth and fifth teachers work in a mainstreamed program in a private day school. This setting is interesting for two reasons: (1) instruction is visually oriented, and (2) students with normal hearing are reverse-mainstreamed from public schools to that school for various reasons. Some students with normal hearing are sent by their school district because they may benefit from visually centered activities. These include, for

---

4. Manually Coded English is a system invented to represent morphemic segments of the English language through signs.

example, students who can hear but cannot talk or students who cannot absorb information audiologically and therefore depend more on visual channels. They also include students with normal hearing whose parents are Deaf and use sign language at home, as well as students who are siblings of Deaf students. Both teachers from this school use Manually Coded English. One teacher, who is hard of hearing, had a group of twenty-two students (Deaf, hard of hearing, and hearing) ranging in age from five to seven years old. The other teacher, who is hearing, had a group of thirteen students (also Deaf, hard of hearing, and hearing). Their ages ranged from three to five years old. Both teachers are similar in their story-reading methods. They read and signed almost each line instead of reading the whole passage and signing afterward. Although both consulted their teacher-aide (who is fluent in ASL) on how to tell a story, they produced transcoded versions of the story for this task.

Of the five story readers, only one approached the task as one of dynamic translation, attempting to provide an equivalent of the written English story in ASL. She has achieved a balance of form and content, enabling the children to enjoy both the story and its linguistic form. The other four teachers approached the activity as a sound-based process, relying heavily on the English forms transcoded to signs and relying heavily on the sound-based rhymes and rhythms of English rather than those of ASL. They read the story directly from the book, usually adding signs as they read, trying to some extent to maintain the content in their signs. However, the form was maintained almost exclusively in their voices. Three of the teachers relied primarily on voice intonation for the poetic features of the story and included few ASL strategies in their signing. These stories had no dynamic, formal equivalence for the Deaf students. The fourth did not use her voice, telling the story entirely in signs. She was perhaps the most successful at communicating the content, but she did not include many ASL spatial involvement strategies or poetic features, thus losing one of the primary goals and effects of the story's author. There was little signed rhyme or rhythm in the storytelling of these four teachers. Therefore, this analysis focuses on the use of space in the single translation that achieves a dynamic rather than a sound-based literal equivalence.

TABLE I. *Story's Structure and Author's Involvement Strategies*

Story Structure	Involvement Strategy
Introduction of main character, Peter, and his house	Imagery and detail
Inside of house House has many noises What to do?	Imagery and detail Inner dialogue and ellipsis
Outside of house Goes to wise man Gets advice Follows advice	Narrative Constructed dialogue Narrative and ellipsis
Repeat basic structure five times	Repeated strategies
Inside of house: problem resolved	Inner dialogue

DISCUSSION

Source Language: Original English Version of *Too Much Noise*

BASIC STORY STRUCTURE

The story, *Too Much Noise*, is analyzed by its basic structure and by the repetition of this structure to create the overall effect. The author divides the story into two locations: inside the house, where an old man (Peter) lives, and outside the house, where Peter tries to find answers to a dilemma. The overall discourse structure of the story, as well as the various involvement strategies included, is mapped in Table I.

At the beginning of the story, the inside of the house is very noisy, which disturbs Peter terribly. He complains about the noises that bother him, listing them in the following structured series of rhyming, rhythmic sentences, using words to create visual imagery and detail:

The bed creaked.
The floor squeaked.
Outside, the wind blew the leaves through the trees.
The leaves fell on the roof. *Swish. Swish.*
The teakettle whistled. *Hiss. Hiss.*[5]

After this list of noises, Peter exclaims that he does not know what to do and then decides to ask the village wise man for advice. At this point

5. The italicized words are reproduced from the original book.

the author creates involvement for the children through ellipsis. She does not explicitly state that Peter will get help from the wise man; she just says that he goes to see him. The audience needs to make the connection between seeing him and a possible solution.

Peter leaves the "inside of house" location and goes to see the wise man, shifting to the "outside of house" location. The author does not require the children to make too many connections, however. In the next sentence she uses dialogue to add imagery and detail to the story, showing that Peter asks the wise man for help. Peter tells the wise man about each noise, repeating the "bed creak, floor squeak, leaves swish, teakettle hiss" refrain introduced at the beginning of the story. The wise man advises Peter to get a cow. Peter questions the value of a cow in solving his noise problem but follows the suggestion anyway.

At this point the author does not tell the children that Peter takes the cow home. Rather, she implies that the cow is there by describing its noise, adding it as a new first sentence of the main refrain:

The cow said, "Moo. MOO."
The bed creaked.
The floor squeaked.
The leaves fell on the roof. *Swish. Swish.*
The teakettle whistled. *Hiss. Hiss.*

This is an elliptical shift back to the inside-of-house location. The children again must deduce that the cow has added to the noise by interpreting the description of the cow's noise immediately before the house noises. Again, through this strategy the children are involved in creating the meaning of the story for themselves.

CYCLE: REPETITION OF STRUCTURE

The author repeats the basic story structure, moving from inside the noisy house to outside for help, back inside for more noise, and back outside for more help. The author never provides an explicit physical description of the interior or exterior; these are prototypical locations, without specific physical sizes, shapes, or distances. Thus the children create their own mental representations of noisy houses and the outside where the wise man is. This "outside" does not imply that the wise man is sitting out of doors; rather, it means that he is outside of the mental representation of Peter's noisy house. "Outside" is a very abstract location in this story.

The author repeats the main refrain throughout the story, building on it as new noises are added. The rhyme, rhythm, and repetition of the refrain draw the children into the story, giving them a way to predict what will happen at each stage of the tale. The author builds suspense and involvement by repeating the main refrain, going back five more times to the wise man, following his advice, and attaching more and more noises to Peter's house, each time adding a new (but utterly predictable) sentence to the refrain. Each cycle is introduced with language very similar to that of the first visit, the language changing only at the sixth visit when Peter becomes angry. This change in the structure and rhythm signals the audience that a change in the story is imminent, and indeed the sixth is the final visit. This time the wise man tells Peter to get rid of the animals. The author has the wise man recast the refrain, changing the frame of "get an animal" to "let the animal go":

Let the cow go.
Let the donkey go.
Let the sheep go.
Let the hen go.
Let the dog go.
Let the cat go.

Illustrating Peter's acceptance of this advice, the author repeats the refrain, changing it slightly:

So Peter let the cow go.
He let the donkey go.
He let the sheep go.
He let the hen go.
He let the dog go.
He let the cat go.

The refrain is recast yet a third time, as Peter begins to appreciate the "quiet noise" as he comments,

Now no cow said, "Moo. MOO."
No donkey said, "HEE-Haw."
No sheep said, "Baa. Baa."
No hen said, "Cluck. Cluck."
No dog said, "Woof. Woof."
No cat said, "Mee-ow. Mee-ow."

The author has used repetition and recasting of the main refrain as a major structure of the story, leading the children through the action, providing them with recognizable landmarks for moving in and out of the house location and with subtle changes in those landmarks that let them know the story is building and then coming to an end. The rhyme, rhythm, and repetition are structured to provide a story experience that includes the children in both creating meaning and also enjoyment of the rhymes and rhythm. Thus form and content are equally important to the author in the telling of this story.

The Target Language: ASL and Visual Patterns

BASIC STORY STRUCTURE, REFERENTIAL SPATIAL MAPPING, AND PROSODIC VISUAL PATTERNS

The English story has two main discourse locations: inside Peter's house, which is noisy, and outside his house, where he goes for help to reduce the racket. In the ASL signing, the two concepts are spatially mapped by the signer, who clearly establishes one signing space to refer to the interior of the house and another space to refer to the exterior. The interior consists of the space immediately surrounding Ms. Daniels (Figure 1). The concept of the squeaking bed is signed in the middle left (nondominant) space,[6] with all the signs related to the topic of the bed signed in that area. The concept of the creaking floor is signed in the lower center, with all the signs related to the floor signed in that area. "Leaves swishing on the roof" is signed in the upper right (dominant) area. Although the leaves, trees, and wind are technically outside (physically), the problem they cause is inside the house, and the swishing leaves are signed bordering the house space. Thus this whole sequence becomes part of the inside-of-house space in spite of logical, physical descriptions. The tea-kettle with its sink, stove, and hissing are signed in the middle right (dominant) space.

The first time the signer introduces these noises, she takes great care to explain each entity and the fact that it makes a noise that is intolerable to Peter. She actually signs the objects in the order of bed, tree, floor, and kettle in an alternating space (Figure 1). (This alternation is a use of

6. It is important to note not only the left and right sides but also their relative dominance for the signer. Thus, we describe spatial patterns in terms of left and right and their dominance and nondominance for the signer.

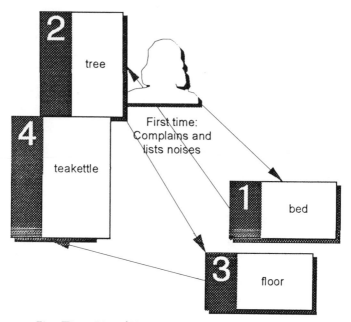

FIGURE 1. *First Time: List of Noises*

prosodic space noted by Valli [1993] and Winston [1993]). This is not the actual order of the story refrain.

The mapping of the interior of the house is not a physical layout; rather, it reflects a mental representation of "inside." This is evidenced by the placement of the various noisemaking entities both inside the house (bed, floor, and teakettle) and out (leaves hitting the roof). Although they are signed at relatively expected heights from a floor, it is not likely that a house would have a bed on the left, a floor only in the lower center, a roof on the upper right, and a sink and stove on the central right. Any truly physical description of a house would have the roof and the floor covering the entire house, with furniture and appliances in between. Thus it is clear that the signer is not trying to establish a realistic description but rather is attempting to evoke the concept of a prototypical house in the space in front of her body. The description and mapping are therefore of an abstract concept rather than an actual physical location.[7] Chunking

7. The other signers who used space at all here set up the house as a physical, concrete description, with the signs for each entity signed in order of height vertically from in front of the face to the level of the floor; they also signed only the sign for the entity, not the entire discourse chunk, at that height. There is no representation of the entire house being filled with noise.

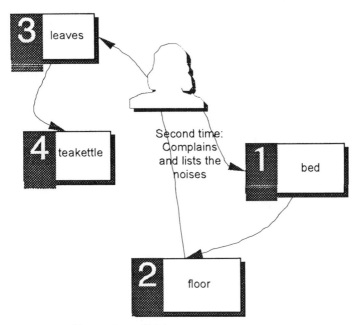

FIGURE 2. *Second Time: List of Noises*

of topics, themes, and ideas that structure the signer's intended meaning constitute an important discourse function of space in ASL. Space does not simply mirror the physical world (Winston 1993, 1995).

Once these entities and noises are established in the context, Ms. Daniels eliminates most of the lexical description and changes her order of mention (using the order of the original English story of bed, floor, tree, teakettle) and the visual movement pattern she created the first time. After the introduction, she consistently signs BED, FLOOR, TREE, TEAKETTLE (Figure 2).

Not only do these entities define the inside house space, they also fill it. The signer moves her hands continuously from space to space, never stopping, sweeping through the full space, creating the feeling of a house full of sounds.[8] These lines are a refrain, and the refrain is a single chunk within the story. Ms. Daniels accomplishes this same effect by her continued movements through the space and her filling of it.[9] The first pat-

8. This is in contrast to the other signers, who all end each utterance with some marked utterance boundary like a pause or a hand drop. They break up the visual pattern being created in the space and lose the sense of rhythm in the process.

9. The other four signers use the center of the signing space and produce more staccato styles of signing. Although they fill the auditory space with their voices,

tern is rather staccato, requiring a full direction change, both in height and side, for each entity. The second pattern is smoother, necessitating a shift of direction in the height but a more continuous flow from one side to the other for the first three items, with only the last sign changing both height and complete direction (from to-the-right to to-the-left). This smoothness of movement creates a more flowing rhythm and visually achieves the effect of the rhyme and rhythm of the English original, which is also smooth lines rather than staccato: each line is said with similar intonation.

Another aspect that creates visual rhyme is the use of handshapes in the creation of the pattern. Ms. Daniels chooses ASL strategies for her handshapes that, through their repetition, create rhymes and rhythm. In addition, she uses handshapes that are simpler and easier to process, reflecting the intended audience of children. For the main refrain, she uses primarily open handshapes (Valli 1993). For BED and FLOOR she uses B handshapes and adds both hands to the squeak sound. For LEAVES and TEAKETTLE HISSING she uses open 5 handshapes. These open, less compact, handshapes are easier to perceive and process, and she repeats them throughout her main refrain, changing them only when she gets to the animals and their sounds, the new information. She uses the sign for each animal, regardless of its handshape: CAT, SHEEP, HEN, DOG, COW, and DONKEY, but she makes sure that the children understand what each animal is by describing it if she thinks they do not understand.

After listing the noises, Ms. Daniels remains in the inside space and presents the next stage of the story: Peter's dilemma and decision to do something. Like the author, Ms. Daniels adds involvement strategies, but, in contrast, she uses inner dialogue to add visual imagery and detail rather than the ellipsis the author used. Peter has a discussion with himself about what he should do and decides that he should go see the village wise man. This inner dialogue, or type of performative, is an involvement strategy that provides a "voice," or in this case, a "body" to the character of Peter, making the story more vivid for the children.

Peter then leaves the house, and the signer shifts from inside house space to outside (Figure 3). Again, in contrast to the author, who uses

---

using English intonation, stress, and volume patterns, they do not produce an equivalent "filling of the visual space" with their signing. The signed rendition is not a dynamic equivalent of the spoken rendition.

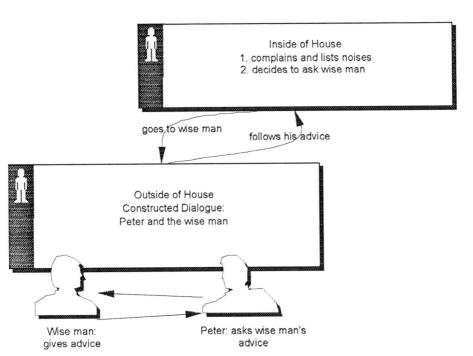

FIGURE 3. *Two Main Spaces*

ellipsis, Ms. Daniels uses constructed action, employing a CL:1 to build this scene for the audience.

Once in the outside-of-house space, Ms. Daniels shifts to constructed dialogue as Peter gets advice, the same involvement strategy the author used. Ms. Daniels maps Peter referentially on the left (nondominant) side and the wise man on the right (dominant) side.[10] As Peter explains his problem, Ms. Daniels reuses the main refrain pattern (first introduced inside the house) within the outside-of-house space, relating the visit to Peter's noise problem. The main refrain is embedded within Peter's constructed dialogue, illustrating the complex overlapping of spatial frames common in ASL spatial mapping. During the constructed dialogue, the wise man provides counsel and Peter questions it ("What good is a cow?"). Ms. Daniels interprets this question as Peter's inner dialogue while in the outside-of-house space. She then shifts to constructed action, showing Peter actually searching for, finding, and taking home the first

10. This follows patterns of constructed dialogue found by Winston (1993) with old information (Peter) being placed on the nondominant side and new information (the wise man) on the dominant side.

animal, the cow. Again, this is an involvement strategy that utilizes ASL spatial mapping; the story's author used ellipsis to imply all of this.

As Peter returns to the inside-of-house space, Ms. Daniels also shifts back to the more central inside-of-house map she created earlier. Ms. Daniels actually shows the cow entering the house space (as do all the animals in turn), an event that would normally not happen. However, the point of this section of the story is the noise itself, so when the cow enters the house, its mooing is added to the earlier house sounds. The cow is not located in any particular spot in the house, but the signing of the mooing, like the signing of the house noises, fills the entire space. Ms. Daniels uses both hands to alternately spell *moo* on each side. Although the choice of handshape is not a compact one (and thus not as poetic as the rhymes for the house noises), it uses movement alternation that is poetic and rhythmic and echoes the spatial structure of the main refrain.

Another repetition within this space is the transposition of the main refrain with the new, added lines; in the English story, each animal and its sound are added first, followed by the old information and finally the main refrain each time. In the ASL rendition, the main refrain occurs first, then each animal is added in order. The animals are not placed in any given spot in the house; they are simply signed within the inside-the-house space. Ms. Daniel's rhythm and rhyme are established by first repeating the more consistent main refrain (the old information), then adding the less poetic, new information. This pattern is repeated throughout the story.

CYCLE: REPETITION OF SPATIAL MAPS
AND VISUAL PATTERNS

After this initial cycle of inside, outside, inside, the English story repeats. Likewise, Ms. Daniel's use of inside and outside space repeats, as does her use of the various spatial structures she has created. After showing Peter complaining about the added noise of the cow, she once again leaves the inside-of-house space and portrays a second dialogue with the wise man about the raucous house in the outside-of-house space.

She then shifts to inner dialogue with Peter, accepting the wise man's advice, then to constructed action to carry it out, bringing the animals home, and entering the inside-of-house space, where, once again, their relative locations become irrelevant, and only the fact that they are noise producers is pertinent. They are each shown with the signing filling up much of the space, often with two hands where one would be expected,

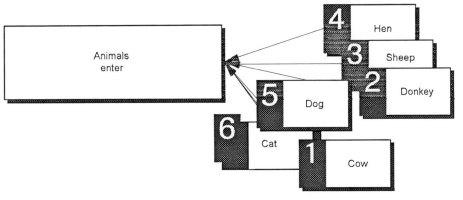

FIGURE 4. *Animals Entering the House*

either simultaneously or alternatingly. Again this pattern of handedness constitutes a rhyming pattern in ASL (Valli 1993).

As part of the cyclical pattern, the animals enter and then exit the house. Their entrances and exits provide further evidence that the mapping of the inside-of-house space is intended to portray a prototypical house rather than a specific location. The animals are brought from the outside-of-house space, and all are entered through a door on the center front left (nondominant) space (Figure 4). However, when they are evicted, they leave to the rear of the space, three to the left rear and three to the right rear, in a pattern of 2, 2, 1, 1 (Figure 5).

The spatial exit points do not correspond with the entrance points. It is doubtful that the old man intentionally threw the animals out in a specific pattern (or that this old house had three doors all leaving from the same room: one, an entrance, and two, exits). It is more likely that the signer is establishing that the entrance and exit of the animals have two clearly separate functions in the story, each signifying a different point. The entrance of the animals marks the addition of noise and the escalation of the problem. Their exit marks the solution to the problem; thus they are mapped differently in the space. (It is certainly possible in ASL to have the animals leave through the same "door" that they entered, but this physical mapping of space is irrelevant to the point of the story.)

Ms. Daniels adds two other prosodic features in the exiting of the animals, that of handshape and movement rhyme. When the wise man is telling Peter to let the animals go, Ms. Daniels begins the refrain with "Let the cow go," signing COW, SEND-AWAY. The sign SEND-AWAY is made with the open B handshape and is signed with the nondominant, left hand only.

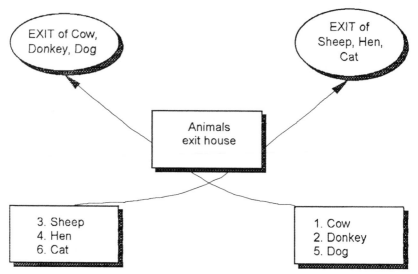

FIGURE 5. *Animals Exiting the House*

The next line of the refrain repeats this syntactic structure, DONKEY, SEND-AWAY, but this time SEND-AWAY is signed by the dominant, right hand only. Ms. Daniels alternates the nondominant/dominant shift for each of the animals, ending on the dominant side. This handshape repetition and the movement alternation creates a striking visual impact within this outside-of-house space.

When Peter returns to get rid of the animals, Ms. Daniels continues this visual pattern to a certain extent but becomes more involved with the constructed action of throwing out the animals and less involved with the handshape and movement rhyme. However, she does use the sign SEND-AWAY toward the end of each animal's exit; furthermore, she employs some alternation of hands, although it is not as striking as in the wise man's original signing. In this section Ms. Daniels focuses more on the detail and imagery of the constructed action of throwing out the animals than on the poetic structures of rhyme.

This structured use of space—from inside to outside and back again—is repeated throughout the story, setting up the recurrent pattern of Peter complaining, getting advice, and following advice. Each of these themes is treated differently in space, but the spatial structure for each theme is repeated several times.

Not only is each separate use of space repeated in order to structure the initial story, but the overall pattern of spatial mapping and prosody is also repeated, in, out, in, out, with the more prosodic, poetic use of space oc-curring inside the house (the refrain) and the more normal use of referen-tial space outside the house to indicate Peter's actions. This shifting from poetic to normal also creates a rhythm that involves the audience, helping them process the story easily and enjoyably.

CONCLUSIONS

Analysis of the use of space both for spatial mapping and for prosody demonstrates that the entire ASL narrative is divided into two main dis-course spaces and that these are further chunked by subspaces that map subtopics in the narrative. The signer uses space to map topics or main points of the story for her audience, mapping concepts such as "inside the house" and "outside the house" without regard to any actual concrete physical description.

A comparison of involvement strategies and linguistic features the au-thor and the signer use shows the importance of the use of space in ASL storytelling (Table 2).

Spatial structuring occurs throughout the ASL story. Each segment of the ASL story incorporates some form of spatial mapping to create in-volvement by the audience. Whereas the introduction of the main char-acter in the English version uses imagery and detail to create involvement, the ASL version incorporates use of space in the constructed action that describes the character.

The discourse location (inside the house) in the original English version creates involvement through imagery and detail; the ASL version intro-duces a spatial map that bounds the inside-of-house space, including the noises that fill it during the story. This space is further patterned spatially through prosodic ASL rhyme features of open handshapes, usually "B" and rhythm of movement in the sweeping pattern created as part of the four original noises. And, whereas the original English uses inner dia-logue and ellipsis to show Peter's dilemma, the ASL version incorporates the spatial structures of inner dialogue and constructed action.

The outside-of-house location is established through narration, con-structed dialogue, and ellipsis in the English; the ASL is spatially struc-tured with constructed action, constructed dialogue, and inner dialogue. The conclusion of the English version includes inner dialogue to create in-volvement; the ASL rendition uses the spatial structure of inner dialogue

TABLE 2. *English and ASL Involvement Strategies in Relation to Story Structure*

Story Structure	Involvement Strategies	
	English	ASL
Introduction of main character, Peter, and his house	Imagery and detail	Referential spatial map: constructed action and narration
Inside of house	Imagery and detail	Referential spatial map: bed, floor, leaves, teakettle
House has many noises	Rhyme	Rhyme: handshape Rhythm: movement contour
What to do?	Inner dialogue and ellipsis	Referential spatial map: inner dialogue and constructed action
Outside of house		
Goes to wise man	Narrative	Referential spatial map: constructed action
Gets advice	Constructed dialogue	Referential spatial map: constructed dialogue
Follows advice	Narrative and ellipsis	Referential spatial map: inner dialogue and constructed action
Repeat basic structure five times	Repeated	Repeated
Inside of house: problem resolved	Inner dialogue	Referential spatial maps: inner dialogue and narration

alternating with narration. Each spatial map, like the English structures, is repeated throughout the story, providing clear indications of the story's structure. The entire structure of the ASL version is spatially mapped.

Each segment of the story utilizes space for its production, shifting among different features of space at various points but always repeating the same strategies in space for the same functions. In the ASL story these spaces map ideas and conceptual entities rather than concrete entities and locations. The signer uses rhythmic and rhyming features of ASL to mold the visual impact of this space. She uses movement contours to define the space, continuous movement to create a rhythm, and repeated movement and rhythm to create a rhyming in the story. This manner of rhyming serves all the purposes of rhyming in any language. It gives rise to a form that can easily accept new information; it helps the audience process the boundaries and the meaning of the chunk more easily; and it creates an interesting, pleasurable experience for the audience, generating involvement by helping them formulate meaning (e.g., expectations of what comes next, predictions of the story's outcome, suspense regarding the series of events). It also involves them by building a repeated visual pattern in the same way that spoken patterns of rhythm and rhyme create a sense of music for hearing audiences. These visual patterns are pleasing to see, especially when they help to add meaning to the story. These patterns, however, occur within a space, adding rhythm and rhyme because they are consciously repeated to produce that effect. They may occur within a referential space, but they are not themselves referential.

Effectively translating a story in ASL requires the same types of spatial chunking that other ASL discourse requires. The signer of this story created visual maps in the space to guide the audience through the main topic and subtopics, repeatedly using these spatial structures in her ASL rendition to produce rhythm and rhyme. The rhythm and rhyme are part of the original and must be part of the translation if the goal of the story-telling is to match the author's aim: to create involvement for the children through the use of sense making and pattern making, regardless of the language. Spatial mapping is an integral part of the entire structure of the ASL version of the story. It helps the audience understand the story through involvement, both in the development of meaning and the enjoyment of the story's form. An understanding of these spatial structures is essential for the production of coherent meaning in ASL.

IMPLICATIONS

This analysis is a preliminary study of the spatial structures used as involvement strategies in a single translated story. As such, it is difficult to draw conclusions about space and its general functions in ASL. However, as one of many case studies, it can add to the growing understanding of the discourse patterns of space in ASL. It corroborates the claim that spatial structures are essential to the discourse structure of ASL and provides an example of the pervasive nature of spatial mapping in the production and comprehension of the language.

Spatial mapping and spatial structures in ASL are a foundation of ASL discourse. More research about the functions of spatial structuring and visual patterns in ASL will add valuable and much needed knowledge in many areas. This research raises many questions for anyone studying ASL, either in the field of linguistics or as a student of ASL as a first or second language. Second language learners include the ever growing group of interpreters who are enrolled in interpreter education programs. It is essential for them to be able to understand the subtle distinctions in meaning of different spatial mappings created by ASL signers; it is equally essential for them to be able to produce coherent ASL renditions that include appropriate spatial structures when interpreting from English to ASL.

Teachers of Deaf students are another group of second language learn-ers who, like interpreters, need to be able to understand and produce the subtle distinctions of spatial structures. Most teachers of Deaf students are hearing speakers of English who have learned some amount of sign-ing or ASL through courses in their university programs and perhaps in-teraction with the Deaf community. As language models for many Deaf children, they can provide a complete language model only if they them-selves are fluent in ASL. Any signed communication method used without spatial structuring will be incomplete and ineffective as a language model.

Parents of Deaf children are another group of second language learn-ers of ASL. Most Deaf children have hearing parents who must learn to communicate visually with their children. An understanding of the visual nature of ASL and the spatial structures necessary to produce coherent, meaningful messages is indispensable in their communication with their Deaf children.

An understanding of the spatial structures of ASL is also essential in the field of linguistics. Much research in spatial structures in ASL has fo-cused on the morphological and syntactic functions of space. In order to produce a coherent and complete account of the functions of space in ASL, the discourse spatial structures must also be accounted for. Further research in that area of spatial structures at the discourse level will con-tribute to a full account of the linguistic structure of ASL.

REFERENCES

Bahan, B. J., and S. J. Supalla. 1995. Line segmentation and narrative structure. In *Language, gesture, and space,* ed. K. Emmorey and J. Reilly, 171–91. Hillsdale, N.J.: Lawrence Erlbaum Associates.

Boyes Braem, P. 1995. Utterance boundaries in sign language. Personal communication.

Emmorey, K., and J. Reilly, eds. 1995. *Language, gesture, and space.* Hillsdale, N.J.: Lawrence Erlbaum Associates.

Hatim, B., and I. Mason. 1990. *Discourse and the translator.* New York: Longman.

Johnstone, B. 1994. Repetition in discourse-interdisciplinary perspectives. In *Advances in discourse processes,* vol. 1, ed. R. O. Freedle. Norwood, N.J.: Ablex.

Klima, E. S., and U. Bellugi. 1979. *The signs of language.* Cambridge: Harvard University Press.

Liddell, S. K. 1990. Four functions of a locus: Reexamining the structure of space in ASL. In *Sign language research: Theoretical Issues,* ed. C. Lucas, 176–98. Washington, D.C.: Gallaudet University Press.

Locker-McKee, R. M. 1992. Footing shifts in American Sign Language lectures. Ph.D. diss., University of California, Los Angeles.

Lucas, C., ed. 1989. *The Sociolinguistics of the Deaf community.* San Diego: Academic Press.

——, ed. 1995. *Sociolinguistics in Deaf communities.* Washington, D.C.: Gallaudet University Press.

McGovern, A. 1966. *Too much noise.* New York: Houghton Mifflin.

Mather, S. A. 1989. Visually oriented teaching strategies with deaf preschool children. In *The Sociolinguistics of the Deaf community,* ed. C. Lucas, 165–87. San Diego: Academic Press.

Meier, R. P. 1990. Person deixis in American Sign Language. In *Theoretical issues in sign language research,* ed. S. D. Fischer and P. Siple, 175–90. Chicago: University of Chicago Press.

Metzger, M. 1995. Constructed dialogue and constructed action in American Sign Language. In *Sociolinguistics in Deaf communities,* ed. C. Lucas, 255–71. Washington, D.C.: Gallaudet University Press.

Metzger, M., and S. K. Liddell. 1995. Constructed action in an ASL narrative. Paper read at Georgetown University Round Table, Washington, D.C.

Nida, E. A. 1964. *Toward a science of translating with special reference to principles and procedures involved in Bible translating.* Leiden: E. J. Brill.

Padden, C. 1990. The relationship between space and grammar in ASL verb morphology. In *Sign language research: Theoretical Issues,* ed. C. Lucas, 118–32. Washington, D.C.: Gallaudet University Press.

Prinz, P., and E. Prinz. 1985. If only you could hear what I see: Discourse development in sign language. *Discourse Processes* 8:1–19.

Roy, C. B. 1989. Features of discourse in an American Sign Language lecture. In *The sociolinguistics of the Deaf community,* ed. C. Lucas, 231–51. San Diego: Academic Press.

Schiffrin, D. 1994. *Approaches to discourse.* Cambridge: Blackwell Publishers.

Tannen, D. 1984. *Conversational style: Analyzing talk among friends.* Norwood, N.J.: Ablex.

——. 1989. Talking voices: Repetition dialogue and imagery in conversational discourse. In *Studies in interactional sociolinguistics 6*, ed. J. J. Gumperz. New York: Cambridge University Press.

Valli, C. 1993. Poetics of American Sign Language poetry. Ph.D. diss., Union Institute, Cincinnatti, Ohio.

Van Hoek, K. 1988. Mental space and sign space. Paper read at Linguistic Society of America, New Orleans, La.

———. 1989. Locus splitting in American Sign Language. Paper read at Pacific Linguistics Conference IV, Eugene, Ore.

Van Hoek, K., F. Norman, and L. O'Grady. 1989. Development of spatial and nonspatial referential cohesion in American Sign Language narrative. Paper read at Stanford Child Language Research Forum, Stanford, Calif.

Wilbur, R. 1994. Eyeblinks and ASL phrase structure. *Sign Language Studies* 84:221–40.

Winston, E. A. 1991. Spatial referencing and cohesion in an ASL text. *Sign Language Studies* 73:397–410.

———. 1992. Space and involvement in an American Sign Language lecture. In *Expanding horizons: Proceedings of the twelfth national convention of the Registry of Interpreters for the Deaf,* 93–105. Silver Spring, Md.: RID Publications.

———. 1993. Spatial mapping in comparative discourse frames in an ASL lecture. Ph.D. diss., Georgetown University, Washington, D.C.

———. 1994. Space and reference in American Sign Language. In *Repetition in discourse-interdisciplinary perspectives,* ed. B. Johnstone, 99–113. Norwood, N.J.: Ablex.

———. 1995. Spatial mapping in comparative discourse frames. In *Language, gesture, and space,* ed. K. Emmorey and J. Reilly, 87–114. Hillsdale, N.J.: Lawrence Erlbaum Associates.

Zimmer, J. 1989. Toward a description of register variation in American Sign Language. In *The sociolinguistics of the Deaf community,* ed. C. Lucas, 253–72. San Diego: Academic Press.

Part 5 Second-Language Learning

An Acculturation Model for Learners of ASL

Mike Kemp

Why do some ASL students learn the target language well while other students struggle? What do the "strong" students have that the weak students do not? For the past few years, educators have been attempting to find the best method for teaching ASL, yet some of our students continue to have problems learning the language. Why?

Schumann (1978) proposed that there are a number of variables that can determine a student's ability to acquire a second language. Schumann's variables include factors of a social, affective, cognitive, biological, personal, input (external stimulation or degree of exposure to language), and instructional nature. This paper will focus on only the first two factors.

Over a number of years, challenges to Schumann's model have arisen (Alptekin 1983; Larsen-Freeman and Long 1991; Maple 1982; McLaughlin 1987). Schumann asserted that the acculturation model is independent of instruction and that instruction plays a minor role in determining a person's potential in acquiring the target language. Other researchers (such as Bowers and Flinders, 1991) have shown that instruction plays a very important role in facilitating second-language acquisition. It seems to be true that instruction, regardless of the methods or approaches used, can serve as a catalyst in developing second-language skills. However, there are occasions when all means of attempting to help students to achieve the desired level of competence have been exhausted. After analyzing the methods and approaches of language teaching that were developed by noted scholars, Robert Blair (1982) developed a list of fourteen assumptions on language teaching. The assumptions explain different points pertaining to language learning. The first assumption is that the teacher can teach only a finite set of vocabulary and grammatical rules, while the student can produce an infinite number of sentences. This may mean that the teacher can do only so much and the rest is up to the student. Educators have disagreed about the students' role in acquiring a second language as just mentioned. The problem is that some students lack important components that can affect their ability to acquire the target language in spite of the efficacy of the teaching method used. The purpose of this paper is to attempt to focus on the acculturation model and how it can affect a person's chance of acquiring American Sign Language as a second language. Readers may be able to gain a better insight into their ASL students and thus adapt their teaching techniques to reflect Schumann's acculturation model. The observations and information pertinent to the factors that we will mention are based on my twenty-six years of experience in teaching ASL.

Let us first introduce the terminology we will be using. *Second language* (as opposed to *foreign language*) concerns a student's capacity to use a language outside of the classroom (Gingras 1978). For example, when a student learns Spanish in the classroom and practices it with members of a nearby Spanish-speaking community, that student is considered to be learning a second language. If there is no opportunity to experiment with the newly learned language outside the classroom, then we consider the language a foreign language. A *target language* is one that the second-language student wants to acquire. A *second-language learner group* consists of people who want to learn a target language. *Target-language user group* refers to a community of people using the second-language learner group's target language as their first language.

The Acculturation Factors Model, according to Schumann (1986, 379), consists of two groups of variables: social factors (external forces) and affective factors (internal forces) brought together to form a major causal variable in second-language acquisition. Schumann asserts that these factors can facilitate success in acquiring a second language.

SOCIAL FACTORS

The social factors that facilitate success in acquiring a second language are:

- social dominance patterns
- integration strategies
- enclosure
- cohesiveness
- congruence

- attitude
- intended length of residence

Social Dominance Patterns

There are three social dominance patterns: dominance, subordination, and nondominance. In terms of political, cultural, technical, or economical reality, the second-language learner group can be either superior or inferior to or roughly on the same level as the target-language user group.

If members of the second-language learner group perceive themselves as superior (dominant) to the target-language group, then they may tend to resist learning the target language. For example, hearing people who felt superior to Deaf people may have been inclined to oppress ASL by referring to English-like signing (Lane, Hoffmeister, and Bahan 1996,159). For example, there are programs in which Signed English is used. The purpose of using Signed English is to make sure that the deaf children are exposed to English per se. In addition, there is a very small number of professors at Gallaudet University who perpetuate the use of simultaneous communication (using signs and voice at the same time) while teaching a class or attending meetings. They say they use straight English because the textbooks they use are in English.

If the second-language learner group feels inferior (subordinate) to the target-language group, they may have difficulty in mastering the target language. For example, the personnel at Gallaudet University's physical plant department (custodians, plumbers, electricians, and so on) may have, at best, only high school education. In my twenty-six years of teaching ASL, I have observed—by watching their eye contact—that they tend to shy away from learning ASL; they are apt to look away when approaching ASL users. In addition, they are inclined not to interact with people who use sign language in any form, whether it be ASL or contact signing (as defined in Lucas and Valli 1992, 39). Physical plant department workers may feel inferior to those around the campus who have more formal education than they do. If so, then this would support Schumann's view of the dominance patterns.

On the other hand, if the second-language learner group and the target-language user group share the same political, cultural, technical, and economic status (nondominance), then contact between these two groups is likely to be more extensive, and such interaction can enhance the second-language learner group's acquisition of the target language. For example, at Gallaudet University ASL teachers and personnel with similar backgrounds have been assigned to various classes on occasion. In addition, the ASL and English Mentoring program has been running for three years on campus and is now sponsored by the Center for ASL Literacy. Fluent ASL users are paired with faculty, staff, and students who need tutorial help in mastering the target language. In exchange, the fluent ASL users get remedial help in improving their writing skills. The outcome of this program is yet to be determined, but, to say the least, the reviews have been positive. The contact between the fluent ASL users and the fluent English speakers/writers is quite extensive, and, predictably, it can reciprocally improve the users' grasp of both languages. In addition, social interaction between the two groups is further enhanced despite the occasional awkward moment. A case in point occurred when an ASL mentor felt belittled by the remark of one of the hearing mentees about her "superior" English. This resulted in a rift between the two, and, without any further discussion, contact between these two individuals discontinued. The incident supports Schumann's view that if there is a perception of superiority or inferiority, interaction between the two parties may well decrease. Success in such a mentoring relationship is based on trust and balance that can reduce the social dominance mentality deterrent to language learning (Anne Marie Baer, personal communication 1997).

Assimilation, Preservation, and Adaptation

Schumann suggested that a person's adjustment to a new or foreign culture and language is determined by three factors: assimilation, preservation, and adaptation.

Assimilation occurs when the second-language group gives up its lifestyle and values and adopts those of the target-language group. This process maximizes contact between these two groups and enhances target-language acquisition.

Preservation occurs when the second-language learner group chooses to keep its own lifestyle and values while at the same time rejecting those of the target-language group. Social distance between the second-language learner group and the target-language user group can be evident and does not help the former in acquiring the target language. This is obvious among hearing people who try to learn ASL. Because Deaf people have their own cultural norms (Lane, Hoffmeister, and Bahan 1996, 124–

73), hearing ASL learners find it difficult to pick up cultural behaviors such as attention getting, passing through two people talking with each other without cutting off the flow of conversation, use of eye contact to maintain attention while signing, and so forth. Hearing people have their own ways of dealing with these issues via the use of sounds. In trying to preserve their own culture, they may divide themselves from the Deaf community.

Adaptation (Schumann [1986] used the word *adaptation* for *acculturation*) takes place when the second-language learner group adapts to the cultural norms of the target-language group and at the same time maintains their own cultural values. This can result in varying degrees of contact between the target-language user group and the second-language learner group as well as varying degrees of acquisition of the target language. Schumann (1986, 379) proposed that there are two types of acculturation. The first takes place when a second-language learner interacts with the target-language user group and maintains constant contact with them, thus resulting in acquisition of the target language. From a psychological point of view, the second-language learner is open to the target language to a point where the language being exposed can be absorbed. The second type of acculturation has the same features as the first, but the learner regards the target-language user group as being different from his or her own culture. In addition, the learner may or may not be aware of a desire to adopt the target-language user-group culture.

The acculturation factor is observable in the Deaf community. Late ASL learners (those who are deaf and grew up in a nonsigning environment) can easily adapt to the cultural norms of the Deaf community if they chose to do so. At times these people maintain their mainstream-American cultural values and also accept the new culture. On the other hand, other individuals have rejected their first culture and immersed themselves into Deaf culture. Contact with the target-language user group is quite frequent, and, as a result, the person is exposed to the new language. The immersion is probably due to the fact that these people discover a new life after spending many years of not being allowed to use ASL at home or in school. There are also cases in which Deaf people have tried to learn ASL but could not cope with the new culture. They have returned to the home culture by discontinuing interaction with the target-language group. An example is provided by the New Signers Program at Gallaudet University. The New Signers Program is offered to incoming deaf undergraduates who did not grow up with ASL. A small number of students suddenly leave the New Signers Program a few days after it begins. Their stated reasons range from "I cannot stand seeing Deaf people making those rubber faces while signing" to "I will lose my ability to speak." Hearing people (i.e., users of spoken language), however, find it quite challenging to adapt to the new culture, especially when they have to learn to make nonmanual signals. Based on my personal observations, I find it a sometimes tedious task when I try to teach the use of nonmanual signals in my ASL classes. For example, if I mention that they show blank faces while signing, my students will make either exaggerated or nonsynchronized facial movements when signing specific sentence types such as questions, assertions, negations, topic-comment, and so on.

Enclosure

Schumann (1986, 381) asserted that enclosure, which means that both the second-language learner group and the target-language user group have a degree of contact, affects second-language learning. Enclosure is high if the second-language learner group and the target-language user group go to the same gatherings such as church, clubs, recreational facilities, and job sites. In short, interaction between the two groups is evident, and the acquisition of the second-language group's target language is expedited. If the two groups go to different gatherings, then the potential for acquiring a second language is minimized. Hearing students have the opportunity to interact with Deaf people at Gallaudet University when taking ASL classes there. The university has a social gathering place where the students can order refreshments. The faculty and staff members at the university are in constant contact with Deaf students who use ASL. These elements provide an opportunity for hearing people to acquire ASL if they want to.

Cohesiveness

If the members of the second-language learner group choose to stick together as a group, they forego the chance of interacting with the users of the target language. Also, if the second-language learner group is large, there will be smaller groups within the larger group. These situations minimize opportunities for acquiring the second language. I have observed that whenever there is a social event (e.g., reception, banquet, etc.), there is a tendency among the Deaf and a small number of hearing people to separate from each other. The hearing people tend to socialize with other hearing people and refrain from using ASL. Communicating without using ASL separates them from the members of the Deaf community. Needless to say, this not only minimizes the second-language learners' chance to master the language, but it also causes the target-language user group (ASL users) to separate themselves from the hearing group.

Congruence

If the second-language-learner group's culture is similar to that of the target-language group, then contact between these two groups occurs frequently. If the target-language group's culture is much different from that of the second-language learner group, interaction is drastically reduced. In other words, the more different a new culture is, the less frequently the second-language learner will attempt to interact. Entering Deaf culture can, at best, be very challenging for hearing people, who are accustomed to hearing voices while interacting with other people; when they interact with Deaf people, the absence of voices can be deafening.

Attitude

If both the second-language learner group and the target-language user group have positive attitudes toward each other, acquisition of the target language will be enhanced. If the attitude is negative, acquisition is hampered. If hearing people manifest a negative attitude toward Deaf people, they have very little, if any, chance of mastering ASL. If Deaf people exhibit an adverse attitude toward hearing people, this outlook prevents them from interacting. There are risks involved when ASL teachers assign their students to go to Deaf clubs or social events sponsored by certain organizations because many Deaf people harbor antihearing sentiments. When they meet Deaf people with such sentiments, even hearing people with a positive attitude will be in for unpleasant surprises and may experience intimidation. On the other hand, there are hearing people who possess a paternalistic attitude toward Deaf members of the community. They may have a tendency to say that they wanted to learn ASL in order to "save the poor unfortunate Deaf people" from possible disasters. This stance may also hamper language learning.

Intended Length of Residence

If the members of a second-language learner group plan to stay with the target-language user group for an extended length of time, the possibility of acquiring the target language is great. This is probably due to the fact that contact occurs on an almost daily basis, thus enhancing mastery of the target language. In addition, because the learners invest much time, they have a further reason to develop their second-language skills.

Deaf people who grew up in a nonsigning environment are likely to pick up the target language quickly if and when they interact with other members of the Deaf community. Students who were educated in oral programs or did not go to a residential school generally enter Gallaudet University or the National Technical Institute for the Deaf intending to be there for an extended period of time. Once they begin to interact with other Deaf people, they quickly acquire ASL.

AFFECTIVE FACTORS

The affective variables that Schumann identified as factors leading to successful second-language acquisition are as follows:

- language shock
- culture shock
- motivation
- ego-permeability

Language Shock

Language shock is prevalent among adults who are learning a second language. They fear appearing ridiculous when learning or acquiring a new language. According to Schumann, adults get "narcissistic gratification" while using their native language. When they are using the target language, the narcissistic gratification is absent, a fact that can affect their performance. A great number of hearing people prefer to use voice while signing; this is called the simultaneous method of communication, or sign-supported speech (Johnson, Liddell, and Erting 1989, 5). Hearing one's own voice while signing may restore to some extent the narcissistic gratification or perhaps simply promote personal comfort. According to Baker (1978, 13–36), if a person refrains from using voice, the quality of signing improves. In addition, research has shown that simultaneous signing and speaking can be overwhelming for many people (Johnson, Liddell, and Erting 1989, 5). Some people are unconvinced that their signing ability is greater while not using voice because they cannot "hear" their own signs. Sign-supported speech may create the perception of clear communication.

Another issue related to language shock is what Schumann termed infantile characteristics. If adults preserve these particular characteristics, their chance of acquiring a second language is enhanced. Children are adept at acquiring second languages because they do not fear making errors. If adults are encouraged to make errors while experimenting with the newly learned second language, the chance of acquisition is further enhanced. For a variety of reasons, adults tend to feel incompetent while using the target language. If hearing adults are uncomfortable using ASL because of the lack of narcissistic gratification and/or infantile characteristics, are they more inclined to use voice while signing? Could it be that using voice while signing is their way of overcoming the sense of appearing comical? If they were greater risk takers, like children, would they have a better chance of acquiring ASL? With that in mind, ASL teachers should be aware of the fact that allowing their ASL students to make mistakes in the classroom is acceptable as long as they are corrected in due time and tactfully. Allowing errors to occur can be an effective way of facilitating second-language acquisition.

Culture Shock

Culture shock occurs when a second-language learner experiences anxiety due to disorientation when entering a new culture (Schumann 1986, 383). A person can be overly dependent on others if he or she feels limited in second-language skills. Headaches, depression, and/or illnesses are symptoms of culture shock. If an adult learner is unable to cope with these symptoms, the chance of acquiring a second language is minimized. A case in point: Hearing ASL learners have encountered culture shock after they completed a class and finally met Deaf people. They tend to find themselves signing and trying to maintain eye contact at the same time. At times their eye gaze will move away from the receiver while they sign. In addition, the hearing people may find it odd to observe that the Deaf people stare at them while communicating. This is only one example that might easily cause hearing ASL learners to experience culture shock.

Motivation

There are two types of motivation for learning a second language: instrumental and integrative (Schumann 1986, 383). Being instrumentally motivated means that a person must acquire a second language in order to keep a job or get a promotion of some kind. They make an attempt to reach the minimum level required for the job. In short, they "learn" and use the target language from 8 AM to 5 PM. The chances of mastering a language for instrumentally motivated people are, at best, minimal.

Those who are motivated to integrate with the target-language user group tend to learn the language inside and outside the classroom. They mainly want to socialize with the target-language user group. For example, a hearing neighbor may want to learn ASL in order to interact with a Deaf family in the neighborhood.

Ego-Permeability

Ego-permeability deals with a person's ability to be flexible and receptive to new concepts, ideas, and changes (Schumann 1986, 384). This is also related to inhibition and is probably one of the most frustrating factors that retards acquisition of a target language. If the inhibition level can be lowered, then ego-rigidity will also be lowered and ego-permeability will be enhanced. Once enhanced, the second-language learner will have the opportunity to practice the target language without the fear of making mistakes or being intimidated by the target-language group. This appears to support the "infantile characteristics" viewpoint.

To conclude, there are factors that can influence a person's ability to acquire a second language. One must keep in mind that no one variable is the determining factor; several factors can overlap each other, thus assisting the process of acquiring a second language. We must emphasize that teaching methods and/or approaches, learning styles, age, tolerance for ambiguity and rejection, and so on are essential in addition to the acculturation variables. ASL teachers have encountered a number of students who are tenacious in trying to acquire ASL as a second language. We must look at those successful ASL students and determine what characteristics they have that could assist weaker students. Once we identify those factors, we should make every effort to assist the weak students in realizing what they need to acquire the target language, which in this case is ASL.

ACTIVITIES TO HELP FACILITATE
THE ACCULTURATION PROCESS

We will discuss the acculturation model as it applies to classroom use. I must emphasize that this is a new concept in ASL pedagogy, and one should bear in mind that Schumann's acculturation model is not the final word at this point. Further research is needed to examine the success of the suggestions that we discuss.

In order to discuss the application, I will group the factors into two categories based on class levels. My own experience indicates that not all the factors can be applied at one level.

Category 1: For Beginning and Intermediate Learners of ASL

This category is designed for students who enter an ASL program with few or no ASL skills. This means that there may be external forces that will influence students' preconceived ideas about Deaf people and the language they use. In addition, one must assume that the students in question will be subject to surprises and, at times, shock. They are probably under the impression that it is very easy to learn ASL (Jacobs 1996, 183).

SOCIAL DOMINANCE

The teacher can assign readings from *Movers and Shakers* by Cathryn Carroll and Susan Mather (1997). *Movers and Shakers* provides information on Deaf people who have made a difference in other people's lives. The book's target population is Deaf students, but I believe that the book can be used in a variety of settings, including ASL classes. For students who may possess feelings of superiority toward Deaf people, this book provides the opportunity to see that Deaf people can and do make a difference in other people's lives. For students who may manifest feelings of inferiority toward Deaf people, the teacher may want to consider inviting several members from the Deaf community to the class. Keeping in mind that diversity is the trend, the teacher should invite Deaf people from different ethnic backgrounds. Because ASL classes are taken by people from various walks of life, it would be helpful if the students are exposed to all types of Deaf people. This will help remove the stereotypes that the hearing students may have about Deaf people. Of course, the teacher must inform the invited guest speakers that they will be talking with very new ASL users. This means that the guest speakers should refrain from using colloquial signs to avoid intimidating the learners of ASL. In other words, the teacher should direct the invited speakers to talk about certain items that were taught in lessons prior to the day the guests visit the class.

ATTITUDE

Attitude is difficult to measure. However, the teacher can at least distribute literature regarding attitude toward Deaf people to the learners of ASL and let them digest the information at their own pace. There is little literature on attitude and Deaf people, but there are a few topics that I believe would help, for example, Betty Miller's paintings on the oppression of Deaf people by hearing people, the history of the 1880 Milan Conference, and Alexander Graham Bell's writings about passing a law to prohibit marriage among Deaf people (Lane, Hoffmeister, and Bahan 1996, 379–407). This may not affect the attitude of the ASL learners, but at least they will learn that there are such sentiments toward Deaf people and their language. In reference to the antihearing sentiments held by a few Deaf people, *Movers and Shakers* furnishes stories about Deaf heroes who helped hearing people. This literature can leave an impression that not all Deaf people have adverse feelings for their hearing counterparts. Hearing people have been encouraged to learn ASL so that they can communicate with Deaf people. However, there is sometimes an invisible line in the Deaf community (Kemp 1992, 77–79) beyond which hearing people may feel not welcomed and accepted. The recently published *Journey into the Deaf-World* provides information pertinent to the feelings of rejection experienced by learners of ASL:

> Sometimes hearing people who are genuinely interested in the DEAF-WORLD and desire to participate in it feel that they are not accepted. In the same way, for example, American expatriates might feel they are not totally accepted in France. But it is not true that hearing people are unwelcome among the Deaf. It's just that Deaf people, like all people, have a need for being, at least part of the time, with others who share the same language and culture, values and concerns. In this regard, the DEAF-WORLD might be likened to a revolving door that spins at its own rate. If you are able to walk in and keep up the pace and, more importantly, are committed to staying the course, then you are more than welcome. Most hearing people, however, only want to go around once or twice and then exit, back to their own circle of friends. The impression that hearing people have—that the door is spinning too fast

for them to join in—is partially accurate, for when Deaf people use their own language among themselves, they use it at their pace. When they behave differently from hearing people, they are following customs of the DEAF-WORLD. The DEAF-WORLD has its own rate of spinning; it may slow down now and then, here and there, for some "outsiders," but when it returns to speed, it is the newcomer's responsibility to keep up. In this respect, is it really any different from any other culture? (Lane, Hoffmeister, and Bahan 1996, 6–7)

In addition, ASL teachers can explain the two views of being deaf: clinical/pathological and cultural (Baker and Cokely 1980, 54; Lane, Hoffmeister, and Bahan 1996, 35) with an emphasis on the latter view.

CONGRUENCE

In "Just How Hard Is It to Learn ASL?" Rhonda Jacobs presented a case for the target language to be considered a truly foreign language (Jacobs 1996, 183–226). She asserted that ASL is very different from English. This supports the congruence argument. Since English is an aurally oriented language, it can be very difficult for ASL learners to switch from the use of their ears and voice to the use of their eyes and hands to communicate. This requires constant eye contact while communicating in ASL. Hearing learners of ASL have found it intimidating when they see a Deaf person constantly looking at them while communicating (personal conversation with my former students). Visual training exercises, such as Mirror Game, Rubber Face, Who's the Leader, and so on (Smith, Lentz, and Mikos 1988, 8), provided by ASL teachers, can help ASL learners to overcome this challenge. These exercises allow learners of ASL to train their eyes on the other person while communication is taking place. What is more, the use of nonmanual signals (Bridges and Metzger 1996) is essential while communicating in ASL. From my experience as a teacher, I have found that the learners of ASL experience discomfort when using these unique grammatical features. The Rubber Game found in *Signing Naturally: Teacher's Curriculum Guide, Level One* (Smith, Lentz, and Mikos 1988) is an activity that helps students learn to use their facial muscles. Hearing learners may be startled when a person taps their shoulder to get their attention (personal observations), and it can be intimidating or misinterpreted as harassment. Information pertaining to Deaf cultural behavior, values, and norms—such as how to get attention, handle interruptions, give listener feedback (back-channeling), and open and close conversation—can be discussed in class via the use of a videotape accompanying the *Signing Naturally* book.

Category 2: For Intermediate and Advanced Learners of ASL

Intermediate and advanced learners of ASL, after taking the lower-level ASL classes, can benefit by participating in the exercises or discussions listed below.

INTEGRATION STRATEGIES

Except for a very few cases, Deaf students from nonsigning backgrounds and/or mainstreamed programs can either assimilate or adapt quickly. One of the most effective ways to do this, based on my experience, is for a student to become friends with an individual Deaf person. This way the Deaf person can introduce the hearing student to his or her other Deaf friends. I once gave this advice to one of my former students. Very much to my surprise, he joined a fraternity that consisted of native users of ASL. When I entered Gallaudet in 1967 and first learned ASL, I became romantically involved with a Deaf woman, which resulted in a rather quick acculturation process for me because I became acquainted with her friends and their friends.

As for hearing learners of ASL, the ASL teacher must caution them to become aware of the invisible line that may exist in the Deaf community, as discussed earlier. The best approach to addressing this issue is to hold classroom discussions.

It must be stressed here that integration strategies are more of a personal matter. No one can possibly teach anyone what to do with their own culture and how to enter another culture. Being aware of these strategies can, at least, assist the learners in trying to negotiate their way into a new culture.

COHESIVENESS

As we have discussed, the larger the group is, the greater the number of intergroups that will be formed. Setting up "silent dinners" can be an effective way to help ASL learners. Silent dinners are sponsored by various programs that offer ASL classes. Arrangements are made with a local restaurant where people can gather and have dinner with members of the Deaf community. Both hearing and Deaf people are assigned to tables. The waiters are informed in advance of the event and, in most cases, are very cooperative. No voices are used, and gestures are generally utilized when communicating with the waiters. If such dinners are to take place, careful planning is essential. The hearing learners of ASL should be grouped with Deaf ASL users in such a way as to have no intergroupings. One possible way to do this would be to assign three hearing learners and two Deaf users of ASL to each table. This type of seating arrangement can provide the ASL learners a chance to interact with members of the Deaf community. Previous visual training (e.g., eye tag) is actually put to use when talking with a group of Deaf people.

INTENDED LENGTH OF RESIDENCE

No one can force another person to stay with the new culture. With that in mind, we need to give some incentives in order to encourage further participation. A program could give substantial discounts to students who want to take advanced ASL classes or purchase advanced ASL books. Certificates could be awarded not at the end of each class but after taking three or four classes. This gives the student a sense of accomplishment after an extended period of time. These are attractive incentives, but I believe there is something else that is more significant. It is the quality of a program that can attract and retain students for as long as it takes to master ASL.

Quality is essential to the survival of a program. Good impressions must be made upon all students who sign up for classes. The program personnel must keep in mind that they are dealing with customers, and their jobs depend on them. If genuine concern is demonstrated to the students, regardless of their ability to acquire ASL as a second language, they may remain with the program and be more motivated to reach the desired level of competence. This, in effect, may prolong the learners' residence.

EGO-PERMEABILITY

Ego-permeability is a difficult factor for teachers to deal with as they help students undergo the acculturation process. Social settings at the end of the course can possibly help students reduce ego-rigidity. Organizing potluck dinners or serving cookies during breaks may psychologically assist the students by putting them in a relaxed state. In relation to infantile characteristics, the teacher can encourage students to risk making mistakes while learning the target language. Discussing inhibitions with students can give them insights about their learning.

MOTIVATION

We cannot teach people how to be motivated or to tell them to pick a certain type of motivation. However, it is possible to ask students why they want to learn ASL. From my experience, reasons range from wanting to improve ASL skills to wanting to become friends with a Deaf coworker. The teacher can group all the reasons for learning ASL into two categories: integrative and instrumental. Once this is accomplished, then the teacher can explain the meaning of these two types of motivation and the implications involved, as discussed in Schumann's paper. It is up to the students to digest this information and to figure out where they stand in terms of motivation for learning ASL.

LANGUAGE SHOCK

Helping students overcome language shock depends on the teacher's personality. ASL students tend to experience discomfort or a sense of looking ridiculous when practicing the language. The teacher must encourage the students to feel good about themselves when communicating in ASL. This can be accomplished by praising more and correcting less. The teacher should also allow the students' peers to correct errors. This is often less intimidating than being corrected by the teacher.

ENCLOSURE

If the learners of ASL share common interests with the ASL users group, then the acquisition process is enhanced. Silent dinners on a regular basis can serve as a catalyst for promoting enclosure between the two groups. It would be helpful for the participants to go through a group-process activity to discover any common interests they may have. For example, the entire party could form dinner-table groups based on who likes sports, literature, sewing, and so forth. These groups could then break up into subgroups (for example, the sports group could be divided into fishing, biking, and baseball), whose participants could share interests.

CULTURE SHOCK

The students can be made aware of culture shock through classroom discussions. Schumann's paper on an acculturation model talks, in part, about culture shock. The teacher can explain to the class about the symptoms of culture shock, such as crying for no reason, headaches, upset stomach, depression, and anxiety attacks. A classroom discussion on the experience of joining a new group—such as when entering college or taking a new job—may help affected students deal with their symptoms. The teacher can ask the students what they were feeling while experiencing something very new.

CONCLUSION

Schumann's Acculturation Model for Learners of ASL should be used as a guide for ASL teachers when teaching the target language. As previously mentioned, Schumann's paper is not the final word. There is a need for research to determine which activities may work and which activities may need to be improved. What we really need is to recognize factors that enhance the acquisition process for strong learners of ASL. This in turn will enable the professionals in the field of ASL pedagogy to furnish such information to other students who are in dire need of assistance in mastering the language.

REFERENCES

Alptekin, C. 1983. Target language acquisition through acculturation: EFL learners in the English speaking environment. *Canadian Modern Language Review* 39(4):818–26.

Baer, A. 1997. Personal communication.

Baker, C. 1978. How does "sim-com" fit into a bilingual approach to education? In *American Sign Language in a bilingual, bicultural context,* ed. F. Caccamise and D. Hicks, 13–36. Silver Spring, Md.: National Association of the Deaf.

Baker, C., and D. Cokely. 1980. *American Sign Language: A teacher's resource text on grammar and culture.* Washington, D.C.: Gallaudet University Press.

Blair, R. W. 1982. A search (1950–1981). In *Innovation approaches to language teaching,* ed. R. W. Blair, 7–8. Rowley, Mass.: Newbury House Publishers.

Bowers, C. A., and D. J. Flinders. 1991. *Culturally responsive teaching and supervision: A handbook for staff development.* New York: Teacher's College Press.

Bridges, B., and M. Metzger. 1996. *DEAF TEND YOUR: Non-manual signals in ASL*. Silver Spring, Md.: Calliope Press.

Carroll, C., and S. Mather. 1997. *Movers and shakers: Deaf people who changed the world*. San Diego: DawnSignPress.

Gingras, R. C. 1978. An introduction. In *Second language acquisition and foreign language teaching*, ed. R. C. Gingras, vii–viii. Washington, D.C.: Center for Applied Linguistics.

Guiora, A., B. Beit-Hallahmi, R. Dull, and T. Scovel. 1972. The effects of experimentally induced changes in ego states on pronunciation ability in a second language: An exploratory study. *Comprehensive Psychiatry*, vol. 13. (As explained in Schumann 1978, 27–50).

Jacobs, R. 1996. Just how hard is it to learn ASL? The case for ASL as a truly foreign language. In *Multicultural aspects of sociolinguistics in Deaf communities*, ed. Ceil Lucas, 183–226. Washington, D.C.: Gallaudet University Press.

Johnson, R., S. Liddell, and E. Erting. 1989. *Unlocking the curriculum: Principles for achieving access in Deaf education*. Working Paper 89. Washington, D.C.: Gallaudet Research Institute.

Kemp, M. 1992. Invisible line in the Deaf community. In *Viewpoints on Deafness*, a *Deaf American* Monograph, vol. 42:77–79. Silver Spring, Md.: National Association of the Deaf.

Lane, H., R. Hoffmeister, and B. Bahan. 1996. *A journey into the Deaf-world*. San Diego: DawnSignPress.

Larsen-Freeman, D., and M. H. Long. 1991. *An introduction to second language acquisition research*. London: Longman.

Lucas, C. and C. Valli. 1992. *Language contact in the American Deaf Community*. San Diego: Academic Press.

Maple, R. F. 1982. Social distance and the acquisition of English as a second language: A study of Spanish-speaking adult learners. Ph.D. diss. University of Texas at Austin.

McLaughlin, B. 1987. *Theories of second language learning*. London: Edward Arnold.

Schumann, J. 1978. The acculturation model for second-language acquisition. In *Second language acquisition and foreign language teaching*, ed. R. C. Gingras, 27–50. Washington, D.C.: Center for Applied Linguistics.

———. 1986. Research on the acculturation model for second language acquisition. *Journal of Multilingual and Multicultural Development* 7(5):379–92.

Smith, C., E. Lentz, and K. Mikos. 1988. *Signing naturally: Teacher's curriculum guide, Level 1*. San Diego: DawnSignPress.

Valli, C., and C. Lucas. 1995. *Linguistics of American Sign Language: An Introduction*. 2d ed. Washington, D.C.: Gallaudet University Press.

Part 6 Language Attitudes

Irish Sign Language:

Ireland's Second Minority Language

Sarah E. Burns

Irish Sign Language (ISL) is the native language of the Irish Deaf community. It is the third indigenous language in Ireland after Irish and English. Over the years, it has been suppressed and subjugated—much like the Irish language—and its use has been forbidden in the schools for Deaf people. More recently, inspired by the Deaf Pride movement in the United States and by the improving status of the Irish language, the Deaf community is demanding that ISL be recognized and used as the medium of education for Deaf children. This paper explores aspects of the Irish Deaf community and its sign language and draws comparisons with the situation of the Irish language in Ireland.

The Republic of Ireland is situated on an island located at the edge of western Europe. The country is made up of the twenty-six counties in the southern part of the island and has a population of approximately 3.5 million people. Ireland has two official languages: Irish, which is recognized as the national and first official language in the constitution of 1937, Bunreacht na hÉireann, and English, which is the second official language. Despite the fact that Irish has official status, it is a minority language in terms of its size and use and, like many other minority languages, has a complex and checkered history.

My sincere thanks to the members of the Dublin and Wicklow Deaf communities; Dr. J. Kallen, Trinity College Dublin; and Dr. C. Lucas, Gallaudet University, Washington, D.C.—all of whom have provided me with unending support and encouragement. Thank you.

This paper will appear in *Visions '97,* a collection of graduate student papers, Department of ASL, Linguistics and Interpretation, Gallaudet University, Washington, D.C. It is based on research carried out for a Master of Science thesis at the Department of Clinical Speech and Language Studies, Trinity College Dublin, 1993–1995, under the supervision of Dr. J. L. Kallen.

Up until the beginning of the seventeenth century, Irish was the main medium of spoken communication used throughout Ireland. A process of decline in the language then began, however, which can be attributed to a number of factors, including the English system of land tenure established during the Tudor reign (1485–1603), which resulted in a considerable body of English- and Scots-speaking foreigners coming to settle on Irish soil, and the Great Famine (1845–1851), when over two million Irish speakers were lost through death or emigration. Gradually, Irish became associated with poverty, isolation, and backwardness. It became a symbol of all that was poor and underdeveloped in Irish society, whereas English was the language of power and status. By the time the Irish Free State was established in 1922, a massive shift to English had occurred, and the remaining Irish speakers formed only 19 percent of the population. The new government undertook the responsibility for the restoration of the Irish language (ÓRiagáin 1988). A broad three-pronged strategy was implemented that remains, in essence, the framework of language policy in Ireland today. Its aims were:

1. to maintain Irish as the spoken language in areas where it was still used;
2. to have educational programs taught through Irish; and
3. to provide the necessary infrastructure or context for maintenance and revival efforts.

To date, the ultimate aim of the Irish language revival movement and government policy has not been achieved. Irish has not been successfully maintained in the Irish-speaking areas, although there are some remaining districts (officially known as the Gaeltacht) where it is used in daily communication. Elsewhere it is estimated that only 5–10 percent of the population frequently use it. In the early 1970s, it was suggested that a diglossic situation, with Irish being used in certain domains, would be a more realistic intermediary step on the road to bilingualism (Comhairle na Gaeilge 1974; ÓMurchú 1970). However, today Irish still does not command any particular domain of language use. Nevertheless, comparing the situation with that of 100 years ago, there have been substantial achievements. Since the 1920s, the number of Irish speakers in the Republic, as recorded by the census, has been rising continuously (Fennell

1981). The considerable corpus of survey data on public attitudes toward Irish and Irish-language policies, gathered since the 1960s, indicates that the majority of Irish people want a bilingual situation in Ireland. Support for a displacement policy has remained low, never rising above 20 percent, over the period when the studies were carried out (CLAR 1975; Irish National Teachers Organisation 1985a, b; ÓRiagáin and ÓGliasáin 1984, 1994). Most success has been in the area of language status and prestige. Undoubtedly, Irish is now perceived in a more positive light. More recently, the growth in the number of Irish-medium schools in English-speaking areas and the establishment of Teilifís na Gaeilge, the Irish-medium television station, in particular, have offered hope for the maintenance of the language.

IRISH SIGN LANGUAGE

The situation of Irish has been well documented. There exists a second minority language in Ireland, however, whose situation a much smaller group is aware of. Irish Sign Language (ISL) is the native language of the Irish Deaf community, made up of an estimated 3,526 members (Matthews 1996). ISL is also used by some of the Deaf community in Northern Ireland. Like Irish, ISL has been particularly suppressed over the years. It can be noted for its small number of users, its poor status compared to the spoken languages used in Ireland, and its lack of recognition, both by society at large and the Irish government. Ignorance about the language prevails, and naive statements regarding it and its community of users can be found in the literature. Examples include the following statements by Griffey (the former director of the only diploma course for teachers of Deaf children in the Republic) and the Irish Department of Education:

Sign language is quite dependent on concrete situations and mime. Its informative power can be very limited without knowledge of a majority language such as English, French, etc. (Griffey 1994, 28)

A manual world is a silent one. It causes social isolation. (Griffey 1982, 257)

Oral communication enables the Deaf child to take his place in the hearing world which is richer in cultural, social and economic experiences and opportunities than the silent and restricted world of the deaf. (Department of Education 1972, 66–67)

The language has suffered from a paucity of linguistic and sociolinguistic research, and there is little published information available. Compared to the study of American Sign Language, for example, which began over thirty years ago, research into ISL is in its infancy, any serious work having begun only in the last five to ten years.

This paper aims to examine the sociolinguistic position of ISL and explore its use by the Irish Deaf community in the wider society and in education. Similarities and differences between Irish and ISL will be discussed along with implications for the maintenance of both languages. The information presented is largely based on interviews of thirty Deaf people from the Dublin Deaf community in 1994. Each interview followed a similar format, although, in an effort to elicit as much spontaneous information as possible, a rigid structure was not imposed, and interviewees were free to digress. Information on the interviewees' backgrounds, their opinions on signing, the status of ISL, membership of the community, and topics such as education, employment, and the media were gathered. The data were recorded in note form. Neither visual nor audio recording equipment was used, again in an effort to limit the effects of "observer's presence" (Labov 1972). Seven of the interviews were conducted through speech alone or a combination of speech and sign. The remainder were conducted through ISL or contact signing. The mode of communication used was the interviewees' choice. Sign language was translated into written English by the interviewer. The interviewees varied in age, educational background, level of hearing loss, and so on. All of these factors are likely to have had an effect on the attitudes and opinions elicited. An individual with a partial hearing loss may, for example, be more strongly in favor of oral methods of education for Deaf children than someone who is profoundly deaf. For this reason, a table detailing background information on each interviewee is provided. In order to protect the identity of the interviewees, they have been allocated fictitious names and, where necessary, the names of places and institutions have been changed.

Introduction of Sign Language to Ireland

In 1846, two Dominican sisters, Sr. Mary Magdalen O'Farrell and Sr. Mary Vincent Martin, and two Deaf students traveled from Ireland to

France to study teaching techniques used there by Catholic educators of Deaf people. After a period of training at Le Bon Saveur school in Caen, Normandy, they returned with a dictionary of French signs and books on teaching the French language to Deaf children. The dictionary had been compiled by the Abbé Sicard, a student of and later the successor to the Abbé de l'Epée, who established the first school for Deaf people in Paris. The sign system that the sisters introduced to Ireland was a mixture of indigenous French Sign Language combined with additional pedagogical signs initially devised by the Abbé de l'Epée in the late 1700s. The sisters, with the assistance of an Irish Vincentian priest, Father John Burke, then adapted the system to suit the English language. Father Burke is said to have translated the French signs into signs that could more accurately express the English language (Griffey 1989, 1994; Le Master and Foran 1987).

In August 1846, St. Mary's School for Deaf Girls was founded by the Dominican sisters. Ten years later, in 1856, a school for Deaf boys, St. Joseph's, was established by the Christian Brothers. The two schools were located within a short distance of each other at Cabra in Dublin, and both adopted the French system of signs. From the time the schools were established to approximately 1946 at the girls' school and approximately 1956 at the boys' school, all pupils were educated using this manual system. The change to oral methods of education then took place, and signing at school was no longer permitted.

Prior to 1846, there are few records of a sign system in use by Deaf people in Ireland. The Dominican Sisters are accredited with having introduced sign language to the country, and the Cabra schools were the first established "Deaf" communities where this language was used. Over the years, it has evolved and changed into the sign language used today by the Irish Deaf community. It seems likely, however, that an indigenous sign system (or other systems) may have been used before this date, particularly where groups of Deaf people came together. There were only a few schools for Deaf people in existence prior to those at Cabra (Matthews 1996). The Claremont school, for example, established in 1816 by Dr. Charles Orpen for Protestant children, "adopted the British system and imposed strict Protestant ethos" (C. Foran 1995). The school remained open until 1971. Some elderly Protestant Deaf people in Ireland continued to use the British two-handed alphabet until relatively recently (personal communication, Barr 1995). Many questions remain unanswered about the origins of ISL and about change that has taken place over the years.

TABLE 1. *Characteristics of Interviewees*

Name	Sex	Age Range	Level of Hearing Loss	Age Acquired Deafness	Deaf Family Members	Age Learned Sign	Where Learned Sign	Member Deaf Community	Marital Status	Deaf or Hearing Spouse	School Attended	Interview Mode
Fiona	Female	40–50	Profound	Birth	Sibling	18 years	Deaf community	Yes	Married	Deaf	Hearing P Oral S	Sign
Paul	Male	20–30	Profound	Birth	None	3 years	School	Yes	Single	—	Oral	Sign
Neil	Male	30–40	Severe/ Profound	Birth	None	7 years	School	Yes	Married	H	Oral	Sign
Aaron	Male	30–40	Profound	Birth	Sibling	11 years	School	Yes	Single	—	Oral	Sign
Michael	Male	60–70+	Profound	18 months	Sibling	7 years	School	Yes	Married	Deaf	Manual	Sign
Craig	Male	60–70+	Profound	3 years	None	5 years	School	Yes	Single	—	Manual	Sign
David	Male	40–50	Profound	Birth	Parents/ siblings	Infancy	Home	Yes	Married	Deaf	Oral	Sign
Joseph	Male	20–30	Partial	Birth	Sibling	4+ years	School	Yes	Single	—	Oral	Speech/ sign
Eoin	Male	20–30	Partial	Birth	Parent/ siblings	4+ years	School	No	Single	—	Oral	Speech
Stephen	Male	20–30	Partial	Birth	None	11 years	School	Yes	Single	—	Oral	Speech
Philip	Male	30–40	Profound	4 years	None	4+ years	School	Yes	Married	Deaf	Oral	Sign
Laura	Female	40–50	Profound	Birth	Sibling	4+ years	School/ Deaf adults	Yes	Married	Deaf	Oral	Sign
Emma	Female	30–40	Partial	Birth	None	14 years	School/ Deaf adults	Yes	Married	Deaf	Hearing P Oral S	Speech/ sign

Name	Sex	Age	Deafness	Onset	Deaf family	Age sign learnt	Where learnt		Marital	Partner	Education	Communication
Hilary	Female	30–40	Profound	Birth	None	4+ years	School	Yes	Married	Deaf	Oral	Sign/speech
Richard	Male	50–60	Profound	3 months	None	6 years	School	Yes	Married	Deaf	Manual	Sign
Anne	Female	40–50	Profound	Birth	None	14 years	School	Yes	Married	Deaf	Oral	Sign
Carol	Female	20–30	Profound	Birth	Siblings	Infancy	Home	Yes	Single	—	Oral	Sign
Eve	Female	30–40	Profound	Birth	Sibling	18 years	School/Deaf adults	Yes	Married	Deaf	Oral	Sign
Iva	Female	20–30	Profound	Birth	None	4+ years	School	Yes	Single	—	Oral	Sign
James	Male	20–30	Profound	Birth	Sibling	4+ years	School	Yes	Single	—	Oral	Sign
Kevin	Male	50–60	Profound	Birth	Parents/siblings	Infancy	Home	Yes	Married	Deaf	Manual	Sign
Tina	Female	20–30	Profound	Birth	None	4+ years	School	Yes	Single	—	Oral	Sign
Gary	Male	50–60	Profound	5 years	None	9 years	School	Yes	Single	—	Manual	Sign
John	Male	50–60	Profound	9 years	None	9 years	School	Yes	Married	Deaf	Manual	Sign/speech
Mary	Female	50–60	Profound	Birth	Siblings	3 years	School	Yes	Married	Deaf	Manual/oral	Sign
Eric	Male	50–60	Profound	Birth	None	7 years	School/Deaf adults	Yes	Married	Deaf	Manual	Sign
Ian	Male	20–30	Severe/Profound	Birth	None	20 years	Sign classes	No	Single	—	Hearing	Speech
Bill	Male	50–60	Profound	Birth	Sibling	10 years	School	Yes	Single	—	Oral	Sign
Adam	Male	60–70+	Profound	Birth	None	7 years	School	Yes	Single	—	Manual	Sign
Luke	Male	30–40	Profound	1.5 years	None	3 years	School	Yes	Single	—	Oral	Sign

P = primary school
S = second level

What Is ISL?

Like all other sign languages, ISL is a visual-gestural system of communication. It is produced by the movement of the upper body and uses the medium of space rather than sound. It is an autonomous, fully functional language. It shares with other sign languages many of the features that linguists have used to define languages as such. It has a rule-governed structure that can be used to represent novel information and create any number of new sentences. Although there are many similarities between the structure and sociolinguistic situation of ISL and other natural sign languages, there are also some differences. In particular, the sociolinguistic environment in which ISL has developed is very different from that of any other sign language and is distinctive to Ireland.

As we have already stated, research into ISL has been extremely limited to date. This situation has recently been improving, and a number of individual studies of the language have been carried out. These include Conway and Veale (1994), Le Master (1990), Maguire (1991, 1993), McDonnell (1983, 1992, 1993), McDonnell and Saunders (1993), and O'Reilly (1993). The most significant research yet carried out has been that of the ISL National Survey and Research Project headed by Matthews and co-funded by the European Social Fund and Institiúid Teangeolaíochta Éireann (the Linguistics Institute of Ireland). Published in two volumes (Matthews 1996 and forthcoming), the work focuses on both the sociolinguistic situation of the language as well as the linguistic analysis of its structure.

Up to now, the lack of linguistic research into ISL has meant that awareness of its status as a true language has been limited. This lack of awareness has been evident not only among the hearing population but also among members of the Deaf community itself. Just as Irish people came to associate poverty and "backwardness" with the Irish language in the nineteenth century, many Irish Deaf people have come to perceive ISL negatively. The term *language* has traditionally been equated with the English language, and, therefore, only spoken, written, or signed versions of English were recognized as legitimate expressions of language (Le Master 1990). Of the thirty people interviewed for this study, twenty-three recognized ISL as a true language, four said that they did not know whether it was a language, and three said that it is always better to sign in English word order. (Each informant has been allocated a fictitious name. The preceding table provides details about their backgrounds). Signed versions of English were termed "grammatical signing" as opposed to the "shortcut way." One informant reported, "I feel that if I'm signing to a hearing person in ISL they will think my level of literacy is below their own or that I'm not fully acquainted with full, good English" (John).

It is only relatively recently that members of the Deaf community have begun to accept ISL as a language: "Now I know ISL is a language but before I did not. In the past you were told you were stupid if you were signing in the wrong order, but there is more awareness now" (Anne). This new awareness follows developments in research into other sign languages, particularly ASL and BSL: "A lot of Deaf did not realize ISL was a language until recently. They saw what was happening in other countries, in Britain and America. They saw that BSL is a real language with its own structure and they began to think it could be the same for ISL" (David). It is clear that a great deal of what has been learned about other minority languages, both spoken and signed, is relevant to the situation of ISL and can be used as a guide to research.

The Relationship between ISL
and the Spoken Languages of Ireland

All children in Ireland are required to study the Irish language. Students attending the schools for Deaf people are exempt from this law, however, and as a result few have any knowledge of the language. ISL and English, the language of the hearing majority, on the other hand, exist in close contact and naturally have an impact upon one another. It is likely that all members of the Deaf community in Ireland are bilingual in ISL and English (spoken, signed, and written versions), at least to some degree. There are many Deaf people who are monolingual in English—for example, those who have received a strictly oral education, perhaps at a hearing school, and who have never learned sign language, but they are generally not considered to be members of the Deaf community. It is possible that there are also Deaf people who are monolingual in ISL, but these can be only very few in number as all Deaf children are taught English at school (signed English up to the 1950s and oral English after that date).

As in other Deaf communities around the world, there is a distinction between the natural sign language used in Ireland (ISL) and signed versions of spoken language (Signed English). The term ISL has been used interchangeably within the Irish Deaf community, however, to refer to both signed English and ISL forms (Le Master 1990). The majority of

Deaf people interviewed for this study did not make a clear distinction be-tween the two, and a number pointed out that there is often confusion re-garding this:

> On a course I gave for . . . , a lot of Deaf people did not realize what the difference is between signed English and ISL. Many thought that signed English meant BSL. These are relatively new terms. In the past, we called ISL "Natural Deaf Sign." (Richard)

> It depends what you mean by signed English. I don't like that term. It is sometimes confused with BSL. I prefer "Manually Coded English." (James)

In addition to this, few Deaf people are equally fluent in both languages and may vary along a continuum such as that offered by Kannapell (1980, cited in Kannapell 1993) for the American Deaf community.

> There is not one Deaf person in Ireland who uses 100 percent ISL or 100 percent signed English all the time. (Richard)

> Of course there is a variety of abilities in ISL, just as there are a variety of abilities in a spoken language among hearing people, but I'd say 80 percent of Deaf people understand ISL. (Philip)

All of the Deaf people interviewed for this study claimed to be bilin-gual to some degree. Some were more comfortable with ISL, whereas others were more comfortable with varieties of English. Twenty-five inter-viewees who said they preferred to use "sign" alone with their Deaf friends reported having to switch to spoken or written versions of English when communicating with hearing people at home, at school, or at work. Those who were more comfortable with English said they switch to sign in the company of other Deaf people. All but three of the interviewees also claimed some knowledge of one or more foreign sign languages: Twenty knew BSL, eight knew ASL, seven knew International Sign Language, and one knew Icelandic Sign Language. The majority of the interviewees, then, claimed to be trilingual in ISL, English, and a foreign sign language, at least to some degree.

Diglossia

In the United States, Stokoe (1972) was the first to identify a bilingual-diglossic situation in a Deaf community. He assigned ASL to the L variety and signed versions of English to the H variety. Griffey (1982) has suggested that the same distinction could be made in the Irish system, with ISL, the L form and signed English, the H. The responses of some of those interviewed support this; for example, Richard reported that "What is said about signed English and Natural Sign Language in other countries for formal and informal situations is true in Ireland."

Many of the interviewees associated signed English with typical H functions (e.g., all formal situations, school, university, court, and television broadcasts). ISL, on the other hand, was often associated with informal situations and "relaxed communication" with friends at the Deaf club. Many attributed higher status and prestige to signed English than to ISL, and the former was often identified with higher educational levels.

> If I'm talking off a platform I use sign supported English, but say when I'm working at the training center the level may be lower so I have to change to ISL to suit their level and learning skills. (John)

> The people who use ISL all the time tend to have poor English skills, whereas those who use signed English tend to have more advanced English skills. (Craig)

Not everyone agreed that ISL and signed English should be distinguished in this way, however.

Developments in the meaning of the term *diglossia* and further study of sociolinguistic patterns have given linguists cause to reexamine Stokoe's characterization of signed English as H and ASL as L in a diglossic relationship (Hawking 1983; Lee 1982; Lucas and Valli 1989, 1992). Similarly, the responses of many of the Deaf people interviewed for this study did not fit this delineation of a diglossic relationship. A number of those interviewed believed that ISL could be used in any situation. One of the interviewees pointed out that ISL is actually used in formal situations and that both signed English and ISL interpreters are often provided at conferences and meetings. Many in fact said they would prefer ISL for all functions.

> ISL is always better in every situation. (Paul)

> For me ISL is always better, signed English is too laborious. (Luke)

One young Deaf man suggested that within ISL itself, there may be both H and L forms—"In the past I thought signed English was for formal situations and ISL for informal, but now I believe that ISL itself can be formal or informal" (James).

The distinction between ISL and signed English is not always clear-cut. The two languages are in close contact and, when any two languages are in contact, spoken or signed, they may borrow from each other; otherwise, mixed, intermediate varieties that share features of both may develop. It is likely that a signing continuum with ISL and signed English at either end exists in the Irish community, similar to those reported in other Deaf communities. People who claim to use "pure" signed English may use features of ISL at times. Referring to the manual English environment in the schools for Deaf people prior to the 1950s, Griffey (1982), for example, admits that the teachers sometimes relied on what she terms "the low version" when they wanted to convey a message quickly. Others who claim to use "pure" ISL may use English for new terminology or to express a concept for which there is no ISL sign.

> I find it difficult to express myself through signed English and I find it difficult to follow interpreters using it. Of course, when it comes to new terminology, for example, for computers, it is necessary to spell out English words. (David)

Signers regularly make decisions about the most appropriate variety of signing to use. From along a continuum, they make choices based on a number of factors such as topic, purpose, and participants. They will take into account whether their partner in conversation is Deaf or hearing. Six people who were interviewed said that signed English was appropriate for use with hearing people (one included those who are hard of hearing or had been deafened), whereas ISL was for use only with other Deaf people.

> Signed English is for when hearing are there. When the Deaf are amongst the Deaf, they use ISL. Of course it depends on the hearing person, for example there are hearing interpreters who know ISL. (Emma)

Perhaps peculiar to the Irish situation, they will also consider the age of the Deaf person. Four of the interviewees identified signed English with older Deaf people and ISL with young people—"There are two generations. The older people are strong believers in signed English. Younger people like myself prefer ISL" (Eve). Those who were educated by manual methods and were at school prior to the proscription of sign are more likely to be comfortable with signed English. Finally, they may take into account both their own attitudes and those of the person they are conversing with regarding their language choice: "It really depends on attitudes . . . signed English is used by people who believe it is better than ISL . . . but ISL is more than just a language, it's part of Deaf culture and identity" (James). It is likely that those who want to make a statement about their Deaf identity choose ISL.

Variation in ISL

Variation is a feature of all languages, and ISL is no exception. Variation was reported by a number of interviewees. Variants seemed to relate mainly to age and educational background, but interviewees also mentioned other factors such as gender and foreign influences.

AGE AND EDUCATIONAL BACKGROUND

When I left school I could understand Deaf of all ages but now I find it difficult to understand the younger Deaf. (Eric)

In the past everybody used the same signs but now because the boys and girls are not allowed to use sign, it means there is a lot of variation. (Adam)

Many of the older Deaf people interviewed who had been educated by manual methods complained that they have great difficulty understanding the signs of younger Deaf people. One man said he sometimes resorts to writing to communicate with younger Deaf people. The change to oralism and the proscription of sign language at St. Mary's in 1946 and St. Joseph's in 1956 led to the development of self-devised gestures among the children (Griffey 1989). Many of these signs have found their way into the adult Deaf community. Without the standardizing effect of sign taught at school, a great deal of diversity has developed.

If they taught sign language at school the teachers could correct the children and keep a standard. (Eric)

GENDER

One of the most interesting features of ISL is that it employs two vocabularies that are commonly identified as "men's language" and "women's language" by its users (Le Master 1987, 1990). Le Master has studied this in detail in her dissertation, "Female and Male Signs in the Dublin Deaf Community." She states that the fact that signers in the Dublin Deaf community have labels for "male" and "female" variation suggests that the variation between male and female signs is greater than the variation within either female signs or male signs. She found that approximately 70 percent of male/female signs were different compared with 8 percent female/female sign variance and 10 percent male/male sign variance. During the 100-year period when sign language was the method of communication employed at the two schools for Deaf children, St. Mary's and St. Joseph's, the pupils rarely had opportunities to interact, although the two schools were not very far apart. The centralization and residentiality of the schools led to great within-gender standardization of signs, whereas the segregation of the schools led to great cross-gender variation. As adults, women were expected to learn the men's signs and then use them with their husbands after marriage. Although women learned the male form of signing, they did not give up their own. The women reserved their female signs for use exclusively with other women (Le Master 1987, 1990; Le Master and Foran 1987). Both Le Master and, more recently, Matthews (1996) report that today gender differentiation is diminishing in the linguistic repertoires of younger signers in the Dublin Deaf community. Instead, there is greater variation within the community as a whole, which was reflected in the responses of the interviewees. None of them mentioned male/female variation; rather, they were more concerned about age differentiation and the effect of language policies in Deaf education.

FOREIGN INFLUENCES

Variation and changes in ISL have often been brought about through contact with other sign languages. French Sign Language, of course, has had the most significant influence on ISL. Today, signs are still in use that are directly derived from the French system, such as the sign for "Friday," which is made with a V handshape (*vendredi*). Later, signs used at St. Joseph's school changed in some cases as a result of contact with schools in the United States (Griffey 1989). More recently, most contact has been made with BSL. Deaf people frequently travel between Britain and Ireland to various sports events and conventions. British television programs for Deaf people, with signers using BSL, are received in Ireland. Many Irish Deaf people who emigrated to Britain in search of employment between the 1950s and 1970s have now returned. All of these factors have resulted in the introduction of some British signs into circulation in the Irish Deaf community (personal communication, Pollard 1994).

Language Planning

Because enormous efforts have gone into restoring the Irish language, language planning is a concept with which the Irish people are very familiar. Most deliberate language-planning efforts in relation to sign language in Ireland have concentrated on corpus planning of signed versions of spoken language. The main impetus for this came from the religious and educational institutions, whose primary objective was to devise methods for teaching Deaf children English. Language-planning efforts in relation to ISL can be divided into three phases, those that took place in the mid-1800s, the 1970s, and the 1990s.

THE MID-1800S

As previously mentioned, the Irish Vincentian priest, Father John Burke, who was said to be fluent in the French language, was given the task of transcribing the documents brought from France by the Dominican Sisters (C. Foran 1994a). In addition, he imposed at least two changes on the borrowed French signs. He modified them so that they could be used to express English rather than French grammar. The signs were also modified to make them more "soft and feminine" for the girls at St. Mary's and more "bold and masculine" for the boys at St. Joseph's (Le Master and Foran 1987). Father Burke's translations are recorded in an unpublished volume that is still in existence today. The volume has recently been transcribed to typed format in order to preserve it and to make it accessible for research (C. Foran 1994b).

THE 1970S

In the late 1970s, a small group of hearing and Deaf people met in order to produce a dictionary that would aid the standardization of signs used within the Irish Deaf community. The Unified Sign Language Committee had at least four main aims:

1. to produce a dictionary of Irish signs that could be used by professionals who work with Deaf people,
2. to make sure that the sign system had all of the signs needed to express every grammatical unit of English,
3. to standardize the vocabulary for use by both men and women,
4. to produce a written record of grammatical signing or signed English for reference.

The committee convened at a time when use of sign had been strictly proscribed at the schools for Deaf children in Ireland. Some people were concerned that Deaf people would forget their grammatical signing and that young people would never learn how to sign "properly." The committee invented new signs for particular English words or grammatical units for which there were apparently no signs available in the old system. In cases where there was more than one sign in use for a given concept, they decided which should be maintained. The majority of signs chosen were male signs. This may have been because signing was used at St. Joseph's for ten years longer than at St. Mary's, and so male signs were dominant in use. Many of the signs were based on the initial letter of the corresponding English word and were usually grouped into classes of related ideas. The signs for the words *busy, do, exercise, practice, serve,* and *work* are identical except for their different handshapes. The work of the committee culminated in the production of *The Irish Sign Language Dictionary* (1979). The dictionary of approximately 2,200 signs became known as "The Blue Book," and its signs are commonly referred to as "new" or "unified" in contrast with the "old" signs used in the schools for Deaf people prior to the introduction of oralism (Griffey 1994; Le Master 1987; Le Master and Foran 1987; personal communication, S. Foran 1994).

THE 1990S

There have been a number of small-scale language-planning efforts in the 1990s. In 1992, the National Association for the Deaf (NAD), in conjunction with the Sign Language Tutors Association of Ireland, published a basic dictionary of approximately 300 signs used by the Irish Deaf community. This dictionary, entitled *Sign On,* was aimed mainly toward hearing people attending sign language classes. There are plans to produce further editions (NAD and SLTAI 1992a, b).

In 1994, a group of Deaf students and sign language interpreters attending a computer-training course in Dublin were experiencing difficulties because of the lack of signs for specialized computer terminology. The students, their teachers, and interpreters met with representatives from the NAD and the Sign Language Association of Ireland (formally known as the Sign Language Tutors Association of Ireland). The most practical signs for certain terms were decided on, and a list of 150 computer words that needed signs were drawn up. A dictionary of these signs was to be published (Coogan 1994) but to date has not been, possibly because of complaints that the signs were "made up" by a panel, reminiscent of "The Blue Book" (personal communication, Leeson 1997).

In the late 1980s, the Irish Deaf Society, in conjunction with Institiúid Teangeolaíochta Éireann (ITÉ), proposed the research program for ISL referred to earlier. Included in this program was a plan to produce a draft of a dictionary, as well as a linguistic and sociolinguistic analysis, of ISL. This was the first and to date the only proposal of language planning in relation to ISL itself, rather than signed versions of spoken English. The project was eventually launched on 7 December 1993 by the ITÉ. The results of the linguistic analysis are forthcoming.

The Success or Failure of Corpus Planning

A high percentage, 83 percent or twenty-five out of thirty, of the Deaf people interviewed for this study felt that ISL should be standardized. Le Master and Foran (1987) note, however, that despite goodwill from the adult Deaf community toward the language-planning efforts of the 1970s, the "reformed language" was not fully absorbed by the community. Similarly, the dictionary *Sign On,* published by the NAD in 1992, has been referred to as a "coloring book" of unemployable signs (IDS 1992). It is difficult to reach agreement on what signs are to be used and what kind of dictionary is to be produced. Many older Deaf people prefer to use the "old" signs they first learned at school and to sign in English word order. Others disagree and prefer ISL.

I would like to see the old signs maintained. Signs like -es, -ion, -ment and -ing are not used so much now. It's a pity because you need good grammar. (Kevin)

I think they should have two dictionaries, one of signed English and the other ISL. They are different languages and should be kept separate. It's up to each individual then to pick which they want to use. (Eve)

Three of the interviewees had reservations about whether ISL should be standardized at all. They stated that variation is natural to sign languages, that it is part of Deaf culture, and that dictionaries actually create more confusion.

You cannot really have a standard. Signs change very quickly, perhaps faster than in spoken languages. It's important to keep the variation. You cannot have a list of correct signs. (Tina)

The Deaf are not interested in a new book of signs, that would just make more signs and more confusion. (Paul)

You can't say the right signs come from a dictionary. You can't impose ISL like that. ISL develops within us and grows up in the younger population and varies with differences in age and background and so on. (Anne)

Although the language planning efforts in relation to ISL have not generally been embraced by the Deaf community, Le Master (1987) suggests that there have been some effects on sign language usage. She states that this is evidenced by the blurring of the link between female and male signs by younger members of the community. Signs previously labeled as "men's" or "women's" signs are now often reclassified as "new" or "unified" signs and are not attributed to either sex. It is likely that as Deaf movements to recognize ISL as a true language gather strength and as research into it continues, there will be increased emphasis on planning and in particular on status planning.

ISL and the Deaf Community

The Deaf community in Ireland is made up of a close-knit group of people who share common goals and meet regularly. Most have a considerable degree of hearing loss, although audiological deafness in itself is not a sufficient condition for membership. Many of the factors that have been identified as significant with regard to membership of Deaf communities in other countries such as Britain or the United States (Kyle et al. 1985; Ladd 1988; Lane, Hoffmeister, and Bahan 1996; Padden and Humphries 1988) are also relevant to the Irish situation.

In a study of the Irish Deaf community, Cradden (1994) concluded that one's identity as a Deaf person is determined primarily by school setting, be it integrated or residential. Schools for Deaf people have traditionally been the sites of socialization into the community. Deaf children in Ireland manage to learn about Deaf culture and acquire ISL at school despite the fact that this is not encouraged by hearing educators. Although twenty-one of the Deaf people who were interviewed for this study had been educated by oral methods and were at school at a time when signing was strictly prohibited, it is significant that eighteen of them said they acquired sign while at school. Two others learned sign from their Deaf parents and siblings, and it is likely that they had a role in passing it on to their peers.

Members of the Irish Deaf community recognize that they belong to a community and have a cultural identity.

> The Deaf have a community, they have their own values, goals, identity, language, and culture. Members identify with this. (Philip)

In addition, they are expected to be involved in community activities. The community in Ireland has numerous formal and informal organizations (e.g., clubs, religious and sports groups, and regional and national associations). The two largest organizations are the National Association for the Deaf (NAD) and the Irish Deaf Society (IDS). These two voluntary bodies provide a range of services for Deaf people and organize various support groups, meetings, and conferences. Most activities and events, however, revolve around the Deaf club. There are many located around the country, the biggest of which is the Dublin Deaf Association with a membership of up to 1,000 (O'Leary 1989). Within the club several groups meet; these include drama group; snooker, table tennis, and bowling teams; youth club; senior citizens group; ladies club; and prayer group. Many Deaf people meet their future partners as a result of socializing within the community, and thus the figures for the number of endogamous marriages are high. The NAD estimates that 95 percent of Deaf people in Ireland marry other Deaf people (personal communication, Keane 1990). This figure matched that of the research carried out for this study—93 percent, or fourteen out of fifteen interviewees who were married, were married to Deaf partners.

It is generally agreed that knowledge of sign language is the primary identifying criterion for membership in a Deaf community. Twenty-nine of the Deaf people interviewed mentioned the importance of this in the Irish community.

> A Deaf person will not be fully accepted if they do not have a good enough level of sign language. Sign language is paramount, if you don't have sign language you will never be accepted. (John)

Partially deaf and hard of hearing people who do not know sign language may not therefore be accepted into the Deaf community although they are audiologically deaf. One informant astutely noted that "the hard of hearing who do not really know sign language are lost in the Deaf club" (David). One young, partially deaf man who said he was not a full member of the Deaf community but who was now learning sign regretted not having learned it at a younger age: "To be a full member ISL has to be your first language and English your second. I wish I had started learning a lot earlier, then I would have been sure of my Deaf identity" (Ian). On the other hand, hearing people who know sign language may be considered members of the community despite their audiological status because sign plays such an important role in dictating membership.

Anyone can be part of the Deaf community, even hearing people, as long as they aspire to being able to communicate with Deaf people in their language and respect the Deaf as a linguistic minority. (Ian)

It is accepted that sign language is the appropriate mode of communication for use at the Deaf club and at events organized by the Deaf community. Some Deaf groups may, however, formally insist on the use of sign. It is the policy of the Dublin Deaf Scout Unit to use sign language, for example, and children who do not want to sign may be asked to leave (Grace 1993). Three of those who were interviewed pointed out that the type of signing used is also important. One profoundly deaf woman who had learned sign after she left school said that she is often mistaken for a hearing person because of her "English-like" signing. In order to be a "true" member, it is necessary to know ISL in addition to signed English. As is the case in other Deaf communities, by choosing to use natural sign language, Irish Deaf people make a statement about their identity and indicate whether they consider themselves members. Through sign they share their daily experiences (McDonnell 1992).

The people who stick to signed English tend to be more isolated and are not really tolerated within the Deaf world. Some others who use signed English are more flexible and change their signing when they are in the company of Deaf who prefer ISL. (Mary)

ISL can express who you are. (Ian)

Sign language shows that you belong to the Deaf world. (Neil)

The Irish Deaf Community in a Changing World

As previously described, the Irish Deaf community is tight-knit, and institutional support is strong. Members meet regularly and participate in various community activities. Some concern has been expressed, however, that the numbers attending Deaf clubs are declining. Tuesdays and Fridays are social evenings at the Dublin Deaf club, but one of the Deaf men interviewed for this study stated that "the Deaf club is like a ghost town on Friday nights" (Aaron).

A report of the annual general meeting of the Dublin Deaf Association (1994) as well as the report of the ISL National Survey and Research Project have also noted the changing social scene. Matthews (1996, 196–97) writes:

> Currently at the largest Deaf club in Drumcondra, Dublin, many Deaf people arrive at the Club, have a look around to meet their friends, and notice that the Club is quiet as most people have gone into the pub next door. So the Deaf person leaves the Club and makes his/her way to the pub next door to join in the conversation and take a drink. And so it emerges . . . that the situation at present leads to Deaf people meeting in smaller groups in pubs in the vicinity of the Deaf club.

Modern technology has had a dramatic effect on the Deaf community. Its focus has been twofold: to provide alternative means of communication and to eliminate the medical condition of deafness. The increased availability of subtitling and closed-captioning of television and video-tapes for home viewing may be one reason that fewer people are attending the Deaf club. Alternative forms of communication such as text telephone (minicom), fax, Minitel, Aertel, and Internet have also become more widely available and reduce the need for face-to-face contact by Deaf people. Hearing-aid technology has developed rapidly over the last twenty years, and cochlear implants now bring the promise of a "cure" for deafness. Implantation is an issue that has been hotly debated by the Irish Deaf community (IDS 1993; O'Sullivan 1994). Up until recently, the surgery was not carried out in Ireland, and those few who had implants traveled to Britain. In 1995 government funding was made available, and an implant center was established at a Dublin hospital. A number of individuals, both children and adults, have now had the surgery.

It is difficult to predict the effect these new technological developments will have on the Deaf community in Ireland, the criteria for membership, and the use of ISL in the future. Certainly, there is potential for serious implications, of which the community is very much aware. At present, however, sign language continues to be the most effective means of communication available to Deaf people, and the Deaf club continues to provide a necessary meeting place for direct contact of members of the Deaf community.

ISL and the Wider Society

Irish Deaf people live and function in an essentially hearing world, although as was just described, they have a community of their own. More than 90 percent are born into a hearing household. They attend schools managed by hearing educators, they work for hearing employers, and they are governed by a hearing government. As a result, Deaf people are under enormous pressure to shift to the language of the dominant, hearing majority—English. ISL is subordinate and has minority status in economic, political, and social terms.

HOME

Because most Deaf children are born to hearing parents, sign language is often not the medium of communication at home. Of the Deaf people interviewed for this study, only two, or 7 percent, had Deaf parents. These were the only ones who used sign to communicate fluently with their parents. A further eleven, or 37 percent, had one or more Deaf siblings. Although all of these used sign to communicate with their Deaf brothers and sisters, they did not use sign language with their hearing parents. The majority, then, did not acquire or use sign language at home. Some reported that they had developed "home signs" or used fingerspelling but emphasized that it was not adequate for normal conversation. Neil, for example, said, "I use mainly speech mixed with some sign at home but I could not have a conversation in sign." Two of the older interviewees who were educated by manual methods mentioned their parents' disappointment when they (the interviewees) began to learn sign.

My mother was not happy when I started learning sign language. (Craig)

My parents wanted me to be able to talk and lipread. They had no experience of deafness. (Mary)

Most Deaf children do not share a linguistic system with their parents and are therefore often subjected to repression at home as well as in other areas of their lives.

EMPLOYMENT

Unemployment rates have generally risen inexorably in Ireland since the early 1980s. A report published by the National Association for the

Deaf in 1973 showed the employment rate (9 percent) of Deaf people to be much lower than that of the general population. More recent figures published by the ISL National Survey and Research Project indicate that the number of unemployed Deaf people has been growing considerably. Of the 269 adults who where actively seeking and available for work when questioned in the survey, 32.3 percent were unemployed (Matthews 1996). Traditionally, Deaf people worked as coopers, tailors, seamstresses, laundry workers, carpenters, and so on (O'Leary 1989). Many of these traditional areas of employment are now becoming obsolete. Today, employment placements for Deaf people are frequently not in keeping with their abilities. A job survey published by the National Association for the Deaf in 1989 indicated that most were still employed in manual labor: 17 percent were in "general factory work," 14 percent worked as carpenters, and 12 percent were machinists/pressers (NAD 1989). Matthews (1996) reports that of those he surveyed only 1.6 percent had managerial or executive jobs and that there are no Deaf doctors, solicitors, dentists, psychiatrists, or members of government in Ireland.

The majority of the Deaf people interviewed for this study were despondent about the limited employment opportunities available to them. They described how they have to accept jobs they do not want and find it extremely difficult to move from one job to another. Many of those interviewed reported difficulty in obtaining promotions.

> Job opportunities for the Deaf are very disappointing. Many have to do jobs they don't want to do. (Aaron)

> There's a ratio of 1 to 10,000 Deaf to hearing in Ireland. It's easier for an employer not to pick a Deaf person. (Paul)

> There are many clever Deaf but few have good jobs. (Kevin)

> I worked for sixteen years in the bank. I never got a promotion and I could have done the job. The only thing I can't do is answer the telephone. I saw younger people coming in and getting promoted, but not me. (Emma)

> I worked for six years in the same job and never got a promotion. I didn't feel equal with the hearing people. (Eve)

In 1977 the government introduced a quota scheme for the public service and set a target of reserving 3 percent of jobs for people with disabilities (Department of Health 1984). For the first time, some Irish Deaf people were recruited by special competition but with equal opportunity for advancement and promotion within the service. However, two civil service employees who were interviewed for this study pointed out that, for Deaf people, promotion continues to be rare.

> Promotion in the civil service is rare because you need to be able to use the phone, go to lectures, and meetings and so on. (Hilary)

> In the Civil Service if you have the qualifications on paper the same as hearing people they have to promote you, but the exams are in English which is not the first language of all Deaf people. (Luke)

Generally, Deaf people work with and are supervised by hearing people. Rarely do these hearing people have any knowledge of sign language, and communication often breaks down.

> At work the boss is not interested in learning sign. He just writes things down and wants me to get on with the job. (Aaron)

> Difficulties arise because of problems with communication. Often this leads to confusion and misunderstandings. Now I insist everything is written down for me at work. (Fiona)

Interpreters who could provide access to the English language are often not made available to Deaf employees. The first register of sign language interpreters was established in Ireland in 1996. At present, there are ten trainees and five qualified interpreters listed on it (personal communication, Leeson 1997). One woman who was interviewed had worked for over twenty years for a government department, and it was only recently that the department had agreed to provide an interpreter for her at meetings. Another interviewee said, "The only problem is real access to communication. There is no other problem. It's not a question of a Deaf person's ability, it's just a problem of access" (James).

A small number of the Deaf people interviewed were optimistic about the future.

> Years ago Deaf people worked in jobs like tailoring, shoemaking, and carpentry. Now things are different, there are more diverse job opportunities. (Michael)

> In the past there was nothing for the Deaf, just an apprenticeship as a tailor and so on. But now it's great with training for different things. (Adam)

In general, however, it seems that in Ireland—as in other countries—Deaf people are in a subordinated position compared to their hearing colleagues at work. They are likely to be underemployed, have factory jobs, be more poorly paid, have considerably less chance of promotion, and be supervised by hearing people.

POLITICS

From a political viewpoint, Deaf people in Ireland are also in an inferior position when compared to the hearing society. Hearing people control government policy making and legislation. ISL has not been given official recognition by the Irish government. An Irish member of the European Parliament, Eileen LeMass, was responsible for presenting a report on "The Official Recognition of Sign Languages" to the European Parliament. In June 1988, members of the Parliament voted unanimously to pass the resolution. The implications of this resolution will affect the situation of all sign languages used within the European Community, but it will take a long time to become fully apparent in society. The resolution will have to be developed by the Commission and go to the Council of Ministers for approval before going back to Parliament for ratification. Member states will then have two years to adopt it before it can become law. It is the responsibility of each member state to encourage their own government to recognize their sign language. As yet the Irish government has not done so (personal communication, LeMass 1991; NAD 1988). This contrasts with the situation of Irish, which is recognized as the first official language of Ireland. The European Union of the Deaf is presently carrying out a survey of all sign languages used within the European Union. The results of this research will be used in efforts to have Parliament recognize the sign languages of the Union.

THE MEDIA

Initially appearing in October 1988, "Sign of the Times" was the first magazine program for Deaf people to be broadcast on Irish television. More recently, it has been replaced by a program called "Hands On," which airs once every two weeks for a half-hour. Since September 1992, Deaf news-readers have been signing a short summary of the news that is broadcast at peak time each evening. Members of the Deaf community are well aware that, by having sign language channeled through this very powerful broadcasting medium, the status of the language is considerably advanced (NAD 1992; O'Leary 1989). However, many argue that it is not enough and that the length of time sign language is shown on television should be increased (IDS 1993). Others add that the type of signing used on television is not appropriate and that ISL rather than signed English should be used (IDS 1993). Among the Deaf people interviewed for this study, there was disagreement about this. A number of Deaf people complained that they have difficulty following the "News for the Deaf." Some wanted ISL. Others preferred a signed version as close to English as possible.

> It's difficult to understand the signs used on TV. The presenters should use ISL but they don't and I can't understand their signing and either read the subtitles or turn it off. (Paul)

> I want as much text as possible, not just reflected information. I don't want to get information by bits and scraps. If I was watching ISL I wouldn't be sure if I got it all. (John)

Fifteen of those interviewed said that ISL should be used, eight said signed English, one said a mix of ISL and signed English, and one said it should depend on the formality of the program.

> It depends on what the situation is. If it's formal, then signed English but if it's a more relaxed studio discussion then it should be ISL. It depends on formality. The problem with "Sign of the Times" is that it is so broad, there's no precedent for what signing should be used. (Ian)

Five people did not offer an opinion on what kind of signing should be used for television broadcasts, saying that they rarely or never watch television.

RELIGION

"Deafness from birth causes spiritual starvation unless education is available" (Griffey 1994, 22). Indirectly, by way of the education system, religion has had an important influence on the situation of ISL. In Ireland, there has always been considerable involvement by religious groups in special education. It was seen as an evangelizing or missionary enterprise. McDonnell (1991, 102) cites from the first annual report of the National Institute for the Education of Deaf and Dumb Children of the Poor in Ireland, which stated that Deaf people had to be rescued "from the depths of more than heathen darkness to the glorious light of gospel Truth." It was with this objective that the Church undertook the responsibility of educating Deaf children. As mentioned earlier, the Protestant Church opened the first school for Deaf children in Ireland in 1816. Thirty years later, two Dominican Sisters traveled to France to study teaching techniques used by Catholic educators there and are credited with introducing sign language to Ireland.

Many people believed that an understanding of the English language was necessary in order for Deaf children to be able to receive and fully understand the importance of the sacraments of the Catholic faith. As a result, all classes emphasized signed and written versions of the English language (Le Master 1990).

When my parents asked why my brother couldn't get an oral education at the school for the Deaf they were told that the boys were all to learn sign so that they could learn the Word of God. (Mary)

Religion, then, has played a significant role in the history of ISL and in the development of policies regarding language in schools for Deaf children in Ireland. Without the influence of religious orders, it is unlikely that the "signes méthodiques" would have been imported from France into Ireland and that the residential schools for Deaf children, the first recorded Deaf communities in the country, would have been established so early.

ISL and Education

Education is one of the principal issues debated by Irish Deaf people. Although similar to the situation in other countries, the intellectual abilities of Deaf children have not been found to be any different from those of their hearing peers; studies have shown that the overall level of achievement of Deaf children is of limited performance in oral communication, with low levels of attainment in reading and writing. One study found the average reading age of a sixteen-year-old Deaf child in Ireland to be between eight and nine years (James, O'Neill, and Smyth 1991). Another study carried out in 1993 found that in the previous fifteen years, only thirty-nine Deaf students attended or were currently enrolled at third-level colleges. This constitutes a severe underrepresentation of Deaf students in higher-level institutions (O'Reilly 1993). Educational and language policies implemented at schools for Deaf children are therefore of considerable concern to a great majority of Deaf people.

Language Policy up to the 1950s

From the time of the establishment of the Cabra schools in the mid-nineteenth century up to the 1950s, all Deaf children in Ireland, including the moderately hard of hearing, were educated through sign language (Griffey 1982). Ireland may be unique in the world in that sign language was used over such a long period. Following the resolutions of the Congress of Milan in 1880, oralism had been introduced into most other European countries and into the United States by the early part of the century. Ireland's late transition to oralism may have been the result of the emphasis on religious instruction discussed earlier. In addition, there was an enormous emphasis on the teaching of written English. A teacher was not given responsibility for a class until he or she was proficient in the use of manual communication. Griffey (1994, 23) states that "the spoken word was never used even though some of the pupils had residual hearing. Speech was considered a distraction for the reader of manual communication." Teachers and pupils were expected to sign in English word order at all times (Griffey 1982, 1994). In spite of this, it was not always the case that signed English was used. Griffey, a teacher at the school for Deaf girls during the period this policy was enforced, reports, "As a young teacher I was expected to sign in conventional English at all times—the order of signs being the same as that of words . . . yet I found that among themselves the children resorted to non-linguistic forms" (1982, 256).

A number of the older Deaf people interviewed for this study, who were at school at this time, also reported using natural sign language rather than signed English, particularly outside the classroom setting. In fact, some of these older Deaf people stated that natural sign was used by not only the pupils but also the teachers on occasion.

> When we were in class we used signed English, we signed in sentences, but once we were free we used natural sign amongst ourselves. (Craig)

> At the time I was in school we were taught through signed English but if we didn't understand something the teacher would explain it in natural sign language. (Michael)

> The Christian Brothers used ISL to explain things even though they were teaching through manual English. (Eric)

The main aim in teaching language at this time, however, was to help the children read and express themselves in correct written English. Griffey (1994, 25) states that "signs were to be only a means towards a more important end. The end was to acquaint the pupils with the written word as the principle source of their language for social communication."

Language Policy from the 1950s

The language policy employed at the schools for Deaf children changed dramatically during the 1940s and 1950s. Educators were influenced by what was happening in other countries and by the demands of parents and former pupils. Parents became more involved in the education of their Deaf children at this time and began to demand that they be taught to speak and lipread. Those who could afford it were sending their children to schools abroad. A survey of the attitudes of former pupils indicated that 95 percent wanted Deaf children to be given the opportunity to learn to speak (Griffey 1967, cited in Griffey 1982). In addition, developments in the field of electronics following World War II meant that hearing aids and audiometers were becoming more powerful and more widely available. As a result, oral methods of education were introduced, and the use of sign language was totally banned. A number of new schools and units with an exclusively oral philosophy were set up around the country. Teachers were advised to exclude all supplemental manual communication and to place greater emphasis on speech input, sound-perception training, and the use of any residual hearing (Griffey 1982). The use of sign was considered appropriate for use only with children who had additional handicaps (Department of Education 1972), and it became associated with "oral failures."

Implementation of the Policy

As we have mentioned, the oralist ideology embraced a very strong antisigning bias. It was believed that the use of sign would impede the development of speech and lipreading. These were considered essentials for Deaf children so that they might take their place in the hearing world. As a result, every effort was made to eradicate signing among the pupils (McDonnell and Saunders 1993). A number of different strategies were employed to do this.

PUNISHMENTS

Children who were found using sign were punished in a variety of ways.

Mostly you would be slapped but also they would deprive us of treats, like sweets and cake. Sometimes you would be put in the corner. It was very strict. It's difficult to remember now, it's so long ago. I often felt embarrassed and ostracized. (Anne)

It was around the middle of the 1970s when I started school. We weren't allowed to use sign and we were told it wasn't normal, that it was filthy. We were slapped if we were caught using it. (Carol)

Other penalties the interviewees mentioned included being fined and students' being told to keep their hands behind a chair.

SEGREGATION OF ORAL
FROM SIGNING PUPILS

A second strategy employed in efforts to prevent pupils from signing was the segregation of those who signed from those in oral programs (McDonnell 1992; McDonnell and Saunders 1993; O'Reilly 1993). Pupils who had already begun their education in the manual mode were allowed to continue, but they were kept separated from the "oral" children as much as possible. This was aimed at enhancing the status of speech and lipreading and diminishing that of signing. The children were told that, if they signed, their speech would deteriorate and they would never learn anything. Elitist attitudes were fostered among the oral pupils, whereas signing pupils were labeled in a negative way (McDonnell and Saunders 1993). The effects of segregation often lasted long after the pupils had left school.

In my class there were some who were very good at speech and others who were very bad. This led to a lot of tension and this was carried over after we left school. On the football team for example, although we were all playing on the team together, after a match we would separate into two groups. Each group would jeer the other and blame each other for things that happened in the match. (Luke)

REMOVAL OF DEAF TEACHERS

Prior to the introduction of oralist methods, there had been a sizable proportion of teachers at the two schools for Deaf children in Dublin who were Deaf themselves. These Deaf teachers acted as role models and would often teach sign language to incoming students. In 1956, the Department of Education introduced a requirement for certification as a teacher of Deaf students. A teacher could obtain certification only through a university education. This excluded—and continues to exclude—the great majority of Deaf candidates, as one of the prerequisites for entry to the teacher-training colleges is knowledge of the Irish language. Students attending the schools for Deaf children are exempt from a law requiring all children in Ireland to study Irish.

Up to the 1950s there were Deaf teachers in Cabra; after that the department stipulated that Deaf people must have hearing qualifications. Most Deaf people couldn't go through the hearing system. (Ian)

Today, only a few noncertified Deaf teachers are still employed at the schools for Deaf children. There is just one Deaf teacher on the staff of St. Mary's School for Deaf Girls who has met the Department of Education requirements as a certified teacher. She received her baccalaureate degree from an American university, enabling her to bypass the Irish language requirement. She then returned to Ireland to receive her teaching credentials from an Irish university (Le Master 1990).

It is also noteworthy that because Deaf children are not taught either written or spoken Irish, they are excluded from participation in a major part of their culture as citizens of Ireland. Discussions regarding the issues around the use, revival, and maintenance of the language are an important aspect of the daily lives of Irish people. In this sense, Deaf people can be considered "tourists in their own land."

The Survival of ISL

The aim of the language policy in Deaf education in Ireland has been to bring about a total shift from the use of ISL to English. In spite of this, ISL has survived. Deaf pupils managed to maintain a signing community at school although they knew it was against school rules and that they ran the risk of being severely punished (McDonnell and Saunders 1993). Sign language became a secret code that they used "under the table." Deaf herself, Saunders describes how the pupils secretly acquired signs from peers (some of whom would have learned sign natively from Deaf parents) or from other signers in the school environment. She states:

We learned signs from other Deaf children. We met adult Deaf workers in the laundry and learned signs from them. We made up our own
signs too, related to events in our lives. For example, our sign for
Easter was the same as our sign for April. (McDonnell and Saunders
1993, 256)

In a review of her experience as a teacher of Deaf children in Ireland over
a period of thirty years, Griffey writes that, "It was obvious that all pupils
were more interested in manual communication than in speech signals.
They were visually orientated. They were poor lipreaders, because they
were thinking in manual communication as they used speech" (1982,
258).

McDonnell suggests that Deaf pupils continue to sign because they
have no other reasonable means of communication. In a study of the communication patterns of pupils in a school for Deaf children in Dublin, he
found that although pupils with profound hearing loss placed the achievement of good oral language skills at the top of their list of priorities, non-
vocal communication predominated in settings outside the classroom
(McDonnell 1992). Saunders supports this: "In school everybody signed.
No matter how we tried not to sign with our friends it was impossible.
We had to communicate, there was no other way" (McDonnell and Saunders 1993, 256). ISL then, like other sign languages, has survived its
greatest threat because spoken English cannot meet the needs of most
Deaf people.

Attitudes of Deaf People regarding Education

Among the thirty Deaf people interviewed for this study, there was
widespread agreement on certain issues pertaining to the education of
Deaf children. Without exception, all agreed that sign should be taught
to profoundly Deaf children. All but one of the interviewees stated that
there should be more Deaf teachers of Deaf children. Deaf teachers were
considered essential as role models for Deaf children and in particular for
teaching sign. Hearing teachers are not presently required to know sign
language. Ten people pointed out, however, that Deaf teachers would
need to have appropriate qualifications that are often difficult for Deaf
people to acquire. There was also agreement that Deaf children should be
given the opportunity to learn English, both spoken and signed versions.

It is a Deaf child's right to learn English. (Michael)

It was recognized that Deaf people live in a hearing as well as a Deaf world and that therefore it is necessary for them to learn English. Some older Deaf people regretted not having had the opportunity to learn speech when they were at school. There were obvious differences of opinion, however, on what kind of signing should be used in the classroom and on how much emphasis should be placed on each of the two languages, ISL and English.

The differences of opinion among the interviewees were found to vary along a continuum with ISL and signed English at either end. Some expressed strong views that ISL is the first language of Deaf people and should be used with Deaf children from an early age in education. Others disagreed and felt that, if a Deaf child is to acquire good English reading and writing skills, the medium of education should be signed English. Many of the older Deaf people who were at school at the time when manual English was in use felt strongly that it is the best medium of education and results in higher levels of literacy.

ISL is okay for relaxed times such as in the evening but children need to learn English and should be taught signed English at school. (Kevin)

Signed English should be used for the sake of education, children can adjust to ISL when their education is over. (John)

Years ago there was a high standard of English among the Deaf because children were taught signed English at school. (Michael)

Deaf children will write the same way they sign. They need to learn to associate sign with the written word. They should always sign in signed English. If they sign in signed English they will think in English. (Gary)

At the opposite end of the continuum were those who believed that a bilingual education would be best for Deaf children, with ISL recognized as the native language of Deaf people and English taught as a second language. A total of twenty-four people stated that ISL should be used in the classroom, and six of these referred specifically to bilingualism.

Bilingualism is the best method of education. Speech and sign should be kept separate instead of teaching the two languages together. Geography and history and other subjects should be taught through ISL and English through speech and sign. (Tina)

Children should be taught all subjects through ISL and even home-work could be done on video. English should be a separate part of the curriculum. (Laura)

One man pointed out that bilingualism is not a totally new system but was used to some extent in the Cabra schools prior to the 1950s.

Bilingualism is not a new system. It was used here in the past. If you ask any of the older Deaf they will tell you the Christian Brothers used natural sign language to explain things, so you see it's not really new. (James)

Despite this, many of the interviewees were aware that it will be some time before bilingualism can become a reality in schools for Deaf children: "There must be recognition that ISL and English have their place in the classroom. That's not going to happen in Ireland for a long time" (Ian).

Present Policies

The most recent policy to be introduced into education in Ireland is the integration of children with disabilities in special schools into mainstream schools. Traditionally among Deaf people, special schools have provided the institutional bases for the acquisition of sign language and ensured that ISL is passed from child to child through the generations. Official government policy regarding all forms of special education is now in favor of integration (Department of Education 1993; McGee 1990). This has brought with it a new threat to the Irish Deaf community and the maintenance of ISL. Twelve of those interviewed were opposed to this trend and said that Deaf children should be educated in special schools where they would be exposed to Deaf culture and sign language. The remainder felt that integration may be suitable for some Deaf children, depending on their level of hearing loss and the facilities available in hearing schools. (At the time these interviews were carried out, the media uncovered a story of cases of child abuse at one of the residential schools for Deaf children in Dublin. Many of the adults interviewed spoke about it outside of the interview context. It is likely that this affected their attitudes toward residential and special schooling for Deaf children, and as a result the numbers opposed to integration may have been smaller than would have otherwise been expected.)

The number of Deaf students attending the two schools in Cabra has been decreasing dramatically over the past twenty years. There were 752 pupils enrolled in the 1979–80 school year, 543 in 1989–90, and 460 in 1993–94 (Swan 1994, cited in Matthews 1996). More Deaf students are entering either mainstream schools or special programs for Deaf children within the mainstream setting. It remains to be seen how the figures will change in the future and how much an affect any further increase in integration will have on the maintenance of ISL.

In 1972 the committee who prepared the report, entitled "The Education of Children Who Are Handicapped by Impaired Hearing," recommended that "the schools for profoundly Deaf children should adhere to their present policy of providing an exclusively oral education for all pupils capable of making adequate progress through the oral medium" (Department of Education 1972, 85). Today, although official policy has not been changed, the more extreme antisigning strategies have disappeared. Some schools for Deaf children have even introduced modest sign language programs into their mainstream curricula (McDonnell and Saunders 1993). Compared to other countries, Ireland is perhaps at an advantage when it comes to reintroducing sign language into the classroom because the period of time between its proscription and reintroduction was much shorter than anywhere else. However, in many areas of education, signing is still regarded with fear and suspicion. No investment has ever been made in ISL to establish the merits or drawbacks of using it as a more appropriate medium of instruction in the schools for Deaf children (O'Reilly 1993). The topic of bilingualism remains largely at the discussion level although there is one small school in Cork that has been using ISL and following a bilingual philosophy since 1987 (Matthews 1996). Significantly, the views of Deaf people themselves have never been seriously taken into account.

The dream and the hope of the Deaf is that signing be given the same status as oral language; that signing should mean signing in our language; that information on Deaf culture and the history of Deaf people and Deaf experience be part of the school curriculum; that books written by the Deaf, about the Deaf or about growing up as a Deaf person be in the school library. (McDonnell and Saunders 1993, 260)

ISL has been maintained and remains a living, changing language despite the efforts of the hearing, English-speaking majority to remove it. During the late 1980s and 1990s, Deaf people in Ireland have been inspired by the DeafPride movement in other countries, and a number of important initiatives have occurred. There has been an increase in research and publications. A number of Deaf people are presently studying linguistics and Deaf studies at Trinity College Dublin and Maynooth University. Some training has been provided for interpreters. Among the public at large, there is a growing awareness of the Deaf community, and there has been a dramatic increase in the number of hearing people attending sign language classes.

There is no room for complacency, however. ISL is in a position of grave inferiority compared to both of the spoken languages used in Ireland. The following list of ongoing needs was compiled following the interviews with the members of the Dublin Deaf community:

Further research and publications
Training for interpreters
Official recognition of ISL by the Irish government
Use of ISL in the education of Deaf children
Increased awareness among both Deaf and hearing people regarding ISL
Additional ISL classes for hearing people
A Deaf studies center in Ireland
Deaf people to be trained and responsible for decision making in all issues relating to deafness, particularly in research and education

There are a number of parallels that can be drawn between the positions of ISL and Irish. Both are used by a small number of people compared to the dominant language, English. Both have histories of suppression and subordination and have been accredited poor status. The negative attitudes toward both languages are now gradually changing, and they are becoming more highly valued by their users.

There are also numerous critical differences between the two languages. Irish has official recognition and the ongoing support of the Irish government; ISL does not. It is required by law that Irish be taught to all children in Ireland; there is no such requirement regarding ISL. Over the past twenty years, there has been an increased interest in an all-Irish-medium of education, and over forty Irish-medium schools controlled by Irish-speakers have been established in English-speaking areas; Deaf adults have no role in the running of the schools for Deaf children, and very few are employed in them. Irish can be effectively channeled through the media: television, radio, newspapers, and other publications; ISL is a visual language and therefore can gain exposure only through the visual media. Radio is completely inaccessible to Deaf people, and access to the print media is limited by their knowledge of the language in which it is written.

It may seem that in many areas ISL is at a distinct disadvantage in comparison to Irish and that the prognosis for its maintenance is extremely poor when expressed in terms of community resources such as schools and the mass media. However, there is a critical factor that has been responsible for the maintenance of ISL: Irish Deaf people desire that it be maintained because it plays two important functions in their lives. First, use of ISL is a defining and nondisposable part of being "ethnically" Deaf and belonging to the Irish Deaf community. Irish, on the other hand, is a meaningful but disposable feature of the ethnic identity of the Irish people. Its decline has not resulted in a loss of identity for them. Second, and perhaps more significantly, ISL is the only reasonable means of communication available to Deaf people in Ireland. It survives because monochannel oralism is too difficult for the daily communication needs of most Deaf people and because they cannot achieve the hearing identity so fervently sought by those who aim to suppress their language. Paradoxically, the function ISL plays in the lives of its users has also been a limiting factor in its spread. Sign languages are first and foremost of attraction to people with severe and profound hearing loss, and ISL is therefore destined to remain largely the language of a limited population of Deaf users.

The two minority languages of Ireland can benefit from each other. The Irish language revival movement has always had the support of the Irish government. It seems imperative that if the status and the domains of use of ISL are to be increased, the Deaf community too will need the recognition of the government and the necessary funding and infrastructure it can provide, specifically in the areas of research, education, and the media. Doubtless, ISL will continue to be maintained as long as there are biologically deaf people who need to use it to communicate and as long as these people come together to form a Deaf community. It can be postulated that if Irish were to play such a critical role in the ethnic identity of hearing Irish people, it would be in a highly unassailable position.

REFERENCES

Comhairle na Gaeilge. 1974. Towards a language policy. In *Advances in language planning*, ed. J. A. Fishman, 519–26. The Hague: Mouton.

Committee on Irish Language Attitudes Research (CLAR). 1975. Report. Dublin: Stationary Office.

Conway, A., and T. Veale. 1994. A linguistic approach to sign language synthesis. In *Proceedings of H.C.I., 1994*, 211–22. Cambridge: Cambridge University Press.

Coogan, L. 1994. New signs for computer age. *Link* (summer):8.

Cradden, J. 1994. "I'm Deaf too": Deaf identity, education and the Dublin Deaf community. Ph.D. diss., Department of Communications, Dublin City University.

Department of Education. 1972. *The education of children who are handicapped by impaired hearing*. Dublin: Stationary Office.

———. 1993. *Report of the special education review committee*. Dublin: Stationary Office.

Department of Health. 1984. *Towards a full life: Green paper on services for disabled people*. Dublin: Stationary Office.

Dublin Deaf Association. 1994. Clubscene. *Contact* 93:19–20.

Fennell, D. 1981. Can a shrinking linguistic minority be saved? Lessons from the Irish experience. In *Minority languages today*, ed. E. Haugen, J. D. McClure, D. Thomson, 32–39. Edinburgh: Edinburgh University Press.

Foran, C. 1994a. Fr. John Baptist Burke, C. M., 1822–1894. *Contact* 93: 16–17.

———. 1994b. *Transcript of the 1847 manuscript Irish Sign Language dictionary*. Dublin: Dublin Deaf Association.

———. 1995. Dr. Charles Orpen, 1791–1856. *Contact* 98:12–13.

Grace, T. 1993. Scouts honour. *Irish Deaf Journal* 5(26):17–19.

Griffey, N. 1982. From a pure manual method via the combined approach to the oral-auditory technique in educating profoundly Deaf children. In *Proceedings of the international congress on education of the deaf: Hamburg, 1980*, vol. 1, 255–64. Heidelberg: Julius Groos.

———. 1989. A history of sign language with special reference to Ireland. Adult Education Course for Tutors of Sign Language, Maynooth, Ireland. Typescript.

———. 1994. *From silence to speech*. Dublin: Dominican Publications.

Hawking, J. 1983. A re-examination of sign language diglossia. *American Annals of the Deaf* 128 (1):48–52.

Irish Deaf Society. 1992. Quotes at education seminar organized by the Deaf. *Irish Deaf Journal* 5(24):10.

————. 1993. Irish Deaf Society congress workshops. In *Proceedings of the I.D.S. second congress* (November 1993, Trinity College Dublin). Dublin: Irish Deaf Society.

Irish National Teachers Organisation. 1985a. *The Irish language in primary education (teachers attitudes)*. Dublin: INTO.

Irish National Teachers Organisation, Market Research Bureau of Ireland. 1985b. *The Irish language in primary schools (public attitudes)*. Dublin: INTO.

James, T., E. O'Neill, and J. Smyth. 1991. Reading achievements of children with hearing impairments. *Link* (winter):4–6.

Kannapell, B. 1993. *Language choice – Identity choice*. Burtonsville: Linstok Press.

Kyle, J., B. Woll, G. Pullen, and F. Maddix. 1985. *Sign language: The study of Deaf people and their language*. Cambridge: Cambridge University Press.

Labov, W. 1972. *Sociolinguistic patterns*. Philadelphia: University of Pennsylvania Press.

Ladd, P. 1988. The modern Deaf community. In *British Sign Language*, ed. D. Miles, 27–43. London: BBC Books.

Lane, H., R. Hoffmeister, and B. Bahan. 1996. *A journey into the Deaf-world*. San Diego: DawnSignPress.

Lee, D. M. 1982. Are there really signs of diglossia? Re-examining the situation. *Sign Language Studies* 35:127–52.

Le Master, B. 1987. Female and male signs in the Dublin Deaf community. In paper presented at the Fourth International Symposium on Sign Language Research, Lappenranta, Finland.

————. 1990. Female and male signs in the Dublin Deaf community. Ph.D. diss. Dept. of Anthropology, University of California, Los Angeles.

LeMaster, B., and S. Foran. 1987. Irish Sign Language. In *Gallaudet encyclopedia of Deaf people and Deafness*, ed. J. V. Van Cleve, 82–84. London: McGraw-Hill.

Lucas, C., and C. Valli. 1989. Language contact in the American Deaf community. In *The sociolinguistics of the Deaf community*, ed. C. Lucas, 11–39. San Diego: Academic Press.

————. 1992. *Language contact in the American Deaf community*. London: Academic Press.

Maguire, F. 1991. A user guide for Irish Sign Language research. Ph.D. diss., Trinity College, Dublin.

————. 1993. *Sign languages: An introduction to their social context and their structure*. Dublin: Center for Language and Communication Studies, Trinity College Dublin.

Matthews, P. 1996. *The Irish Deaf community*, vol. 1. Dublin: Institiúid Teangeolaíochta Éireann.

————. Forthcoming. *The Irish Deaf community*, vol. 2. Dublin: Institiúid Teangeolaíochta Éireann.

McDonnell, P. 1983. Social context and language usage: Implications for children with impaired hearing. In *Language across cultures*, ed. L. Mac Mathuna and D. Singleton, 141–53. Dublin: Irish Association of Applied Linguistics.

————. 1991. Vested interests in the development of special education in Ireland. *Reach* 5(2):97–106.

————. 1992. *Patterns of communication among Deaf pupils*. Dublin: Sociological Association of Ireland, National Rehabilitation Board.

————. 1993. Building blocks of ISL. *Irish Deaf Journal* 7(27):6–8.

McDonnell, P., and H. Saunders. 1993. Sit on your hands. In *Looking back*, ed. R. Fischer and H. Lane, 255–60. Hamburg: Signum Press.

McGee, P. 1990. Special education in Ireland. *European Journal of Special Needs Education* 5(1):48–63.

National Association for the Deaf 1973. *Information about the young adult Deaf population of Ireland*. Dublin: NAD.

————. 1988. Sign gets thumbs up from Euro Parliament. *Link* (autumn):3.

————. 1989. Job survey. *Link* (autumn):15.

————. 1992. "Signs of progress" news for the Deaf. *Link* (December):5.

National Association for the Deaf, and Sign Language Tutors Association of Ireland. 1992a. *Press release, sign language dictionary project*. Dublin: NAD.

————. 1992b. *Sign on*. Dublin: NAD.

O'Leary, J. 1989. The Deaf's great hunger for their rightful place in society. *Link* (autumn):2–5.

Ó Murchú, M. 1970. *Language and community*, Comhairle na Gaeilge Occasional Paper 1. Dublin: Stationary Office.

Ó Riagáin, P. 1988. Bilingualism in Ireland 1973–1983: An overview of national sociolinguistic surveys. *International Journal of the Sociology of Language* 70:29–51.

Ó Riagáin, P., and M. Ó Gliasáin. 1984. *The Irish language in the Republic of Ireland 1983; Preliminary report of a national survey*. Dublin: Institiúid Teangeolaíochta Éireann.

————. 1994. *National survey on languages 1993: Preliminary report*. Dublin: Institiúid Teangeolaíochta Éireann.

O'Reilly, J. O. 1993. The hearing impaired equal opportunities in higher education in Ireland? Institutional and student perspectives. Ph.D. diss., National University of Ireland, Dublin.

O'Sullivan, N. 1994. The cochlear implant controversy. *Irish Deaf Journal* 8(31):6–7.

Padden, C., and T. Humphries. 1988. *Deaf in America: Voices from a culture.* London: Harvard University Press.

Stokoe, W. C. 1972. Sign language diglossia. In *Semiotics and human sign languages,* 154–67. The Hague: Mouton.

Unified Sign Language Committee. 1979. *The Irish Sign Language dictionary.* Dublin: NAD.

Index

Lexemes used with pinky extension, 7, 9–11
Lexicalized loan verbs in BSL, 54–55
Liddell, S. K., 171, 185
Liddell, S. K., and R. E. Johnson, 141
Lillo-Martin, D., and E. Klima, 171–72, 176
Linguistics
    ASL acceptance by linguistic community, 110
    spatial structures in ASL, 208
Linguistics Institute of Ireland, 240, 249
Local-level policy on education of deaf children, 116–18
Lucas, C., 5

Maguire, F., 240
Mainland China, 63–64
Mainstreaming. *See also* Least Restrictive Environment (LRE)
    American deaf students, 107–8, 122–23, 126–28, 130–31
    Irish Deaf students, 266
    reversed mainstreamed classrooms, 184
Malayalee English, 60–62
Malay language, 61–62
Male vs. female signs in Irish Sign Language, 245–48
Mandarin language, 64–66, 72. *See also* Chinese language
Mann, Horace, 105
Manually Coded English (MCE), 192–93, 242
Mapping in storytelling, 183–210
    ASL and visual patterns, 197–205
    involvement strategies, 187–88, 191, 200–201
    methodology of study, 191–94
    reading stories aloud, 189–90
    referential spatial mapping, 185–86, 188, 190, 197–202
    repetition of structured use of space, 202–5

rhythm and rhyme, 186–97
source language of story, 188–89
structure of story used in study, 194–202
teachers in study, 191
theoretical framework of study, 185–90
translation of story into ASL, 189–90
Maravcsik, E., 48, 50
Marriage of Deaf partners in Ireland, 251
Martin, Sr. Mary Vincent, 236–37, 259
Mathematical symbols in Taiwan Sign Language, 72
Mather, S. M., 167, 188
Matthews, P., 240, 246
McDonnell, P., 240, 258, 264
McDonnell, P., and H. Saunders, 240
Media
    Irish Sign Language, programs in, 257–58
    See Hear! (BBC television magazine program for deaf people), 44–45
Meier, R.
    eye-gaze research, 171–72, 176
    referential spatial mapping research, 185
Metzger, M., 185, 188
Metzger, M., and S. K. Liddell, 185
Milan Conference (International Congress on Education of the Deaf), 105
Morphology
    nonmanual adjectives and adverbs in tactile ASL, 27–29, 35
    tactile ASL, 19
    verbs in BSL, 51–54, 56
Movers and Shakers by C. Carroll and S. Mather, 223–24

Nahuatl verbs borrowed from Spanish, 48–50, 52

Wilcox, S. E., 41
Winston, E. A., 185, 188
Word-search repairs, 148, 150–51,
  158–63

Yau, M.-S., 48
Yiddish language, 61–62

Zimmer, J., 5, 188
Zone of Proximal Development
  (ZOPED), 111